The ACCOUNTING PROFESSIONAL'S ENCYCLOPEDIA of LOW COST & CREATIVE MARKETING STRATEGIES

The ACCOUNTING PROFESSIONAL'S ENCYCLOPEDIA of LOW COST & CREATIVE MARKETING STRATEGIES

Allen R. D'Angelo

Archer-Ellison Publishing Company
Winter Park, Florida

**The Accounting Professional's
Encyclopedia of Low Cost &
Creative Marketing Strategies**
by Allen R. D'Angelo

Copyright © 2001 by Archer-Ellison Publishing Company

ISBN 157472-350-2

Library of Congress Catalog Card Number 2001116532

Published by

Archer-Ellison Publishing Co.
P.O. Box 5795
Winter Park, FL 32793
407.678.5999

DEDICATION

I have written this book for accounting professionals with an entrepreneurial spirit. This is for those who are teachable and possess a passion for performing their service with superior competitive excellence.

For new professionals, may this book put you on your pathway for marketing success for a lifetime.

For those accounting professionals who have been in business for no more than three years, may this book become a marketing arsenal for you.

For professionals who have been in business for years and years, may this book awaken you from even one iota of slumber long enough to put a little zest back into your business.

For everyone who still believes that American Entrepreneurism does indeed free those who partake of its virtues and disciplines, may this book remind you that selling one's services with enduring excellence and responsibility contributes significantly to the foundation of our free market system.

TABLE OF CONTENTS

INTRODUCTION

This book presents marketing guidelines and ideas for promoting the practice of the typical accounting professional. The author makes no claims about the legality, or regulatory acceptability of any ideas or discussions presented herein. The author mandates that all accounting professionals reading this book must request a written opinion from the Department of Business & Professional Regulation and the appropriate division of the state which certifies accounting professional regarding any and all marketing or advertising method(s) discussed in this book to make certain that any aspects of the material presented herein do not run afoul of any state or federal law(s) or rule(s) set out by such regulatory authorities. Check extensively with all appropriate federal and state regulatory governing boards, agencies and private legal professionals before applying ideas from this book to your accounting practice.

We have presented an example below of one CPA/Attorney's receipt of a state opinion regarding the use of a CPA/Attorney designation in print advertising and other marketing methods.

DEPARTMENT OF BUSINESS & PROFESSIONAL REGULATION

Jeb Bush, *Governor*   Cynthia Henderson, *Secretary*

June 14, 2000

████ ██████ ██████
████ ███████
████ ████████ ███████ ██████
████ ████████

Dear ████ ████████:

At a Board meeting on October 28, 1999, the Board of Accountancy considered your request for an opinion relating to 473.302 (7), F.S. definition of practicing public accounting and 61H1-24.001, FAC, Advertising and determined as follows:

A CPA/Attorney may use the CPA/Attorney designations in advertising if he is an attorney and a Florida CPA that holds an active license.

If however, the firm performs any of the services set forth in 473.302 (7) then the firm (including sole proprietors) must be licensed as an audit firm.

The attorney designation is not considered a specialty designation. Therefore, the asterisk is not necessary unless specialty designations (such as CFP, CMA, etc.) are also used.

Please keep in mind that this opinion is based solely on the facts set forth in your letter and is not intended to be an opinion of general applicability. Furthermore, we have not conducted an independent factual investigation to determine whether other relevant facts do or may exist. We have not determined whether any aspects of these transactions run afoul of any law or rule other than those specifically mentioned herein.

Sincerely,

DIVISION OF CERTIFIED PUBLIC ACCOUNTING

BY:_____
        ████ ██ ██████
        Division Director

MPW/jc

–1–

QUICK MARKETING TIPS
FOR YOUR ACCOUNTING BUSINESS

In this book, I have included the best marketing ideas I have personally tested in accounting businesses over the last ten years. Each idea is explained with enriching detail in the chapters of this book. Don't undervalue any of these ideas—you must carefully test each of them in order to see how well your adaptations of my ideas will work for you. Here is a foretaste of what is to come in the remainder of this book:

DEVELOP MORE INTERACTIVE MARKETING APPROACHES

- Create an e-zine, an e-mail newsletter, that goes to your clients throughout the year to give them powerful tips and suggestions that save them time and tax dollars. Freely give tax-saving ideas and valuable time-saving tax preparation tidbits. Include investment portfolio management tips, if you offer financial investment advice. Your e-zine should mention your Internet web site, if you have one, and you should have one.
- Develop a web site that enables your clients to submit their accounting files (i.e. Quickbooks and Quicken files) to you from your home page. If you give financial advice, allowing your clients access to a myriad of recommended e-trading websites on your web pages will create value for your clients.
- Conduct special information nights and seminars that cater to your high-end clients. These special events do not have to be expensive. Some accounting firms have had success with renting banquet halls, catering dinners, and bringing in special speakers to talk about topics that add value for their clients. You can offer mini-seminars in your conference room entitled, "The A-Z Start-up Business — How To Set Up Your Small Business Correctly From The Beginning." You can charge or run the events for free.

- Create Cross-Promotion Teams. Select three to five other noncompetitive professionals who service the same kind of clients. You may decide to team up with a marketing consultant, an attorney, and an insurance salesperson specializing in estate planning working for a large insurance company, and a financial planner. Create a team with these professionals. You can swap client lists, write letters of referral for each other to each other's client base, create a cost-shared advertising program, and share other marketing costs in profoundly simple and highly valuable ways.
- Give yourself a 12-week challenge to increase exposure within your local community in several new ways. Consider conducting seminars for your local Small Business Development Council and Chamber of Commerce. Write several articles for your local newspaper on important issues related to your area of specialization— i.e. small business issues, decreasing tax burden of retirees, and other hot topics. By increasing your promotion effort in one short explosive burst (12-weeks) you will create lasting relationships with others in your community who are poised to help you market your business.
- Start increasing the quality and frequency of messages about what makes your services different to your present clients. If you decide to publish high-quality booklets or a magazine for your market, be sure to include something in it that has high retainable value. One way to do this is to send information that fits in a standard file drawer and looks like a file folder — such as a laminated file folder that lists valuable information for tax preparation with your name on it. Perhaps the file folder could be sent monthly to your clients. Include valuable information on recent changes in tax laws, with a list of services you provide to help manage those changes. Maybe the folder can serve as a monthly tax organizer with tax-savings reminders and ideas about easy ways to organize tax-related paperwork. Use your creativity to determine the specific client applications you can use to create a valuable packet to be retained by them, thereby reminding and inspiring more use of your services throughout the year.

- Develop a creative mastermind group. Put together a group of other business people from noncompetitive industries, consisting of trusted friends and colleagues, to work together to share best marketing strategies. Meet to exchange marketing ideas every week or two. If you're able to visit another city outside of your present market(s), make an effort to develop relationships with other accounting business owners there. Consider meeting with them regularly to discuss how to improve each other's businesses. Each of you will benefit dramatically from the shared experiences of fellow group members.

SIMPLE, PRACTICAL, OFTEN OVERLOOKED SUGGESTIONS

- Help your clients find your business location. Make your ads and client communications clear regarding how to find your office. Make your location crystal clear by using a map and reiterate your address in all of your ads. Make your phone number jump off the page. Don't make it time consuming for clients to find your location.
- Spread the word that you're interested in developing new clients, and don't hesitate to ask your existing clients to tell their friends about the value they have received from you. Clients tend to feel really wonderful when they can give you the help you ask for in the form of referrals.
- Set an advertising budget and stay within the guidelines. Barter your services with the media in exchange for advertising, when possible.
- Develop marketing and media consistency. Follow-through with your marketing plan by buying enough ads and facilitating consistent exposure of your message to your primary target market. People have to see an advertisement seven to ten times before they take action.
- Volunteer to work with local charities. Be certain that your promotional objectives are met in the process. In exchange for your time, which is a form of sponsorship, ask for cooperative publicity, or a caption mentioning your "sponsorhip" in advertisements promoting the activities of the charity.
- Become active in local networking groups and business associations. Join committees. Make everyone on your committee familiar with you and your business philosophy. It will reflect on you.

- Create a publicity-based event for charity. Consider conducting a golf tournament for a good charity and enlist leaders in your community to participate.
- Take media representatives to lunch and write them frequently informing them of all the wonderful newsworthy activities and charities you are involved with.
- Carry your business cards everywhere. Hand them to people with whom you engage in conversation. Give out five cards per day. This will put about 100 of your cards into the hands of new potential clients every month. That's 1200 extra potential clients per year. Put an irresistible offer on your business cards that guarantee each client a unique level of value, care, and an enjoyable experience.

–2–

FOCUS YOUR MARKETING
ON THE KIND OF CLIENTS
YOU WANT TO ATTRACT

When you think about the different kinds of clients you could possibly attract to your business, you realize that the opportunities are quite staggering. For many accounting professionals there appear to be so many options that strategic vision may become marred by confusion. Your business system will barely survive or completely thrive depending on the level of client specificity you build into it. As a business owner, your choices may often appear staggeringly plentiful.

You may elect to service small businesses, attempt to attract Joe and Sally six-pack, work with down-sized employees on 401k program decisions, find self-employed folks, work with rich clients on estate planning, work with big businesses, or choose one or more of these options.

Some accounting professionals open their own businesses because they feel everyone needs tax and bookkeeping services. Their strategy is to attempt to attract anyone and everyone to their business. However, as you will see in this book, this is exactly what creates the biggest problem because not everyone is "in" your market.

A fundamental, but very important distinction that makes your business unique is the type of clients your business tends to attract and the distinct reasons "why" they are attracted to you. Your target market consists of that special group of clients you service extraordinarily well. This is usually one or more segments of potential clients who will buy, or have a unique interest in you, your services, and the unique ways you deliver them. It's important to differentiate between attracting merely anyone in your local area versus attracting the unique people who are in your specific target market. Notice that I described your target market as that "special group of clients you service extraordinarily well." This is an important key because there are many kinds of clients who will never understand and appreciate what you do and how you do it. It can be very costly and futile to attempt to market to clients who simply do not make an appropriate match with you or your business. Your aim is to create a marketing system that powerfully influences the right groups of people in your target market to hire you to perform your services.

Your aim is to capture as many target clients as possible—those best suited or predisposed to appreciate and receive the most from the unique business experience that you offer. Your role as marketer is to simply make it easier for those in your target market to discover you and do business with you. Underlying this idea of appealing to the appropriate target market is the reality that you must put the "why" into your marketing in order to attract the right people in the first place. You must give your target market the right reason "why" they should and will do business with you. It is really that simply. When you make begin connecting with the right target market by explaining the most appropriate and self-serving reason why they should contact you, the results are often astoundingly pleasing.

PROFILE YOUR TYPICAL CLIENT TO SELECT YOUR TARGET MARKET

You should continually identify, redefine and clarify who your primary target market is. I am certain that you have given this considerable thought at some point in the development of your business and have already begun to focus your energies on the people you want to attract. The best way to be certain that your target market strategy will be successful is to analyze your existing customer-base. The concept here is that if you identify the kinds of clients you tend to attract, and upon which your business has been built, then you can use that as a model for future success to attract more of those kind of clients. I am surprised that so few business professionals apply this idea of modeling their present clients. Modeling will help you confirm whether you have successfully attracted the kinds of clients over time that you initially set out to capture. In essence, you can use that information to build a better business system, one with fewer leaks. In my mind a leaky business system is one that wastes resources on marketing because it doesn't capture an optimal number of high probability clients during each month that it is implemented.

CASE IN POINT...

Do you think it's an accident that Sara McMillian, an accountant, who spends most of her time networking in local Business

Women's Associations, attracts a lot of clients who are young professional women in their mid 20's to late 40's?

Do you think it's by chance that bookkeeper John Waller, who spends time giving free seminars for small businesses throughout his community, attracts mostly small businesses? In fact, 90% of his clients are small business owners.

Both of these accountants have deliberately thought about the kind of clients they would like to attract. They have focused their energies astutely by selecting their target market carefully. If you look at your client list and you don't notice a specific pattern based on the type of clients you attract, then you have probably settled for what I call "A & E" clients — that's "any and every" client that comes along. There's nothing wrong with that. It just doesn't help you create an easily repeatable marketing system.

It will help you tremendously to take time to learn more about your present clients. You must discover what types of clients have chosen you out of the vast array of accounting and bookkeeping services in your area. You must clearly discover why they have selected you. Often I find that unless you ask your clients why they elect to give you heir business over competitors, then you may be surmising incorrectly.

When we talk about the type of clients that you tend to attract, we must touch upon the demographics and lifestyle characteristics of your customers because it's will be helpful to you to visit a few basic marketing concepts, even if you think you have mastered them already.

DEMOGRAPHICS

Demographics concern the characteristics of your target market including age, income, gender, marital status, number of children and other objective characteristics. Why is this important? Because once you are able to describe your target market with explicit detail, you will exclusively focus your marketing efforts on your high-probability targets, first. How else would accountant, John Waller, know he is better off conducting small business seminars to obtain clients, rather than run newspaper ads for his services? It is because he knows the kind of clients he wants to attract, as well as the best and cheapest ways to find droves of them. Which, by the way, is what most of the chapters of this book will reveal.

To determine the demographic profile of your target market, analyze your current clients either by observation or by having them fill out simple questionnaires, asking them five or ten basic questions while in your waiting area during their next appointment. Tax season is a great time to do this because many clients you normally don't see throughout the year suddenly reappear for tax help. Tax season gives you a prime opportunity to get to reconnect with them to discover new needs.

Here is a sample of the kind of demographic questions you can ask your clients using a questionnaire:

- What is their age range?
- What percentage are male/ female?
- What is their range of income?
- What percentage are single? Married?
- What percent have children?
- What geographic location do they live in (by zip code)?
- What need do they have for my product or service that other people in my market don't have?
- Anything else you think is appropriate.

Once you have the answers to these questions, you'll be able to generate a simple profile of your clients. Your client-base profile may look like this:

- Small business owners — mostly male (or female).
- Ages 25 to 45.
- Average household income level of $35,000 to $65,000 per year.
- Most live within a ten-mile radius of your office.

This research will give you insights about possible people-groups that you are not currently making a marketing effort to capture, but should be. After analyzing your clients, you may realize that your initial business goal was to attract more medium-sized business clients than you have actually captured. Becoming aware of your need to refocus on that goal is imperative in striving for excellence in the future.

LIFESTYLE INFORMATION

In addition to demographic information, lifestyle information will help you make better marketing decisions. Lifestyle measures include attitudes and mind-sets, activities, interests and opinions. Typical questions you can ask your clients to determine lifestyle information deal with reading and media viewing habits, interests, opinions, consumption patterns, attitudes, hobbies, personal likes and dislikes and so on.

Analyzing your current customers to identify these issues can be challenging. However, collecting information about your clients' attitudes, interests and opinions and other lifestyle issues, you will help you begin to discover new ways to market to more people. Once you learn more about your current clients, you will also discover new ways to reach and capture more people who are similar. It's that simple. For example, if you know that your clients tend to drive a certain make of SUV, you can easily rent a mailing list of similar SUV owners in your area. This simple action helps you screen and capture potential clients who may have a similar lifestyle, and income base as your present clients.

Once you have created a profile of your typical target client, the difficult part is over. Now you have a tool to focus your energies, because you have identified a specific, definable, market niche of potential clients. It is best to define five to seven specialized niches that will later guide your marketing and media buying strategies.

If you still are not certain that you see any special patterns emerging through this process, or if you have a start-up business then, simply select several groups of clients that you feel you have a connection with. If you have always been especially motivated to work with small businesses, have your staff join every local organization that caters to entrepreneurs. You can create a special marketing program to include all of the niches that you select.

IDENTIFY OPINION LEADERS WHO WILL ATTRACT MORE OF THE PEOPLE IN YOUR TARGET MARKET

Once you select niches to focus your marketing efforts on, make an effort to identify as many opinion leaders' clients as possible related to each niche market. An opinion leader is anyone who has a strong influence within a niche market. Some accountants give special opinion leaders free services because of their powerful influence in bringing in other clients.

HERE'S ANOTHER GREAT EXAMPLE...

Sara McMillian looked at all of the local business organizations that catered to women to find opinion leaders. Then she decided to become an opinion leader herself by joining the leadership of several associations.

In order to find opinion leader networks at local clubs and organizations, she became involved in key organizations and befriended a committee chairperson who she knew would tell others about her accounting services. She gave them vouchers for free consultations to convince them of the quality of her services and worked to gently persuade them to talk to others about her.

USE THE POWER OF CLIENT FOCUS TO IMPROVE YOUR BUSINESS

Let's have some fun with this idea. Perhaps in the past, you primarily used special price offers as the only way of inducing clients to patronize you. Or maybe your best marketing effort was to run a yellow-page ad. Imagine that this effort attracts a sufficient number of clients during tax season and a few of these clients have spun off into regular monthly payroll and bookkeeping clients.

After reading this book you decide that it is time for a change. You decide to rethink your business to attract a different caliber of client. You determine that if you try to attract a more upscale clientele and charge accordingly that you will probably work fewer hours and have much more satisfaction in the process.

After analyzing your clients by observation, chatting with them a bit, and conducting questionnaires, you realize that most of them have something special in common. A significant number are very successful business owners. You crunch all the numbers and determine that most of your cash flow and profits have indeed been derived from this special group. Scrutinizing your own location, which is near a business district, you make the decision to spend more time trying to attract more members of this elite group of business professionals from your area.

Your research reveals something of their determination to be successful, which tells you that receiving accurate financial feedback about their businesses is necessary in order for them to make precise and accurate decisions. You understand that most of them view their business as a "means to an end" which, to them, means having greater freedom, more time to spend with their family, to travel, and to have fun in other areas of their lives. You also recognize that they are overworked, extremely busy, and have little time left to spend in meetings with advisors unless it's absolutely necessary.

Gathering this information increases your sensitivity to their needs. This process helps you rethink your business so that you can better customize it in unique ways for your target market of small business owners.

You decide that you will reshape your accounting and bookkeeping service to better serve small business owners. You create an Internet web site that allows small businesses in your area to connect with your new accounting/small business resource center. You hire a computer whiz to create a CD-ROM program that logs clients onto your Internet web site. The program has fill-in forms, questions, and helps small business owners perform cash-flow and other important analyses, which improve their decision-making. You provide small business owners with valuable information on your web site, such as how to minimize their chances of being audited by the IRS. You give a series of financial investment strategies to help business owners manage and protect their present and future investments. You offer to conduct a free analysis that will save clients 20% or more on normal expenses.

By focusing intently on the distinct needs of your unique clients, you begin aligning your marketing efforts with your unique business attributes that have attracted them to begin with. This process helps you strengthen your business system, weed out less profitable clients and focus your marketing strategy.

You discover more of their needs, which reveals other opportunities for you to add value to their lives through your business.

More certainty is created as you continue to employ this strategy. If you neglect to make this foundational marketing decision of "client focus" then it will be made for you by chance or by competitors. But you can always mitigate these forces by simply deciding to focus on targeting a specific clientele.

Now it's time for you to make a decision to select a specific target market. You must create your client profile, identify opinion leaders within your market, and think about the self-evident marketing methods that your client-focused strategy reveals to you. Then you will be one step closer to obtaining a further clarified understanding of the results that wise marketing will bring to your business. Great marketing begins with the enlightenment that client focus contributes greatly to your program.

–3–

CREATE A SLOGAN
— A UNIQUE SELLING PROPOSITION —
FOR YOUR ACCOUNTING BUSINESS

Your Unique Selling Proposition (USP) is the core pillar that supports most of the marketing you will ever implement. It has been called your "elevator speech." Imagine that you are in an elevator on the seventh floor of a hotel. A stranger who is riding along with you asks you what you do. You have less than a minute to tell this person the reason your business is different from any other accounting business. What are you going to say? This is far more than a mere academic exercise. If you cannot pass the elevator speech test in practice, then you are probably not able to clearly communicate your primary "point of difference" to your potential business clients. This will mar the clarity of your message to new clients. If this is the case you will unknowingly impair your existing client's ability to tell others what makes your services and your business different, thus hampering your word-of-mouth efforts. Stated another way, by quickly and completely explaining to your clients the specific value that you give, you will fully equip them with the words needed to tell others about the uniqueness of your accounting services. Then your clients will be more likely to become miniature "word-of-mouth" messengers empowered throughout your city to do your most valuable marketing for you. More importantly, you will be able to create a phrase, a slogan, that communicates your point of difference through each of your marketing efforts.

In this session we will look at your competitive challenge, the importance of discovering your uniqueness, the two questions that lead to your USP, and how to write your USP in a compelling way.

YOUR COMPETITIVE CHALLENGE

Your USP is a statement or slogan that tells people why your business is unique. In a world where your clients can easily hire a competing firm to replace you, marketing becomes very important. The world is getting smaller and whether you like it or not, your competition is increasing.

Owning and managing your accounting or bookkeeping firm is not easy when you consider that your competition is always nipping at your heels. To compete successfully, you must offer services and products that no other business offers, or do it in a way that's competitively unique. You must be able to clearly and quickly communicate your uniqueness. You must discover and invent the things that make your business different and then telegraph this message compellingly to your market.

Challenge yourself to discover what your firm offers that no other accounting or bookkeeping firm offers. Conduct competitive research to determine how your business differs from that of your competitors'. When you do you will be on the road to becoming a market leader.

During several consultation sessions with me one of my accounting clients could not figure out how to identify a significant point of difference from her competitors. She racked her brain day and night for a few weeks trying to figure this out. Finally, she decided to craft a point of difference based on elite service. She decided to look at the specialized needs of her 25 top clients and then brainstorm the most unique ways to deliver the best services for each client need. These people were her highest paying clients. She asked each of them to tell her what other things would delight them aside from the good work she did for them. They mentioned going to cultural events, golfing and other fun events they could attend with the money she saved them. My client used all of this information to her advantage. She started rewarding her best clients with tickets to plays and classical music concerts. She also began sending special coffee-table books on topics that interested them, such as golfing. The result was that her best clients valued her for taking the time to support their special interests. Systematically, she asked if they would provide her with four referrals to other clients whom they felt would be pleased to be treated as they had been by her firm. Her clients responded warmly and overwhelmingly. She increased her business by 300% in six months in the first stage of creating her USP. Her unique appeal of "helping clients do the fun things they love with the money and time she saved them" became the basis of her USP/slogan.

Once you invent and discover your uniqueness, then a statement or slogan must be created emphasizing the distinctiveness of your accounting firm that sets it apart from all others. Your USP is a description of the primary unique benefit your business offers to clients. Your USP is the main reason that clients patronize your business and not your competitor's.

You have probably invested a great deal of your own effort and personality into your business. Perhaps this is reflected in the way your offices are decorated and designed. Notice how the services you offer reflect your own unique ideas. The way you care for your customers. The way they respond. Your business is unique. You are, too!

Every client has a distinct advantage and receives a distinct benefit upon entering your establishment, and the experience your business provides is compelling enough to make you different from your competitors, and clients do not hesitate to tell others about it.

In your competitive local market you have no choice but to offer your prospective clients and present customers a highly unique experience. Give them an advantage that is so distinctive— so far above and beyond that of your competitors—that they will have less motivation to do business with your competitors and more incentive to visit you.

There are two primary reasons that you need a USP. First, to help you understand how special your accounting and bookkeeping service is from your client's perspective. Second, to help you communicate the advantages and the outstanding ways your accounting and bookkeeping services really perform for clients. Your USP helps clients understand, appreciate, and continually rediscover new service dimensions of your business.

STAGE ONE: DISCOVER WHAT MAKES YOUR BUSINESS DISTINCTIVE AND ABSOLUTELY UNIQUE

Your USP can be based on superior quality, selection, service, expertise, years in the business, convenience—or any special quality that separates you from other competitors. Pinpointing this is the essence of what your Unique Selling Proposition must be about.

If you are not sure about what makes your business distinctive from your competitors, then this indicates one of two things:

(1) You offer your clients a unique set of advantages and benefits; however, you never identified them yourself, and you are not clear on what those advantages and benefits are.

(2) You offer your clients no unique advantages, and you are simply fortunate to obtain their business in the first place. If this is the case, how do you plan to keep your clients? Whenever a competing business offers your clients an advantage, then they can take your clients from you.

Sometimes accountants and bookkeepers mention that their location is a primary advantage. Location certainly can be an advantage. If your business is located in a business center, your clients may benefit by convenience of location.

But what happens when a competitor opens a business near you? In a location just as convenient as yours—with a fresher appeal; new marble office designs, or maybe faster service?

Often convenience through location alone can quickly become a low-level advantage. You need to consider how to create strong customer loyalty. For your business to thrive and not just survive, you must give clients an incredible advantage. The unique advantage you give must be so excellent that they are willing to drive out of their way to visit and pay whatever is necessary to receive your services.

STAGE TWO: ASK YOURSELF TWO KEY QUESTIONS THAT LEAD YOU TO YOUR USP

You want to bring your clients to an understanding that doing business with an accounting or bookkeeping firm other than yours would be an irrational, unthinkable choice. This is the goal of your USP.

To achieve this goal, start by understanding your clients better than your competitors. Find out what advantage, benefits, results, comfort and protection your clients want the most from your business. Maybe your clients want 24-hour service. You may discover that clients feel safe because you have spent time educating them on the processes you use, or have given them a realistic picture of what their specific outcome will be. Perhaps this makes them feel more comfortable or better protected. If this is the case, "comfort" and/or "protection" could be the basis of your USP.

You must identify an important unique benefit your clients are not receiving from anyone else but are receiving from you.

There are two important questions you must ask yourself and your clients (in person or in survey format) to help you fully discover the uniqueness of your business and to facilitate writing your USP.

Ask yourself:

> **Question One:** What superior advantage, benefit, or improved result does my business offer to my clients?
> **Question Two:** What superior benefit or advantage or increased result am I giving clients that is so subtle that my clients are not even aware of it (and by not making them aware of it, am I doing them a disservice)?

Your task is to make the distinctiveness of your business known to your present clients in multiple ways. So that's why I always tell my consulting clients that everything—brochures, business cards, all ads, and every marketing effort—must be an elaboration and further explanation of your USP.

STAGE THREE: WRITE YOUR USP OR SLOGAN

A strong USP must create a compelling advantage. The better your USP, the less you will have to be concerned about competing on price. When your business gives better service than other accounting businesses, and your clients are fully satisfied, then price-based competition is no longer the key to your success.

Take the answers to the two questions above, and begin crafting them into a statement that reflects the main advantage your accounting business provides. Below are some examples that demonstrate how your USP might be constructed.

USP EXAMPLES

- *Blue Bell Ice Cream:* "We Eat All We Can, And Sell The Rest."
- *A California Law Firm:* "Provider Of Modestly Priced, Fixed-Fee, Non-Rip-Off Legal Services That Anyone Can Afford."
- *An accountant could use this* "We're Your Tax Burden Reduction Specialists."
- *An accountant could use this* "Guaranteed To Reduce Your Overall Expenses By 15% Or More."
- *An accountant could use this* "Finding Funding For Your Start-up Business Is Easier Than You Think."
- *An accountant could use this* "Investment Advice That You Won't End Up Paying For Later."

As you read these examples, did you feel a sense of excitement, or wonderment, or what I call "wow-factor" rise within you? That is the way you want your clients to feel when they read or hear your USP. You want them to know immediately why you are different. A good USP enables them to understand your difference at a higher level. This makes clients tend to "connect" with you much more quickly.

Once you are finished writing your USP and testing it on a few bright clients, use it liberally in the rest of your marketing collateral—in business cards, letterhead, radio-television-newspaper publicity, yellow-page ads, print ads—and in every way that you advertise your business. Put your USP into everything you do in order to promote your business. Let everything your business does become an extension of your USP. And remember: Never promise something that you cannot deliver.

Now you have the key skills you need to craft a USP that is based on the one primary point of difference that separates you competitively. Build your business on it. Expand and enhance your services in the light of it. Make it a real part of your entire business. Then, communicate your USP to your clients and, of course, don't forget to practice it on your next elevator ride.

–4–

COMMUNICATE ENHANCED VALUE PROPOSITION STATEMENTS (VPS)

Value, in the sense that it is most widely used in marketing accounting services, is specific and subjective to your clients. Value represents the perceived advantages, distinctive benefits, and special performance characteristic that you and your accounting firm offer that create unique experiences for your clients. The value of your services will be translated into the maximum price that your client is willing to pay you for your services.

The starting point of all of your marketing should be on the clear and realistic communication, definition, specification and articulation of the precise nature of the value that you will deliver to the client. I call this your value proposition.

As an already successful professional, you know that different clients bring different requirements and perceptions to each consultative session and interaction. However, by looking closely at the common value preferences of your clients, you will see an absolutely unique and powerful pattern emerge. You will be able to create groupings or segments of clients who share common desires for certain kinds of service qualities and values. For example, let's say you have analyzed the quality and value preferences of your clients by grouping clients who have shared common characteristics and have discovered the following patterns:

- Ten clients want you to create a powerful written plan to cut costs or boost sales
- Twenty clients retain you for quick but enriching solutions via telephone consultations
- Five clients hire you regularly to conduct in-house seminars for their staff

Searching for the patterns of desired value amidst your present clients gives you a basis for tremendous marketing growth. Here are your three primary aims in enhancing your value proposition:

YOUR FIRST AIM:

To discover and identify the value preferences of your clients that are hidden amid the present chaos of your business. Then, match the kinds of values your clients want most with a specific value-enhanced service.

WAYS TO APPLY THIS IDEA

Make a list of the value preferences of your current clients. Call a sample of clients by phone suggesting that they spend 20 minutes allowing you to conduct an in-depth interview, asking questions to improve the quality of your service. The questions should uncover the value preferences of clients.

Your interview questions might include:

- What do you value most about the service we provide?
- If we enhanced the value of the service we give you by 10 times, what would that consulting intervention experience be like? Please elaborate.

YOUR SECOND AIM:

To create well-clarified value propositions that you can articulate and communicate to help clients treasure and understand the enhanced value given through your services. Use them in ads, brochures, on the phone and in face-to-face client situations to communicate the precise kind an quality of value you give.

WAYS TO APPLY THIS IDEA

Look at the notes you took from your in-depth client interviews and "hunt down" the hidden values that your clients talked about. List the advantages and then convert them into Value Proposition Statements (VPS's). Your list and corresponding enhanced Value Proposition Statements might look like this:

- Creating a written plan that boosts sales or cuts costs because it makes the client feel safer during times of turbulent financial crisis.

Corresponding Enhanced Value Proposition Statement:
"The plans that we create for you give a constant flow of certainty. You will feel safer in turbulent times, you and your people will have the strong sense of protection and of being safely surrounded by the best ideas, advice and strategies. Our plans will teach you what needs to be done. You'll know exactly how to do it. By doing it day after day your people will get better, become more efficient and your business will grow stronger."

- Allowing clients to contact you for service by phone because of the need for quick answers in times of chaos.

Corresponding Enhanced Value Proposition Statement:
"This program gives you access to my ideas 24 hours a day. When you need priceless idea gems and cost-saving information about how to deal with a technical problem, you can call me and I'll be there to guide you, help you focus, and sort through the chaos that robs you of your productivity. Your business will be back on track for good by creating three new systems that will guide your decision making. I will then give you all the access you need and my best on-the-spot instant solutions by phone consultations. You will experience freedom, clarity, and total focus."

- Conducting in-house seminars for the staff of your clients to continuously analyze and upgrade productivity levels.

Corresponding Enhanced Value Proposition Statement:
"My training gives your staff new skills to help them evolve and progress, consistently surpassing all past and expected future capacities. The kind of training that I perform starts with the most complete analysis of your staff's performance, which you will not find anywhere in your industry. I will customize a training program that systematically upgrades employee skills to more

advanced levels of technical proficiency. I will encourage and motivate your staff to enthusiastically apply at least 95 percent of the new skills that they learn or I will not accept payment for my services. My training will be advantageous and will induce your staff to take on new patterns of progress and professionalism in representing your business every day."

YOUR FINAL AIM:

Use the value-base that you have worked hard to develop within the pool of your present clients. You must attract more groups of clients who share the same kinds of value preferences.

Here is an easy, yet powerful process for attracting more clients with similar value preferences as your present clients:

STAGE ONE

Meet with all your present clients systematically. Take clients to lunch or meet at their office to present them with a value summary of past services performed and to confirm their rating of each service you have performed in the past. Your value summary should list all of the value-enhanced services that you performed for each client, including comments from letters of praise that were sent. The value summary should also have room for a score that the clients can fill in to measure their level of satisfaction for each point on a scale of 1 to 10.

The point of Stage One is to solidify in the mind of clients three foundations. First, this communicates to the client that you care very much about enhancing the quality of their experiences with your business. Second, you are reminding your clients of all the enhancements you have given to them. Third, it helps you see which value-enhanced services are most important to them and how to expand them.

STAGE TWO

With a complete understanding of all of the enhanced values that each of your clients want, begin sorting the value summaries that you developed in Stage One. Sort the summaries into groupings based on the similarity of value preferences. When you finish Stage Two, you should have five to seven groups of clients with common value preferences.

STAGE THREE

Create a simple and logical strategy to find more clients from each of the value preference groups. Model your present clients from each value preference group by asking yourself how you attracted them in the first place. Look back on what marketing methods you used to attract them to your program. Determine which associations they belong to, where more similar clients are likely to be found. Make a marketing ideas list for attracting more people from each value preferences group.

STAGE FOUR

Identify and list the newest and best marketing methods that will successfully help you to attract more potential clients using your preference groups. For example, knowing that you want to attract potential business consulting clients who value the quick speed of your telephone consulting services might lead you to connect with businesses who already appreciate fast technologies, such as telephone conferencing services, internet providers, etc.

Your aim in communicating enhanced value statements in all of your marketing approaches is to position your business in the minds of your clients based on the kind of value that you give to them. You may also use enhanced value statements as special tools to make present clients aware of the special magic they experience when doing business with you.

—5—

POSITION YOUR FIRM TO STAY AHEAD OF COMPETITORS

Your firm must develop a "share of mind" of the market you serve. This means all of your marketing messages must continually promote your "point of difference." As we have discussed earlier, the primary unique advantage or benefit that you offer must be so enticingly extraordinary that it causes people in your market to clearly understand what makes you different. Over time you will begin to earn a special position in the collective mind of your target market. In this session we will discuss the basics of your positioning challenge. Your challenge is to have a different position from your competitors in some special way. Below we will create your Five-step Positioning Plan.

THE KEY TO POSITIONING

The people in your target market are probably oversaturated with advertising and marketing information already. Your marketing messages may not get noticed. Those who see your advertisements will identify a need and categorize your business in their minds, or ignore your message completely. The key to positioning is to stay ahead of your competition by finding a special hole in your market and filling it in an exceptionally unique way. A hole is a void. It is an area of need, which is pressing, and is either not being fulfilled by competitors, or ineffectively being fulfilled.

People in your market will often select attributes—benefits and advantages—that are associated with a particular accountant. When they think of this particular professional, the attributes they have associated with him or her emphasizes the reason for selecting them. When a client needs to receive a particular kind of service, the firm associated with that attribute usually comes to mind first.

When people are in the market for someone to help them with pre-retirement issues, one particular accountant may "pop" into their minds ahead of all others—the one who has established a reputation of expertise and trustworthiness in that area—and no other accountant is usually considered.

YOUR FIRM'S POSITIONING CHALLENGE:

Study your competition. Really study the other accounting and bookkeeping firms in your local market and try to figure out what primary unique positions they are battling for.

If you study your local market carefully, you will discover that most accountants and bookkeepers in the market tend to compete on price or some other generic attribute.

Let's look at the Positioning Grids below. Think of the grid as a map of the way your local market views accountants and bookkeepers. Just for this example, it may help you to imagine that you are about to start your business for the first time and enter your market as a brand new accountant or bookkeeper.

If you look at Positioning Grid A, you will notice that accountant 1, accountant 2, and accountant 3 all compete on low price, and they are tax-service-only firms. Then accountant 4 enters your local market, just before your business opens. Accountant 4 gives clients a little more service than the other accountants and charges a premium price for the extra service. Accountant 4 has a distinct position in the local market. Accountant 4 is different in some way from all the other accounting firms.

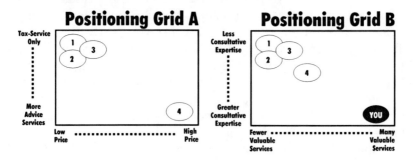

Now look at Positioning Grid B. You decide to change the rules of the local marketing game a little. You open a full-service accounting firm in your local area. You hire retired business experts, a start-up business counselor, tax-auditor, negotiating specialists, you give extensive advice on mutual funds and securities, and you create something similar to a business consulting-services firm. You emphasize your firm's expertise on helping entrepreneurs become wealthy and successful in business and in life. Thus you are taking on a more holistic approach to business. You begin to use every idea presented in this book to promote your firm as the premier business and financial services accounting firm and you offer this new expertise to your market.

You spend a lot of time educating potential clients about how your new services will benefit them and how they can enhance their lives by revisiting your business and also obtaining fresh information on your web site. You position yourself as an expert tax and financial specialist while promoting your staff as competent, educated professionals. You speak at local business luncheons sharing your expertise on business accounting, and are always adding extra information about the variety of services your business gives.

As you can see in Positioning Grid B, your market begins to understand that your firm is the accounting firm to visit in order to experience your new business and financial service expertise.

You have created a unique position in your special market by educating your market and meeting more of their needs than your competitors. By demonstrating your expertise and unique services you have begun to carve out a special position in the mind of your target market.

Now, if your price is fair for the service you give, if you attempt to "wow" your clients by over-delivering the value they receive and packaging that value in a special way, then you're going to build a unique reputation in this new position. You will have put your business well on the road to successfully positioning yourself in the mind of your market.

Of course it is imperative to mention that you can create a special positioning strategy for more than one market. If you analyze your client base, you will discover that most of your clients— approximately 75% to 85%—already come to you for a very specific reason. Understanding this you put yourself in the best position to capitalize on this by formally using this "reason" as the basis of your positioning strategy. You will in a short time begin attracting more clients who already identify with the "reason," but had no idea that any professionals had this expertise to help them. When you start formally promoting this aspect of your image people simply have a better understanding of what it is that you can do for them.

FIVE STEPS TO POSITIONING YOUR FIRM

1. Make a list of the firms that are competing for your target market. Consider including other types of indirectly-competitive businesses, such as tax attorneys, business consultants, if you also offer similar services. Try to be somewhat broad in scope.

2. Next to each competitive accounting and bookkeeping business, outline its position. What kind of clients do they attract (ages, incomes etc.), how is each one different from the other competitors?

3. Use this grid to plot each business. The bottom axis of the grid must contain a measure, like price, or speed, *but it must be the main way that the firms in your specific local market tend to compete.* The other axis must be the service attribute that is *most important* to the clients in your local market (See Position Grid A and B)

4. Find a unique niche in your market and fill it. Think about repositioning your business in your market by offering something that your clients value that is truly different and unique. It might be as simple as offering clients dinner when they visit (i.e. pizza and soda) during tax season, or you might decide to enhance other aspects of your business in more elaborate ways.

5. Describe your niche in a detailed, but short, phrase, such as: "The accounting firm that helps you make more astute security investments." You might want to rework your USP to make it better in the light of the new insights you have received in this session on positioning. Or perhaps you will decide to do the opposite by creating your positioning strategy around your preexisting USP. The choice is yours.

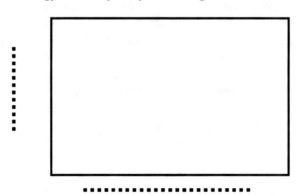

Remember that a good positioning strategy takes time to fully implement. But now that you clearly understand your positioning challenge, and have the tools for implementation, you will soon be miles ahead of your nearest competitors.

Your aim is to now break down your positioning strategy into definable steps that your business will take to gain the new position that you have set your sights on. I suggest that you continue to think about your primary positioning goal as you read the rest of this book. You will discover hundreds of potential steps and ideas that you can use to gain a more clearly defined position in your market.

–6–

POSITION YOURSELF AS AN EXPERT IN YOUR LOCAL MARKET

Understanding which aspects of your skills, talents and knowledge are most valuable to potential clients will give you a competitive edge. If a large number of people in your market are hungry for your expert knowledge on the topic of "keeping more of the money you make," then discovering this is exceptionally valuable to you. Simply stated, you can translate your understanding of this market need into tangible marketing programs that highlight your expertise at the center of the message. This suggests radio interviews on business radio; a column in local publications, speaking programs at local association meetings, television news interviews and much more. All of your programs would then be centered around your highly-focused message of "keeping more of the money you make," which would make a great unique selling proposition.

You must learn how valuable your personal talents, time and resources are to your clients, and in order to create an effective marketing program. Fully understanding your professional worth and finding the hot expertise-based topics that your market is hungry for helps motivate you to give something back to your community.

Whether you acknowledge it or not, you certainly know more about your special expertise, than the vast majority of your local clients do, and probably at a far higher level than most of your competitors. Now is the time to expand community awareness and knowledge of your expertise to the highest level possible.

Why subordinate your expertise? Why hide it? Why not promote yourself within your local market with greater respect to obtain higher recognition of your expertise in new ways? It's time to reveal, communicate, and share it in bold new ways.

Doing this means turning your expertise into outward public communications that you initiate to reach out to your local market on a consistent basis. You must obtain coverage in your local media to become differentiated from your competitors. Consider speaking at special public events. Submit articles to your local newspapers and magazines. Publish your ideas in newsletters and magazines in your industry—perhaps even beyond your local geographic market. Organize and articulate your expertise in a plain, simple and easy-to-apply ways. Consider have a ghostwriter help you organize your ideas into articles, chapters of a book or a booklet in your area of expertise. You can distribute information to your market in many forms. If your business specializes in giving clients greater security by assuring them that you will reduce their tax burden systematically, then publish your ideas on your systematic formula that reveals to clients whether they are candidates for your services. You must dedicate your efforts to establishing your expertise, and educating and informing your public in new ways.

The key to establishing your expertise is by educating your clients to apply your ideas in ways that give them a clear, distinctive and valuable advantage. This makes your advice worth listening to because it serves the best interest of your target market. When you find a profoundly interesting message that instantly appeals to your market, then people will appreciate you for your knowledge and associate this expertise to your business. When you disseminate a message that is real—one that helps people in your market save money, make money, create a simple plan for sending one's children to college without hardship, etc., this engages the attention, respect and acknowledgment of your market.

Another way that you can develop a higher level of expertise in your local market is by creating a credible, information-rich newsletter or short-run magazine that goes to your clients and other key people in your market. I know many business owners who do this via e-mail (called an e-zine) as well as with a printed and mailed newsletter. Each issue must contain well-written highly targeted articles that create tremendous value for potential clients. You can offer expanded versions of the same newsletter articles to local newspapers. If you develop an excellent relationship with a local editor, you will be able to convert your newsletter articles into regular column topics consistent with your business mission. Consider using your newsletter as a cross-promotion vehicle by highlighting other noncompetitive businesses in exchange for their client mailing lists.

Here are six surefire ways to become a leading expert in your field or local market:

1. Read everything that you can get your hands on to stay on top of the industry trends, developments and forecasts. Subscribe to trade journals covering your area of expertise. Look for ideas that are valuable to your specific market. Synthesize your research into a simple, workable, results-producing plan that you can share with your market. Your own experience-based advice will usually be unique and is better than reiterating the ideas of others.
2. Consider having a professional ghostwrite a book for you that you can share with the press, local newspapers, trade journals, consumer magazines. Offer to give the publication to local bookstores in your area and allow them to sell the book and keep all of the money for themselves—just for promoting the book.
3. Create a special report. You can have organizations give it out as a bonus or let them sell it for pure profit. One financial consultant created a publication for businesswomen on how to invest for success and gave copies to the local Chamber Of Commerce and Small Business Development Council to distribute. She positioned herself as an expert financial consultant.
4. Put on seminars throughout your market. Cooperate with other businesses that reach your market by holding seminars at their facilities. For example, work with Small Business Development Councils and Chamber of Commerce Small Business entities, etc. You can conduct free or low cost seminars on how to save money on taxes. Begin hosting regular breakfast and lunch meetings at a restaurant to speak on your most valuable topic.
5. Approach local radio and television talk show producers to see if they are interested in interviewing you on your topic of special expertise. Mail or fax news releases about your availability and how your expertise profoundly helps their listeners. Purchase time on local radio stations for fifteen-minute or half-hour shows.
6. Continuously send out publicity releases about news, trends, and law changes—how these developments will impact people in your area—to all local publications.

-7-

POSITION YOUR BUSINESS AS THE PRIMARY INFORMATION RESOURCE IN YOUR SPECIALTY

Here's a market niche that is crying to be filled. Reposition your company as the source for specific information—as the firm with a special expertise in your local market or on a special topic—and you'll be amazed at the increase in business that results. Associate your personal expertise and qualifications with your firm. Tie your expertise and the strengths of your firm together strategically.

First, do some homework. Read everything you can get your hands on to keep abreast of vital trends, developments, and forecasts that relate to your specialty and local market.

Write a book or report that you disseminate through press releases and trade journals. Make the publication available free to anybody who wants it. It can also be distributed for free, or sold by people who own local bookstores.

Approach bookstores, and offer to allow them to sell your publication and keep all the money for themselves—just for showcasing the book. If it's a report, you can have it given it out as a bonus, or have them sell it for pure profit. You're getting all the free publicity you could hope for—and the only costs are your writing- and printing-expenses.

Put on seminars throughout your area—either free or for a low cost. You could team up with other business experts, who have complimentary products or services and who are noncompetitive with you, to organize the seminars. For example, as an accountant, you could get together with a financial planner, an attorney, and a management consultant, and cooperate to conduct seminars on how entrepreneurs can protect and increase their wealth in the year 2000 and beyond.

Buy time on radio stations for half-hour shows. In fact, you can get on radio talk shows at no cost simply by calling them and applying. You can become the keynote speaker at all sorts of organizational meetings. You can host regular breakfast and lunch meetings at your facility (or at a restaurant) on the subject that you're an expert in. You can publicize yourself and your information product.

If you become widely recognized as an authority (and this takes time) you will instill confidence in your customers. This is a form of branding. In other words, It's a powerful method of "brand recognition," which automatically leads customers to you and your accounting services. One obvious way to do this is to title your company under your name. Use your picture in your ads and sales literature. However, when you make yourself a personality, follow through with superb service and quality, otherwise, negative word of mouth will rapidly decrease your image. An alternative more impersonal strategy is to promote your brand of business—almost as a franchise—that delivers it's own unique form of expertise.

Start sending out lots of press releases. You'll have reporters calling you. Start a local, regional, or national telephone information hotline service. You can have a free, informative recording. At the end of the recording, you could make a proposition similar to the following: "If you want more information, call this number and talk to one of our consultative specialists."

You can create a web site that promotes your business as the primary source of information in your area or subspecialty. You can create an e-zine—a newsletter by e-mail—to give fast updates on your area of specialty. Conversely, you could have a paid hotline that gives valuable advice that you can sell to people. It's inexpensive to run and can generate leads for your business.

Every business has untold opportunities to educate. For example, a stock-brokerage firm should educate prospects about its services, the investments it has available, its financial strength, the number of people it employs in research to help the client, the trading staff, special expertise of key employees and other interesting and helpful facts. Beyond the standard research reports it should have books and reports that teach and encourage stock-and-bond investing. The firm could have a book for large investors entitled, "How to Manage Your Own Private Mutual Fund," or a book for small investors entitled, "Why You Should Buy Mutual Funds And Not Try To Manage On Your Own." Beyond that, there are thousands of interesting articles to reprint and books to give away that can be effectively employed as lead generators.

As you probably know, it's troublesome to receive a call from a telemarketing trainee trying to clear the road for some stockbroker or a brassy guy asking intimate financial questions in the first thirty seconds of the conversation. But if I ordered their free book, I've got to listen to what they have to say, because they have expert information to share and I want to receive it. That's human nature.

—8—

RESEARCH THE REAL NEEDS OF YOUR CLIENTS

Far too often I see accounting business owners and managers deciding which issues they think their clients will be most concerned about. They attempt to anticipate which services their clients will like best. They guess at which marketing messages will work best. In doing this they try to anticipate their clients' needs and wants without confirming any of their own impressions. You pay a heavy price when you do this because you risk losing touch with your clients. You risk losing your connection with clients when you assume too much or think you know more about what they really want or need than you actually do. The solution to a lot of marketing problems tends to surface when you interact with the people in your market. This requires you to take time to really listen to and connect with the people you serve.

As an expert business marketer, you have an obligation to find out what your clients really want and need from you. How should you do this? Here are a few very simple marketing approaches you can use to maintain a connection with your clients.

CONDUCT CLIENT INTERVIEWS

This method is very simple to do: It consists of continually asking your clients directly what they want and need. You will call them up. You will visit with them. When they visit you, you will ask their opinions of your service and what else they would like to experience through your business. Mail your clients a five- or six-question survey form that asks them what else they want from your business. Create a survey form on your web site to elicit new needs.

LEAD A FOCUS GROUP

Conduct a focus group, consisting of several clients, who can help you become connected to their needs and obtain feedback on how you are performing. Don't hesitate to ask your clients what specific services you should add, or extra-special touches, to completely create a "wow" experience for them. One accountant conducts focus groups every three months consisting of five-to-seven clients. During the focus-group meetings, he acts as a moderator in a high-powered brainstorming session. He simply encourages the clients to use their imaginations to think up ways to improve the experience that they have with his business. These sessions have been very fruitful. Some of the ideas that have surfaced include giving away ad space to his clients in highly productive publications. He has a very interesting arrangement with a prestigious local magazine. He barters ad space with the magazine and it actually costs him nothing.

HIRE A MYSTERY CLIENT

Another productive, but less used way to learn more about your clients is to hire a "mystery client" to receive services from you and your staff. A mystery client is a friend or paid researcher who visits your business undercover and then provides objective feedback on the quality of the service experience. During the service encounter, have the mystery client ask other clients in your waiting room why they selected your firm, or what they feel is the biggest need your firm fulfills for them. Have your mystery client ask questions of your staff that gives you specific answers. Then, if you feel comfortable, consider paying the mystery client to go undercover to competing accountants to do comparative research there. The results will change your outlook about your business entirely.

Armed with the new perspective these methods yield, you will be empowered to make improvements to your present services. You will obtain the knowledge necessary to optimize your business, tailoring it for your target market in ways your competitors have never thought of. You will simply see new opportunities that your competition probably will never see because you have taken steps to get outside of the myopic box that they are still inside of. You will be able to effortlessly make the dynamic changes required to attract more clients with less effort. You will dimensionally apply the insights you receive from your research into your firm's appearance, presentation, offerings, services and into your marketing approaches.

The results of your marketing efforts will increase, once you clearly understand what your market really wants from you. It would be a waste of effort to try to be all things to all people. This is like trying to study for an exam by reading and memorizing everything on the topic of the exam. A better approach would be to narrow the topic by selecting to study only the important things that you know will be on the test. And if you could study only the topics appearing in the actual test questions then you would score a perfect 100% on the exam. In your business your clients create your test—they know what they are looking for in an accounting firm—so they always have the answers you need to your most pressing marketing challenges.

This is the kind of power that market research gives you. It will take the guesswork out of your marketing completely if you use it. This means that your promotions and ads will embrace this newfound and enlightened understanding of your clients' world and what it means to live in it. This will cause you to improve your marketing approaches dramatically. Your new direct mail letters and postcards will contain a profoundly fresh sense of empathy, sincerity and understanding of the real hopes, wants, needs, problems and desires of the people in your market. When people begin to discover that you understand them at a higher level, they will respond to you, your offerings and all of the other inducements you will be sending to them.

My promise to you is that if you research and satisfy the real needs of your clients you will engage their interest in your business in a unique way. It will be as if they have a new static charge that attracts them toward your business for newfound reasons. All that you must do is carefully listen to your clients and make small changes in your business to give them more of what they want as time continues. You will become a private investigator, whose job is to uncover the real needs, desires, and aspirations of your clients. You will discover that some clients who stopped patronizing your business will sense a new excitement and some will return to you. Others who may not have thought of your business before may begin to become interested in you. Why will this happen? It will occur because you will be learning and addressing the true issues that your clients feel are most important to them.

After researching the needs of your clients you might discover some issues that you had based your selling propositions or marketing methods upon that were unknowingly meaningless to your clients. And you may find that you have unintentionally ignored the issues which were most important to them. This whole client research process is like playing hide and seek to find client needs—it is like a game in which you both win. Once you find their unique needs and satisfy more of them, you and your clients win together.

Researching the real needs of your clients will transform your business in a multitude of ways if you will diligently do everything I have described in this chapter.

–9–

INCREASE YOUR USE OF PROMOTION ACTIVITIES THAT CONSISTENTLY YIELD BETTER RESULTS

Here I will give you the simplest and most practical way of optimizing your marketing program in a very short time. The strategy is a three-step method that requires you to track all of your marketing methods and select the methods that out-perform all others consistently. As easy as this sounds I am always surprised to discover how few firms take the time to determine which of their marketing methods yield better results than all others. At my marketing seminars I tell my participants that for the same investment of time, dollars and effort, they could just as easily implement a marketing approach that yields 10 clients or 110, for the same investment of resources. It is not uncommon for some accountants to continue using marketing methods that yield mediocre results while simultaneously underutilizing more successful methods. I explain that it is time to make a decision to cut the mediocre methods from their program, and stress the importance of remixing the resources that have just been freed from mediocre marketing into more successful methods. I give you the same advice.

You improve your results by running your most successful marketing methods more frequently, or perhaps creating larger ads, and/or employing an array of marketing- intensifying strategies that we will discuss in this chapter. If you are testing a new marketing method, do so on a very small scale and pay for increases out of your profits. Now this might sound like common sense to you and I, but I am perpetually perplexed by how few business people attempt to aggressively increase the use of their most successful marketing methods. This session will reveal the foundation for identifying your most successful strategies and rechanneling your resources to intensify your use of them so that you will get better results faster.

If you take a close look at the marketing activities that work best for you business, you'll probably discover that most of your best clients came to you by word-of-mouth. Word-of-mouth occurs when your clients tell friends and relatives about your business. They use your services and are so pleased with them that they tell more people. It is not uncommon for accounting firms to enhance their reputations and attract a larger number of dedicated clients by referrals. However, when you ask accounting business owners how much of their resources are used to invest in referrals, they usually say none. Therefore, their primary marketing activities are out of "common sense alignment" with their basic business generation strategy. Make certain that you align your marketing investment with the areas that most of your clients tend to come from. This give your marketing results an instant lift.

I want you to pinpoint where the bulk of your clients come from. Have you ever taken time to find out how most of your clients first learned about you and what brings them in for subsequent service? If special promotions in your local newspaper have been most effective in bringing in new clients, why would you continue to spend resources on other low-producing forms of promotion?

Maybe you are not completely clear about which of your promotion efforts have been most successful in attracting clients. Now it's time to put a solid tracking system into your business system. I want you to trace your results from the origins of your marketing investment to your media choices and the responses from actual clients. This means taking time to ask each client how they heard about your firm, what brought them in and why they picked you over competitors.

This topic often astounds me because so many business owners never take the time to learn which of their promotion tactics have worked best in the past. They simply do not know for certain which ones to increase. Some make the same marketing mistakes for months or years because they do not attempt to track their results to determine which efforts work best for them.

STEP ONE: ASK YOUR CLIENTS THE "MILLION-DOLLAR MARKETING QUESTION"

Your must determine how most of your clients first learned about you, and what motivated them to hire you. So, the key question you must ask all of your clients is, "How did you first learn about us?" I call this the Million Dollar Marketing Question. The power of this simple question is amazing because it helps you track which of your marketing methods work best. It gives you fresh decision-making insights about which methods you must scrap and which you must keep. You must continue to ask clients what influenced them to hire you after their initial visit—thereby giving you a complete picture of which of your marketing messages and media strategies works best.

You will gain another important benefit on a completely different level by asking the Million Dollar Marketing question. You will show your clients that you really care about them because you considered them important enough to ask how they learned about your business.

STEP TWO: CAREFULLY CONSIDER THE ANSWERS YOU RECEIVE

Next, write down all of the responses to the question about how your customers first discovered you.

Take a good look at your list of responses. You may feel surprised by the some of the client-generation recurring patterns that you discover in the responses. It's usually such a wonderful learning experience to tally your responses as you determine how most of your clients first learned about your business.

Some walked in because they were visiting the office next door. Some many have discovered your ad in a local newspaper. Some may have learned about you because friends referred them. If they are regular clients you may discover the specific cues that tend to remind them to come back. All of the insights you receive are highly valuable to you. Be an investigator. Have fun discovering what has influenced your clients to hire you.

If you have never asked your clients these simple, insightful questions that track their in-roads into your business, then you will surely be in for a pleasant surprise. You may even be shocked to discover how much you didn't know about how your clients locate you.

When I ask accounting and bookkeeping office managers how they have attracted most of their clients, most of them say they are not sure. I usually ask them to start tracing this information with their clientele. After they do this they normally tell me that 70% to 90% of their best clients come through referrals. That's when I sit back and ask them a demystifying question, such as, "If referrals are a huge part of where your business comes from, then how much of your money, time and energy do you spend on generating referrals?" Usually they will look at me and say, "None" or "Little". That's when I begin to get really excited about the tremendous opportunities that my client is about to discover. Usually once I convince my client of the value of tracking client flows and readjusting marketing decisions, I'll say something like; "Can you see the power of aligning your marketing efforts with the natural force of referral marketing that has already been a catalyst for increasing your business?" The typical response is, "Absolutely." Astute business owners and managers understand the power of aligning their marketing actions with their growth strategy.

Don't miss out on this incredible, but very simple idea. Take time to learn more about how you are attracting your clientele.

STEP THREE: FOCUS YOUR MARKETING EFFORTS ON YOUR MOST EFFECTIVE STRATEGY

If you identify that the majority of your business results comes from something other than where you spend most of your time, money, effort, and emotional energy, then you could likely boost your business dramatically in only a month or two by realigning it. I want you to redirect your efforts, your attention, your energy, your promotion dollars, your time, and all of your other resources toward the marketing methods that are already producing the highest results for you.

One accountant discovered that 90% of her clients came to her because of her print ads in a local newspaper. She was also buying radio commercials which she never tracked. We tracked the responses for all of the media she used and determined that the radio pulled very little business for her. I mentioned the obvious to her, that perhaps she should transfer the money she would otherwise invest in radio and television to other kinds of print ads. She made that simple shift and it gave her a higher level of effectiveness for the same level of media-dollar investment. It's so simple and so effective. It's common sense marketing that you can use immediately to obtain compelling results in your business.

–10–

FINDING NEW TARGET MARKET OPPORTUNITIES FOR YOUR BUSINESS

Opportunities to expand the scope of your marketing efforts already exist all around you. I am confident that this chapter will challenge you to profoundly improve your marketing approach by opening your eyes to a profitable client capture opportunity that you may have never thought of.

It utilizes a special seven-step need-finding system. You may want to go through the seven-steps several times for practice before finalizing decisions to make significant changes to your business.

I have discovered that many innovative business owners who demonstrate a unique flair for creatively marketing their businesses seem to understand this seven-step process intuitively.

STEP ONE: THINK OF YOUR BUSINESS AS IF IT WERE IN A BROADER MARKET

If you ask most accounting and bookkeeping business owners which market they serve, they would probably say the "tax-return/ bookkeeping services market." But if you really look at what the most successful accounting businesses are promoting, it is not the service itself. It is often a very specific value-added benefit outside of the generic features of the service. Value-added benefits include things like prestige, your unique expertise, and your ability to pamper clients in a unique way, or give extra fast service.

In looking from a broader perspective, I recommend that you look at things such as your personal talents, your dreams, and your gifts for the special elements that you should expand upon in creating a truly different business experience for your clients. If instead you focus only on generic service aspects that others can easily copy, then your "uniqueness" will not sustain you for long. Your aim is to look at the qualities of the services you offer and try to add more valuable things to them. This helps you take your business to an entirely different "level." You can more easily see opportunities to add extra bonuses and value-added aspects by choosing broader market from which to think about your business. Looking at your business from a broad market perspective helps you set a new pace for yourself. If you are used to thinking about your business narrowly and solely in terms of the accounting services you offer, you'll miss seeing the opportunities that a broader market perspective provides.

For example, if you decided to take your business into the "small-business services market," your newly-selected broad market, would open up a whole new set of possibilities. You would create special relationships with other small business suppliers, seminar providers and perhaps with others folks who have unique inroads into this special area. Or, if you have decided to focus on the "financial services market," you would broaden the scope of the products and services you sell, which would open up entirely new spheres of clients to you. Consider this, operating from a broad market perspective would give you a strategic marketing platform from which you could sell more services to your present client base and attract new sets of clients altogether. This gives your business an immediate bounce from existing marketing efforts to sell the new services. For instance, you could enclose a piggyback circular about your new services in direct mail pieces that are intended to remind clients to visit for tax services. It is a double-whammy. We'll talk more about using the piggyback idea in different ways in a later chapter. For now, since you are already investing in the mailing, why not use it as a marketing vehicle to sell additional portions from your delectable menu of services. Making this shift to a broader market will usually help you identify and harvest more profitable opportunities.

The key here is to simply broaden your view of the market you are in so that you can uncover more of the needs that the people in the market have. It is mostly a perspective shift. This is your first step toward "outside of the box thinking" about the marketing of your accounting and bookkeeping business. Fresh perspectives do breed new opportunities.

STEP TWO: LIST POTENTIAL CLIENT NEEDS

Brainstorm with your buddies, staff, and clients to create a list of as many client needs as possible. Again, try to think as far "outside of the box" as possible on this step because later on you will have more innovative things to put back "inside the box."

Make a list of as many relevant client needs as possible from the perspective of the broader view of the market. Brainstorm to obtain an exhaustive list of potential client needs. Even if an idea seems crazy, include it in your list. Write it down. Exclude nothing that comes up. Keep the creative juices flowing as you expand your list. Your list should be four to five times larger than the example below.

To stimulate your thinking a bit more try asking yourself why people buy services and products in the broad market you have selected.

For example, if your broad market is the small business market, ask yourself, "Why would people in the small business market buy more services?" or "What extra needs would they have that you might fulfill?" Your list should be even more expansive than the following "small business market needs" list:

I strongly suggest that your give your clients a survey over several months to help you expand this into an exhaustive list of actual client needs.

NEED TO:	
TRACK EXPENSES	HAVE ZERO NSF CHECKS PER MONTH
CREATE ACCURATE CASH-FLOW PROJECTIONS	SPEND LESS TIME ON PAYROLL
CREATE A FINANCIAL PLAN FOR CHILDREN'S FUTURE	OBTAIN A TAX REFUND FASTER
FIND SOURCES OF START-UP CAPITAL	SELL A BUSINESS
LEARN HOW TO CREATE A MARKETING BUDGET	IMPROVE WAYS TO PROMOTE BUSINESS ON THE INTERNET
LEARN HOW TO USE AN ACCOUNTING PROGRAM	NETWORK WITH POTENTIAL CLIENTS
WRITE A BUSINESS PLAN	IMPROVE CASH-FLOW
OBTAIN CREDIT-CARD MERCHANT STATUS	FIND WAYS TO CUT OVERHEAD
CONSOLIDATE DEBT	CREATE ADS FOR PRINT MEDIA
CREATE SYSTEMS TO RECEIVE PAYMENTS	CREATE USER-FRIENDLY COMPUTER NETWORK SALES ASSOCIATES
COMMUNICATE IN SECOND LANGUAGE	CREATE A SAVINGS PLAN
FIND SMALL BUSINESS-FRIENDLY BANKS	OBTAIN GOVERNMENT GRANT MONETIZATION
COLLECT RECEIVABLES MORE QUICKLY	CREATE A PLAN TO RELEASE DEBT SOONER
CREATE A PLAN TO RELEASE DEBT SOONER	CLEAN UP BAD CREDIT

STEP THREE: FORM "SUB-MARKETS" USING THE NEEDS LIST

Start this step by selecting five to seven of the most pressing specialized needs from the list. Choose those that you think are most important to clients and very specific. Some find it useful to imagine that they are a client as they begin to rank needs. You will use your top five to seven specialized needs as the basis for different sub-markets.

Group similar or related needs with each of the first specialized needs you've identified. For example, small business owners have a "need to obtain start-up capital", and that's pretty important. So we'll put that one down first, below. Next, cluster other related needs with this first specialized need under it—i.e. to obtain start-up capital. Do this for each of the top five to seven specialized needs. This is called need clustering because you identify a specialized need and a cluster of related needs that go with it. See the examples of clustered needs below:

STEP FOUR: GROUP SPECIALIZED NEEDS

Continue to group specialized- and related-needs together until you exhaust your list. And it's okay to put them under more than one specialized need category, if you think that clients presenting that specialized need also have similar ones. Once your needs list is exhausted, you should have five to seven sub-markets. Think of each of these groups as new clusters of clients with very

SPECIALIZED NEED:	RELATED NEEDS:
NEED TO FIND START-UP CAPITAL SOURCES	NEED TO FIND SMALL BUSINESS FRIENDLY BANKS NEED TO CONSOLIDATE DEBT NEED TO CREATE A PLAN TO RELEASE DEBT SOONER NEED TO OBTAIN GOVERNMENT GRANT FOR MONETIZATION NEED TO WRITE A BUSINESS PLAN
NEED TO CREATE USER-FRIENDLY COMPUTER NETWORK SALES ASSOCIATES	NEED TO LEARN HOW TO CREATE A MARKETING BUDGET NEED TO LEARN HOW TO USE AN ACCOUNTING PROGRAM NEED TO CREATE SYSTEMS TO RECEIVE PAYMENTS NEED TO COLLECT RECEIVABLES
NEED TO CREATE A FINANCIAL PLAN FOR CHILDREN'S FUTURE	NEED TO CREATE ACCURATE CASH-FLOW PROJECTIONS NEED TO HAVE ZERO NSF CHECKS PER MONTH NEED TO COLLECT RECEIVABLES NEED TO IMPROVE CASH-FLOW NEED TO LEARN HOW TO USE AN ACCOUNTING PROGRAM NEED TO CREATE A SAVINGS PLAN

Need to spend less time on payroll	Need to learn how to use an accounting program Need to find ways to cut overhead Need to track expenses Need to improve cash-flow
Need to clean up bad credit	Need to have zero NSF checks per month Need to create accurate cash-flow projections Need to track expenses Need to improve cash-flow

specialized needs to whom you can send highly-targeted messages about your firm.

STEP FIVE: NICKNAME THE "SUB-MARKETS"

Review the specialized need groups and assign a nickname to each one based on the importance of the characteristic specialized need.

STEP SIX: THINK ABOUT WHY PEOPLE IN EACH SUB-MARKET BEHAVE AS THEY DO

This step alone could take an entire book. The more that you observe, research, and interact with each sub-market segment you identify, the better your marketing program will become because you will understand the needs of the people in that niche intimately. That's the key to successful marketing. You must learn as many details as possible about them. Find out what they read, which web sites they visit on-line, what they buy and how they

NICKNAME:	SPECIALIZED NEED:	RELATED NEEDS:
Start-up Entrepreneurs	Need to find start-up capital sources	Need to find Small Business-friendly banks Need to consolidate debt Need to create a plan to release debt sooner Need to obtain government grant monetization Need to write a business plan
Sales Crews	Need to create user-friendly computer network sales associates	Need to learn how to create a marketing budget Need to learn how to use an accounting program Need to create systems to receive payments Need to collect receivables
Family Financial Planners	Need to create a financial plan for children's future	Need to create accurate cash-flow projections Need to have zero NSF checks per month Need to collect receivables Need to improve cash-flow Need to learn how to use an accounting program Need to create a savings plan

EMPLOYEE-RICH BUSINESSES	NEED TO SPEND LESS TIME ON PAYROLL	NEED TO LEARN HOW TO USE AN ACCOUNTING PROGRAM NEED TO FIND WAYS TO CUT OVERHEAD NEED TO TRACK EXPENSES NEED TO IMPROVE CASH-FLOW
CREDIT AWARE CONSUMERS	NEED TO CLEAN UP BAD CREDIT	NEED TO HAVE ZERO NSF CHECKS PER MONTH NEED TO CREATE ACCURATE CASH-FLOW PROJECTIONS NEED TO TRACK EXPENSES NEED TO IMPROVE CASH-FLOW

buy it, etc. Write down your ideas and take careful notes about each of these special sub-market segments.

STEP SEVEN: ESTIMATE OF THE POPULATION OF EACH OF THE SUB-MARKET SEGMENTS IN YOUR LOCAL MARKET

Find out how many people from your local area fit into each sub-market segment. Try to estimate the size of each sub-market segment. This will give you an indication of which has the greatest potential. Larger segments—those with more people spending more money—are usually great places to start promoting first. Consider some of the special ways you might select to reach each sub-market with your message as you put some numbers to your estimates.

CONCLUSION

Now you have a way to organize your marketing efforts in a more specific way around the needs of several niche segments of clients. You should create highly targeted marketing—with unique offers, messages and separate mini-marketing efforts—for each segment of clients that you have identified above.

Keep in mind that in order to service newer sub-markets, you may need to take on more equipment, services, resources, staff members, and possibly larger or totally new facilities. Consider these capacity issues and the degree to which you want (or don't want) to remake your business to accommodate them. You may decide to begin your effort by targeting only one sub-market and then add extra segments to your plan later. I know that you will always use conservative caution and plan your growth far enough in advance because that's how smart people in your field tend to work. And in my opinion, you must be among the brightest in your industry if you are studying how to improve your marketing efforts by reading this book. Select only a handful of those in your field have sought to study how to improve the marketing systems of their businesses.

–11–

ANALYZE YOUR GEOGRAPHIC MARKET
FOR NEW OPPORTUNITIES

This session is all about improving your business by finding more clients through geographic marketing analysis. Here we will perform a very simple geographic assessment by modeling your present client base. Then we'll determine if your present marketing efforts have been aimed at your geographic hot spots, which are areas offering excellent quality, high-probability clients. If you determine that you have not been hitting your geographic hot spots with messages about your firm, then I will give you some suggestions for doing so. If you have already been marketing using geographic analysis, then I will make some suggestions for improvement.

I do not know how you chose your present office location. I hope that you performed some kind of analysis to determine how compatible your office location would be with that of your target clients. If you didn't, I am certain that your experience at your present location has since caused you to form some very astute conclusions about the quality of your initial location decision. Whether you are near of far from your clients, you can always improve your ability to find untapped opportunities geographically because there is potential business all around you.

Interestingly, geographic and demographic information about your target clients tends to overlap. Even common sense tells us that your wealthiest clients usually live in the wealthiest neighborhoods. Better business clients lease more upscale offices.

While these issues are basic they are also important. One of my clients, an accountant, had a terrible time trying to bring clients into his office because he had moved to a select location which was inconvenient for many of them. In order to retain them after he moved he literally had to hire extra staff to visit clients in their homes. This was time-consuming and costly, however he soon learned that it gave him a tremendous competitive advantage. How so you ask? While his staff was performing tax-related services for his clients in their homes, they gathered a lot of information about the clients' neighbors. Through this information gathering process, they developed a very clever and highly successful referral system that added 80% more clients in one tax season by asking each client for referrals to their neighbors.

Think about the geographic location of your business. Do the business districts and neighborhoods in proximity to your office contain your target clients or do most of your clients reside further away? Perhaps you feel that it's not necessary for you to be in close physical proximity to your market. While this could be true, you may have overlooked some other opportunities that geographic marketing analysis will uncover.

You must become very familiar with the zip codes, business districts, housing developments, telephone number codes (first three digits after area code), Standard Industrial Classification Codes and other geographic indicators of your main target clients. Many accounting professionals simply look at the kind of clients from which the bulk of their business is derived to determine their target clients. They closely study the geographic indicators associated with their target clients to create several carefully crafted profiles that can be used to create geographic maps of their business territory with overlays depicting where the bulk of their clients exist.

Your first challenge is to find you're geographic market "hot spots"—places with high concentrations of potential clients that closely resemble your best clients. Again, the easiest way to determine those hot spots is to model your current client list. By examining where your existing clients live and work you can be sure there are many others like them in the same geographic areas.

Here is a simple five-step plan that will help you to analyze your geographic market for opportunities to find more clients who are like—as in, "modeled" from—your present clients:

- **Step One:** Look at the current client list in your computer database or customer mailing list. Sort your list by client zip codes and run counts to determine how many reside in each zip code. If you do not have a list of clients you can do a quick informal survey to begin building your database.
- **Step Two:** Obtain a map of your city and county that is subdivided by zip code. Make sure the map shows the zip

codes for each area with a clear delineation of streets. You can obtain a map of zip codes for your area at your local library. Ask a local reference librarian for a map of your city with a zip-code overlay.

- **Step Three:** Sit down with both your map and your client list. Count the number of clients you have attracted from each zip code. Put this number, with a circle around it, in each of the zip code subdivisions on a copy of your map. Then, locate the street locations of your clients.

- **Step Four:** Put a large red dot indicating where your business is located on the map.

- **Step Five:** Now stand back and look at the patterns. Look at the zip code areas containing the largest number of clients. How close are they in proximity to your business? What percentage of all of your clients do they represent? What is the average and farthest distance clients have traveled to work with you? How many, or how few clients do you pull from short- and long-distance locations? Based on this information try to determine where the "hot spots" are for your accounting business. Locate the clusters of streets and specific subdivisions where your clients reside, or if they are businesses, note the commercial districts on the map. You may notice that certain geographic areas seem to pull more clients. If this is the case think about the factors that have contributed to attracting these extra clients. Try to isolate all of contributing variables related to your place of business and the location of your clients.

This simple five-step procedure should give you some insights about your market from a geographic vantage point. Perhaps you will observe certain geographic areas which are lagging and decide that opportunities for increasing your efforts to market are better there. Or maybe you will consider a different approach altogether. After some thought, you may decide to focus your marketing efforts on the geographic areas where your marketing has been performing better. My point is that you now have another marketing tool—another way to organize and execute the delivery of your marketing messages—so that you can implement a better geographic marketing strategy.

With your geographic analysis completed you must choose specific business districts, neighborhoods and/or streets where you will make a stronger effort to disseminate messages about your accounting services. Here are some suggestions for putting your message out into your geographic hot spots—many of the ideas presented here are discussed in greater detail later in this book:

- Send a series of letters to your present clients in the geographic hot spots which contain the most clients asking for neighborhood referrals. Perhaps you will select three to five different geographic hot spots within which to begin your campaign. Consider asking clients in these areas outright for referrals to neighbors in their area. Tell them in the letters that you would appreciate learning about other potential clients in their area. This strategy tends to work well to stimulate word of mouth because you already have a high concentration of clients in that hot spot. It will be likely that one person may have up to three or four people in their neighborhood recommend your services to them. This strategy allows you to saturate that hot spot with word-of-mouth in favor of your business. (See chapter on referrals for more ideas)
- Take a few day trips through several neighborhoods or business districts where your best clients live. As you are driving, ask yourself, "In which of these neighborhoods do I have the greatest potential for promoting my business first?" Start with the areas in which you feel that you have located a large enough base of prospects with a high probability of becoming your clients.
- Consider using doorhangers in hot-spot areas with a very special and enticing offer to try your accounting services. (See chapter about doorhanger promotions for more ideas) You may decide to hire high school students to place doorhangers on office doors of small businesses in primary "hot spot" areas, as well. Perhaps you will decide to test setting up a small temporary satellite office in a high traffic area — with large banners during tax season.
- Send out postcards with your web site address (URL) to targets in these areas. Another great idea is to contact a local newspaper serving a hot spot area to put a free standing insert or one-page newsletter from your firm inside their newspaper deliveries. You could also buy a small highly-targeted mailing list of

residents only in your hot spot areas. Instead of mailing to everyone in your city you could send more mailings to a few hot-spot neighborhoods with special offers for prospects to try your services. This provides you with a targeted and focused saturation marketing strategy in an area with higher-probability potential clients.

The insights you will receive from geographic analysis will be very revealing. Consider new and exciting ways you might like to test and combine many of the other enriching marketing ideas present throughout this book in conjunction with your geographic analysis to generate more business from your "hot spots."

–12–

EXPANDING THE LIFETIME VALUE
OF YOUR CLIENTS

The concept of Lifetime Value is so empowering for marketers of accounting services because it reveals the real worth of developing long-term relationships with your clients. In this session we will look at the power understanding Lifetime Value gives you to expand a client's value to your business by marketing at a much faster rate than most of your competitors.

You already know that you must invest time and money wisely to obtain clients. I submit to you that until you appraise the true worth of your most valuable asset—your customers—you will never really know how much of your resources to invest initially to capture each client. This is a huge problem amidst business owners today. At seminars I usually mention the problem of intangible asset-value management that most business owners present during consultations. Frankly, so many business people today just don't have a clue about how to manage intangibles. Thank heavens accounting professionals tend to profoundly understand the intricacies of managing intangibles. And in spite of that you still probably have more hidden opportunities to convert intangibles into cash by employing smarter marketing tactics.

The most valuable long-term intangible asset that you have is your present base of loyal clients. While you may strongly agree with this statement, you may still have taken fewer actions, investments and efforts than are necessary to optimally expand the value of existing clients to your business. Actually, you are probably missing many easy opportunities right now. Most people are never aware, of course, that missing these valuable opportunities creates incongruity in their business, which usually results in cash-flow fluctuations and other related problems. Solving the overall problem is fairly simple. It requires giving you a thorough understanding of the marketing options that are available to you to acquire more clients sooner and once the become clients expanding their Lifetime Value to you.

You already understand that you have to invest something to capture more clients. Perhaps you think about this investment as a series of advertising expenditures, whether they are yellow-pages ads, direct-mail letters, or other marketing efforts. The key question becomes "How do you make the decision about how much you should invest to obtain a client and how much is too little or too much?" The answer lies in calculating the Lifetime Value of your specific clients, which we will cover in this chapter. For now, I will define the Lifetime Value of a client as the total level of profit a client generates for your business over the life of their relationship with you.

The best way to illustrate this concept is to share a story about how one accountant doubled his business in six-months using several simple, but practical, applications of the Lifetime Value concept. I had an accountant whose name was Stan. Even though you may not be in the same situation as Stan, I think his story will spark your interest in applying the idea of Lifetime Value to your business.

Stan is an excellent tax accountant. I hired him several years ago; he did a great job. By the time January of the next year came around, I called Stan because it was time to worry about my taxes again. You know what? Because I had become a friend and confidant, he told me that his business had decreased by 35% during the course of the year. When I drove up to Stan's office I found him sitting there. He knew of my career as an expert marketing advisor. He asked me what he could do to save his starving business.

I said, "Stan, if I could show you a way to double your client base without writing a business plan or spending a dime of your own money, would you be willing to try my idea?" He told me that he absolutely would because it would put him ahead of where he was before all his losses began happening.

We calculated the Lifetime Value of his typical client and concluded that his average client was worth about $750 in transacted business over a lifetime of three years. I asked Stan if he would be willing to invest at least half or more of the dollar value of his first transaction with a new client to capture them, initially. He agreed, but only if it would bring in enough clients to make it payoff. Stan was ready to use Lifetime Value as the basis of his marketing turnaround strategy.

Stan and I sat for about an hour making a list of all of the noncompetitive consultants and other business folks that he knew. And by the time the hour was finished we had a list of about 45 potential, or what I call, Lifetime Value shareholder partners, to help him market his services.

I held this list of partners up so that Stan could see it. I asked him what would happen if half of these partners sent 5 or 6 clients a month to him. He told me that this might add 112 to 135 new clients to his business, on average, a month. Then I asked him if he would be willing to give those partners 50%, maybe 60%, or maybe even 75% or 100% of the revenue on a first transaction-only basis for referring their clients to him. He told me he would have to try it to see if it worked. It did. He got eleven of the partners on his list to refer 165 new clients to him. On his list he had a relative who was a lawyer, several real estate agents, and many other high-potential partners. Five key people referred a total of 85 clients to him alone. They were the heavy hitters of the list. He hired a couple of students to help him handle the extra workload. And guess what happened? He paid out a lot of money from the initial transactions as an incentive to his partners for their referrals in order to capture these clients in the first six-months. But the residual value of these clients was pure profit for him in the transactions and years that followed. He did it all using only one basic Lifetime Value marketing strategy.

Relatively few accounting and bookkeeping business owners and managers have calculated the Lifetime Value of their clients. Once you understand how to measure the value of your relationships with clients, you will be able to craft a more successful long-term marketing strategy. You will understand the value of your clients in a way that few of your competitors ever will.

–13–

LIFETIME VALUE HELPS YOU OVERCOME YOUR TOUGHEST MARKETING CHALLENGE —CAPTURING MORE NEW CLIENTS—

When you calculate your average marketing cost per client it gives you some important insights. If you use my rule of thumb of investing an amount equal at least to the value of your first transaction, you may discover that you are either over-investing, or more likely under-investing in your clients.

Whether you bring in five clients, fifteen, or fifty this week it will cost you the same for your entire marketing effort. It's a matter of "cost" versus "effectiveness." So, if you think like most accounting professionals, the newspaper print ad, the mail-outs, the radio commercial, the television commercial, and any other form of advertising you use must pull above breakeven for the short-term duration of that campaign for you to feel good about it.

Some accounting and bookkeeping firms, like Stan's mentioned in the last chapter, have mastered the art of Lifetime Value marketing. They look beyond each ad campaign. In many cases they use intensified marketing to pull more leads up-front, knowing that the clients will only be profitable on the back end of the relationship. However, before you consider acquiring new clients at, or below breakeven, which I suggest testing, your very first step is to learn how to calculate the Lifetime Value of your clients.

CALCULATING THE LIFETIME VALUE OF YOUR CLIENTS

Let me bring the concept of Lifetime Value to a practical level for you. Let's say a client brings you an average profit of $275 on the first service that you perform for them. He or she repurchases 11 more times that year (once a month) and your average profit on a repeat service is $67.58. After looking at the collective records of your clients' records, you determine that your average patronage life is three years for loyal clients. This means that your average new client is worth $2,640.30 to you during an average three-year span.

I arrived at the $2,640.30 by adding up the $275 initial profit, plus the additional profit of $67.58 on 35 purchases expected for the next three years. If your marketing and advertising costs to attract and successfully convert a client are $130, then every $130 you invest is worth, a Lifetime Value of, $2,640.30 to you.

Wouldn't you be foolish not to increase your investment on the front-end of your business by perhaps giving your staff 25% of the profit on the first transaction for every new client referral that they bring in? Or, like Stan, by creating a standing arrangement to share first-transaction profit for referrals with other non-competitive businesses that share your target clients.

TO CALCULATE THE LIFETIME VALUE OF YOUR CLIENTS:

1. Compute precisely how much customers cost you by dividing your current marketing budget (including location costs - rent, lease, etc. - if you depend on location to attract customers) by the number of customers your collective marketing efforts are now attracting. You can calculate this per year or per month. This is your average cost to capture one customer.

2. Compute any additional costs to convert a prospective customer.

3. Compute how much in sales you average for those prospects that become customers and the cost for converting those prospects into customers.

4. Average the cost to capture a customer (#1) and the cost to convert a prospect (#2) into a client. This is give you the average cost for producing a customer.

5. Subtract the average cost for producing a customer (#4) from your customers' average initial purchase to give you the profit on their first purchase.

6. Compute your average repeat sale; your average profit on those sales.

7. Compute how much additional overall profit a customer is worth to you over their lifetime of patronage by determining how many times most of your customers come back to you per year and multiplying that by the average number of years your clients actually tend to stay with your firm. Be conservative.

The back-end—all repeat sales after a client's first purchase— is where the bigger profits tend to be. This concept is one of the keys to successful marketing. Once a person hires you, it's much easier for him or her to hire you again and again. It's less expensive, as well, because you don't have to invest as much money marketing on the back-end, to bring them in again, as you do on the front-end, to initially attract them.

On the back-end you will resell, up-sell, and cross-sell more existing and new services to your customers. Reselling is simply selling them the same services they bought before, ideally more often than in the past. Up-selling is influencing them to buy a better, more expensive, more sophisticated, or more expensive service than in the past. Cross-selling is influencing them to buy something else that's related to the original product or service. We will discuss back-end marketing, up-selling and cross-selling in another session of this book.

When you consider the total Lifetime Value contribution that is made each time a patron walks through your door, you realize that the opportunity to expand your business is greater. Have fun recreating your basic marketing strategy by using Lifetime Value to connect your business to more clients more rapidly.

ADVANCED LIFETIME VALUE APPLICATIONS

As you now know, key to using lifetime value is to be able to calculate the profits one customer brings you so that you spend just the right amount of money on marketing you obtain that client. If you spend too much to obtain each of your clients, than you are losing profits on waste coverage, or ineffective marketing. If you are spending too little, you are wasting your opportunity.

The most profitable thing you will ever do for your business is understand and ethically exploit the marginal net worth (Lifetime Value) of your customers.

What is the current marginal net worth of your customers? Again, it is the total aggregate profit of an average customer over the lifetime of his/her patronage—including all residual sales— less all advertising, marketing, and fulfillment expenses.

Imagine that your typical new customer brings you an average profit of $75 on the first sale. He or she repurchases three more times a year, with an average reorder amount of $300. Now, with the average patronage life lasting two years, every new customer is worth $975.

I arrived at the $975 by adding the $75 initial profit, to the three additional purchases per year times the two years they remain a customer.

Once you know precisely how to quantify the marginal net worth of a customer, then you must work with the data.

If a customer will be worth $975, and it costs you $30 to acquire him or her, then every $30 you spend is worth $975. You would be foolish not to increase your advertising budget to secure more customers.

You could, theoretically, afford to spend up to $975 to bring in a client and still breakeven during your first two years of maintaining a relationship with that client.

In other words, this is a method to plot what you can afford to spend to acquire a new client. It is a little obtuse and sometimes hard to calculate, but it is a well thought-out scheme and a prudent calculation for you to make.

If you have modest capital, you could still easily justify spending 100% of the profits for your first sale—since every $75 (the first transaction profit average) you spend to acquire a customer means $900 in your bank account over the next 24 months. If you double the number of new customers, you will double the next two years' profits.

Spend everything you can to justify bringing in a customer as long as the cost for doing so is less than what you are earning in the process. If you feel you cannot afford to spend more than the entire initial sale profit for a customer, just remember that you will be making money on him or her in a few months. Start out spending only what your cash flow can justify, but after a quarter or two of reorder profits, step up the ad budget.

Using Lifetime Value has one other advantage—most of your competitors have no idea what a customer is worth. If their marketing budget is a percentage of sales, then during a recession they might cut their budget. If you continue advertising and marketing at your current level, you'll also have their customers.

I ultimately want you to spend less per customer on acquisition cost—so why am I trying to get you to spend more? I am doing so because this is the most lucrative short-term way to get more new customers. After a while, you can start slashing your cost per acquisition.

Everyone wants as many new customers as possible, but almost no one quantifies precisely what a customer ultimately is worth and how much they can spend to acquire one and be profitable.

LIFETIME VALUE: BRING IN CLIENTS AT A LOSS AND STILL MAKE A FORTUNE

Depending upon the various types of clients you serve, a client is worth a certain average dollar amount to you over the period of your association.

If an average client stays with you two-and-a-half years, and each year you charge an average of $2,000, of which you realize $1,000 in profit, then with two-and-a-half years' worth at $1,000 profit, every new client is worth an average of $2,500 in profit. Some will be worth only $500, some will be worth $5,000—working on the basis of averages. Knowing in advance the average worth of a new client, in profit, allows you to work backwards and figure what you can afford to pay to bring in a new client..

If you knew with certainty that a client would be worth $2500, you could actually spend $2,499 and still make a profit. While I know that you would probably seek to earn more of a profit than this, certainly you could afford to wisely invest $100 to $500 to obtain a profitable client. When you understand their worth over the course of your relationship, then you can justify spending more money to bring them in.

It is certainly justifiable to spend at least what they are worth on the first bill. If the first bill brings in $200 in profit, you might justify spending that $200 to obtain the client, give up the profit on that and be delighted to bring them in. At a minimum, you could spend the profit because your service costs you only time. If you have the cash flow, you could afford to spend both the profit and the actual cost of services.

If you gain a client with $2,500 in average profit for every $200 you spend, you still make $2,300. Every time that you spend $200, you accrue $2,300 to your practice over the following two-and-a-half years. Once you understand that, it gives you great flexibility in what you are willing to spend to bring in a new client. You could even hire a sales rep and say, "Every time you bring a new client in, I'll give you 100 percent of the first month's billing."

Lifetime Value is very powerful, but most people do not see it. When you do, you see how much you can afford to spend for acquiring each new client.

You must calculate the time value of money. If you acquire a new client worth $2,500 over the lifetime of purchasing with you, what would you be willing to expend to obtain that client? If you spend $0 per new client, that's a real bargain. If you spend one visit's worth of revenue, or the first billing, that, too, is a low amount compared to their worth over time. Most people do not have that long-term perspective.

FURTHER EXPAND THE LIFETIME VALUE OF YOUR MOST LOYAL CLIENTS

Your most loyal clients provide your accounting practice with incalculable value, not only from a direct remunerative standpoint, but also because of the value of the networks, alliances, and ancillary relationships that are associated with these businesses. If you took on no other task except systematically using your most loyal clients as the basis of all your marketing action, then your practice would obtain geometric growth.

A client's lifetime value is determined by how much they enrich your business during the time the client tends to remain with you. If you are not certain how many tend to stick with you on average over time, then you must find out by researching your business records. If someone is with you for an average of seven years and you gross $5,000 per year for the services you render, then the lifetime value of that client is $35,000. Chances are that if you understand the lifetime value of each of your clients, you will see them as potential $35,000 clients and not $5,000 clients that you are barely breaking even to work with. Taking on this perspective of lifetime value can transform your accounting practice by opening up a world of new opportunities for you to explore.

Here are some of the best ways to further expand the lifetime value of your clients:

- Understand that your initial relationships with new clients will cost you more time and effort because servicing new clients requires more time and learning. In addition, you may be trying to start more initial business relationships by "reducing the barrier of risk" for your newest clients. Some accountants try to obtain more business by giving reduced project costing, special trial inducements and other sampling techniques to capture new clients quicker. While it may at times be a wise strategy to give away more service or time at first to obtain clients, it may be setting your practice up for a long-run reduction in lifetime value. To expand the lifetime value of your clients, consider charging less during the beginning stages of a consultation with high-potential clients. Communicating what your client can expect from you builds a higher level of trust instantly.
- Make special "extra-valuable service" offers to your most loyal clients. Increase the number of services you offer

by 10 percent to 25 percent. This elite group of clients is primed and ready to say "yes" to new overtures to receive even greater value from you. Make one extra presentation per year, and consider presenting an extra seminar in a technical field and subcontract the training out to another firm. (One accountant purchases a new software package per year to add to his list of client services. He hires a new junior accountant to learn the software package and in a few weeks he adds a new list of services to the repertoire of his business.)

- Take a moment to make a special client wish list. Contact each client and ask what services they would love to receive from you if you could make them available. Ask your clients what extra results and advantages are important to them and would instantly hire you to perform on their behalf. Use that list as a springboard for increasing your accounting services' offering and the lifetime value of your most loyal clients.

–14–

SET SALES GOALS THAT TAKE YOU TO THE TOP OF YOUR LOCAL MARKET

Many business professionals ask me time and time again "How can I get from where I am in my business right now to where I want to be?" One of the answers I usually like to share is to embrace a higher level of goal setting. I usually say, "Commit to achieving your higher-level goals no matter what comes your way, and be flexible enough to change your strategy when necessary to obtain the primary result you desire." In this session, I will begin by sharing some of my philosophies on how we tend to think about "success and failure." Then I will give you some simple guidelines for improving your goal setting.

The problem is that most people usually set their "success standards" too high and their standards for "failure" much too low. Perhaps you've been doing this too. If you ever find that you feel frustrated when thinking about the progress you've been making in your accounting business, then you too may be doing this. Even if you feel content about your business performance, I suggest that you consider looking at goal setting from the new perspective I will share here because it will help you achieve more with less stress.

You already understand the value of setting realistic goals that take you step-by-step to new levels of business building. And you have probably learned that by breaking larger goals down into more easily achievable smaller goals that you can achieve them faster and reduce some of the frustrations you may be experiencing with any unfulfilled goals that you have.

Never allow unmet business goals become a psychological sign of "failure" for you. Every one of your experiences in reaching for a goal is a learning opportunity. One of the most difficult things to remember is that even the smallest successes are opportunities to celebrate. And oftentimes we need to learn to enjoy small successes before we will be able to truly appreciate larger successes. If you have fewer clients than you think you ought to have, don't get upset. Instead, celebrate your expertise in being able to acquire the clients that you do have.

Use the goal-setting suggestions that follow to reach to a higher level of business and marketing success. My ideas will work for you no matter how long you have been in business.

Here are my simple guidelines for setting and achieving your marketing goals:

1. SET AN OVERALL SALES GOAL

I would ask you to look carefully at the financial picture of your accounting business. Look carefully at the relationship between your cash flow and your marketing investments— especially during non-tax season. Check to see if your business is breaking even during good times and slow times.

If your business is ever below breakeven, then your first realistic goal should be to achieve breakeven during that lull. If you're above breakeven, then you should pick a realistic goal for increasing your sales to a reasonably higher point above breakeven. I suggest you go through all of the information in this book and then come back to this section and begin by completing the Goal Summary Worksheets that follow this section.

In order to create your new growth goals, begin by setting your projected increase at no less than 5% and no more than 25% in the first year during your marketing improvement program. Always give yourself three months to achieve your first minimal monthly sales increase. Later when you feel more comfortable applying more of my ideas to your marketing program you can set a higher overall sales goal.

Look at your overall sales for last year and try to make some rational conclusions about how much more you think that you can conservatively and realistically increase sales by. You can start by stating your overall sales goal as a yearly sales number in dollars, and/or as a monthly goal.

Your overall sales goal may look like something like this:

To increase our total sales from $7,500 on average per month by 15%, to $8625, on average, per month in exactly 90 days from 5/9/03.

2. CREATE SUB-SALES GOALS

With your new overall sales goal in place, begin thinking about how you will break this down into smaller achievable sub-sales goals. Some accountants organize their sub-sales goals by different categories of marketing or methods of advertising, each of which brings in a certain definable amount of business for them. Others organize their sub-sales goals using categories of revenue streams, which are based on client subdivisions. For example, one accountant does this using the following logic: He says, "80% of this year's revenues will come from my present clients, and then I'll test five new marketing methods to generate an amount equaling the remaining 20% of last year's business revenues, then I'll add two more marketing systems to my business to bring a 10% increase over-and-above what we did last year." Your sub-sales goals help you translate your overall sales goal into a "to-do" list of marketing methods for your business. How you organize your sub-sales goals is entirely up to you.

How will you organize your sub-sales goals to achieve your overall sales goal?

Here are a few thought provoking questions you may find helpful:

- How many clients must I add to my business each day, week and month throughout the year in order to reach my overall sales goal?
- By how much must I increase my average client transaction to achieve my new overall sales goal? Is it too high or too low now? What specific changes must I make to increase it?
- By how much must I increase my average marketing cost per client in order to reach my overall sales goal? How can I fine-tune my marketing investment to "invest more wisely" in my clients? Am I investing optimally per client? How do I know that?
- How can we more effectively up-sell, or cross-sell more, or different services to our present client base in order to increase the average number of services most clients buy? What specific product/service packages should we add to the current mix of offerings that we sell to clients.

Formalize each sub-sales goal by writing it down. Remember to also include a benchmark (we're increasing from X to Y, X is the benchmark) and a time aspect with each sub-sales goal. Here is an example:

OUR FIRST SUB-SALES GOAL IS: To increase the number of clients we service by 15% per month, from 112 clients per month to 128 clients per month, within 90 days (or before 7/27/04).

OUR SECOND SUB-SALES GOAL IS: To test four new marketing/advertising media on a small scale. Since we currently use two ads in local magazines that tend to attract 75 clients per month, doubling the number of ad placements by 8/1/04 will increase business to at least 135 clients per month by 11/25/04.

OUR THIRD SUB-SALES GOAL IS: To create one Accounting Cross-Team that increases our present client referrals from zero to 25 additional referrals per month. To do this we will exchange referrals with a successful tax attorney, a business consulting firm, and a local business- seminar provider on 9/1/04. We expect the extra referrals by the end of the same month.

After you read this book, you will begin to realize that there are many more marketing ideas you will want to use to stimulate your sub-sales goals. Many of them will add tremendous value to your marketing program if you first test them appropriately on a small scale. You can add them to your list of sub-sales goals anytime you want. Add as many sub-sales goals as you like. I suggest that you take it slowly initially, and focus only on your most important sub-sales goals. Use only the marketing ideas that are most compatible with your business philosophy. Setting realistic and easily achievable sub-sales goals is foundational to the continued progress of your accounting business.

3. USE GOAL SUMMARY WORKSHEETS TO CHART YOUR PROGRESS

For each sub-sales goal that you have written, use a Goal Summary Worksheet to list the most important steps you must take in order to reach your sub-goals. Break down your sub-sales goals further into step-by-step marketing "to-do" lists.

Some business owners use this system of goal setting in conjunction with their time management systems. Others use the Goal Summary Worksheet and the list of 10 steps as their "To-do list." Use the worksheets, put the pages in a three-ring binder, and check-off marketing tasks after you have successfully completed each one. With each task you complete you are one step closer to fulfilling your sales sub-goals and overall goal.

See Goal Lists and Goal Summary Sheet below for advanced planning:

Goals List	Date: _____

Overall Goal _____
_____

Sub-Goals	By Date
1	
2	
3	
4	
5	
6	
7	
8	
9	
10	

Goal Summary Worksheet

Sub-Goal Number: ☐

Sub-Goal Description:
_____

Ten Specific steps I need to take to achieve this Sub-Goal:	By Date
1	
2	
3	
4	
5	
6	
7	
8	
9	
10	

–15–

CAPTURE HIGH-POTENTIAL PROSPECTS

One of the most critical starting places for igniting powerful changes in the way you look at your business is in discovering how you "think about" your clients. I want you to ponder how you appraise the value of and manage that group of people that you call "prospects and clients." My goal is to help you identify your highest priority prospects and get you started on the road to maximizing the value of your marketing efforts toward those clients.

This may sound a little extreme—comparing an accountant's approach in marketing to car interiors! But I'll do it anyway! Ever notice how some people have messy car interiors and others have exceptionally clean car interiors? What does your car interior look like? Do you take time to clean it periodically? Do you regularly sort through the buildup of spare change in the ashtray? Or is there junk all over the car? Have you ever been shocked and surprised by a high-ranking colleague, whom you were certain would display an immaculate car interior, and upon getting into the car discovered a minefield of Egg McMuffin wrappers? Have you ever been that colleague? I have. But that was during my first few post-college years! My car is getting much better! If you have been there too, you'll remember at some point you got so tired of your messy car that you just had to take some action to correct it. Right? Usually it was because you had to pick up a friend and you didn't want to be embarrassed by the story your messy car tells about you. Well, the way you manage your clients' relationships is a lot like your car in that you often won't take action to make the necessary effort to make positive changes until you're convinced that you absolutely have to.

I want you to take a series of very specific steps to expand and augment your vision of the value of your clients. Try the following enriching action steps.

STEP ONE

List all of your clients in order of their value to you. List clients in order of the total amount of dollars they have invested with you to date. Add up how much each client has spent with you to date, and use that as the basis for listing your biggest clients first. It is easiest to use a spreadsheet, or accounting program to do this. Make certain that you have listed all your clients by putting the clients who have spent the most money with you at the top of the list.

STEP TWO

Divide the list into 10 equal parts, scanning your list from the top down. This means that 10 percent of your clients will be in each group from the top down. If you have 1,000 clients, you will now have 100 per group. If you have 100 clients, there will be 10 per group.

STEP THREE

Look at your top three groups of clients who have invested the most with you over the lifetime of being your client. Add up how much all these clients have spent with you to date and compare this number to your total sales to date. What do you discover?

STEP FOUR

Stand back and ask yourself, "How well have I managed this first group of my top 10 percent clients?" Are they given special attention? Are they sent more meaningful communications? Have you also sent special gifts that nurture your relationship, such as books or magazine subscriptions on their favorite vacation getaway? If not, why not find some creative ways to connect with their special interests as valued friends and colleagues?

How about your next two groups of clients? Look down from the top at your best 20 percent and best 30 percent top clients. How have you managed your relationships with these clients? What opportunities do you have to obtain more business from them just by asking for it? Probably a lot more than you think.

Also look carefully at the defections — the clients you are losing. Find out what is distinctive about the defectors. Compare your most loyal clients and defectors across every possible dimension. In which ways do they differ? A major bank had dramatically different patterns of client defection. Careful analysis revealed that clients with lower education tended to be more loyal, while those with more education had a lower tolerance for bank errors. Some accountants find that defectors consist of clients who feel that they do not receive adequate results fast enough for the level of resources invested. I want to motivate you to look deeply at your clients to find out what makes them most loyal. Then you can focus on attracting the ones who will become your "star" clients.

The point is that your top clients present you with a whole new set of opportunities you may have never fully explored. You will always release more value back into your business by introducing new services to your best clients first. If you are testing new offers for selling add-on technical services, seminars, and additional training programs or anything else — start by testing your new programs with your best clients first.

–16–

INFLUENCING YOUR BEST CLIENTS TO HIRE YOU MORE OFTEN

In addition to persuading new clients to hire you to perform more services, you must also develop deeper and more profitable long-term relationships with that select group of clients that you call "your best clients." There are only a few of them in your business. These represent the most profitable top 15% to 30% or so of your client base. These are the clients who spend more with you and have bigger Lifetime Values. Your aim is to graduate more existing clients from the lower recesses of your business on up into this category of clients. Your top clients will also be more receptive to your offers to hire you more often.

Think about how much it would benefit your business to shift 10% of your best clients who hire you quarterly to once-a-month clients. If you could persuade more of your best clients to use more of your accounting and bookkeeping services, more frequently, your business would almost automatically grow more profitable. I have seen many accounting professionals increase their businesses by three or four times their original size within a year just by following the methods similar to the ones outlined below.

BUILDING MORE MEANINGFUL CLIENT RELATIONSHIPS BASED ON TRUST AND ENRICHMENT

I view your role as an accounting and bookkeeping services marketer—not as a salesperson pushing products and services on clients—but as one who provides satisfying and enriching services that add real value to their lives.

As you know, your job is to work hard to attract the right clientele. You also know that you must cater to your clients by providing enriching services. As your clients have more and happier experiences with you, they will even want more of your services because they see what you offer as truly valuable. You want your clients to experience superior results, and receive real benefits from hiring your services. They trust you and your staff. They have entrusted to you a critical part of themselves and their lives. Persuading them to express their further confidence and trust in you by purchasing more products and services is often a very easy thing to do. They will become happier with you as they obtain greater results from you. They will feel nurtured by the advice that you give. Your clients already recognize that they receive tangible benefits from you.

Your objective is simple: To drill-down deeper into the world of your clients and pour more value into their lives. You can do this by sending them meaningful communications more often; Offering them more opportunities to grow through the process of education; to create irresistible long-term programs in which they achieve their financial goals; to open up your business and offer valuable products and services to your clients.. Below you will find six suggestions for systematically influencing your best clients to transact more often with you.

SIX WAYS TO INFLUENCE YOUR BEST CLIENTS TO HIRE YOU MORE OFTEN

I have discovered six secrets that consistently release an uncanny power to any businessperson who uses them. They are, in my opinion, when used together, the six prime movers of marketing. I have listed them here and we will look at them in greater depth in the next six consecutive chapters.

1. Communicate personally with your best clients by phone or letter to maintain a solid relationship.
2. Create special events that acknowledge your best clients and make them feel special
3. Develop and offer long-term buying programs that make it easy and fun for your best customers to visit and use your products and services.
4. Use appropriate pricing incentives to persuade clients to try new products and services.
5. Develop a back-end of products and services that your clients can choose from.
6. Promote the products and services of other non-competitive businesses to your clients.

–17–

COMMUNICATE PERSONALLY
WITH YOUR CLIENTS

One of the best ways to foster an excellent relationship with your clients is to communicate personally and interactively with them by phone, letter, and e-mail. The key is to share value-rich ideas and maintain a strong positive connection with them. Growing that connection into a strong bond is the key to creating a long lasting client relationship. The secret is to create a sense of community with your clients.

You bond with your clients by sharing information that relates to their interests. Nurturing them by overdelivering incredible service is another way of doing this. Another key is to perform targeted follow-up by phone or letter to ensure they are happy immediately after you have serviced them. It is just too easy to allow your clients to remember you only during tax season instead of purposefully making your presence continually relevant to them.

A couple of days ago I received a mailing from American Express. I have several different American Express cards for business and for personal use. I receive more wonderful letters, more surprise certificates and gifts, more account updates, more alerts, more communications from them than any other company. And do you realize what this does? This subconsciously prejudices me to want to use my American Express Card over and above the other cards that I carry. This is a very simple but very effective strategy.

An accountant I know owns an upscale practice. She continuously communicates with her clients to increase the quality of their relationships. She has learned that she can more easily stay relevant to her small, home-based business clients by sending them high-quality information. She sends information they can use to get results. She sends printed newsletters, an e-zine (e-mail magazine) with links to articles on her web site containing highly valuable information. On her web site she also places relevant articles written by other small business owners. She sends full-color postcards to clients reminding them to visit her web site when updates are made available. Her e-mail list has grown to 15,000 clients, many more than she can now handle— and now she is selling space advertising in her newsletter to attorneys and other non-competitive service-providers who also want to reach these people. This is a great example of the impact that developing a continuous communication strategy can have on your business. Your clients will think of you as a valuable source of information and ideas.

CREATE A STRATEGY FOR CONTINUOUS COMMUNICATION AND FOLLOW-THROUGH

I have a client who has improved his accounting business by 25% in four months. He calls clients and sends letters He has representatives visit his clients to conduct free analyses to make suggestions for improving cash-flow and cutting overhead. He has a well-targeted strategy. He has five different segments of clients— one segment consists of young families who are in debt to whom he sells a packaged software system to reduce debt. Another segment consists of small businesses to which he sells a consultation-based cash-flow improvement program for a nominal monthly fee. His continuous devotion to using a strategic marketing approach is the key to his success. Constantly communicating with clients will not produce multiplied results unless it is done strategically.

Your continual communications strategy must be ongoing and have a specific purpose. It must be "self-serving" to your clients. Simply telling clients how great your services are will not do the client a lot of good. Creating an exchange with your clients empowers you to discover new needs and to explain more of the need-satisfying services that you have created for them. You have to make certain that you always put your clients' interest far ahead of your own.

When you sit down to craft a letter or create a marketing campaign think of your clients as very dear and valued friends. Think about the privilege of having the opportunity of becoming better connected and acquainted with these friends. You must care about them far beyond their capacity to spend money with you. You must celebrate with them, fully empathize with them, sharing their heartfelt challenges.

If you share this philosophy of continuous, targeted, empathetic communication, you will be tremendously motivated to have your staff pick up the phone, or send letters with special offers to maintain that connection. Think about the special occasions of your clients' lives. The list of special occasions is long and includes—weddings, engagements, graduations, funerals, birthdays, vacations or trips to special places, Valentines Day, Christmas. Why not consider sending a card, small gift, or an e-mail to acknowledge a unique event in the life of your client?

You must document information about these client lifetime events on an index card file or a database program in your computer. Connect with a special phone call or letter before, during, or after these life-changing occasions. Your clients will be happy because you took a moment to think about them. Conduct a little research by looking in your local newspaper for announcements. Find out about special life-changing events by simply talking to clients. If your client says that her daughter is getting married, or is having an engagement party, try to take an interest in this and find out more.

Use every opportunity to connect with your clients in non-self-seeking and non-commercial ways. Send them magazine clippings, notices of tax law changes that impact them, or articles about their personal interests with a note saying, "Bob, I thought this article might help you." Send your best clients top-selling books you think they might enjoy. Show your responsiveness by sending them reminders that you have taken a special interest in them. All it requires is a little bit of initiative and follow-through. Train your staff to "chat with a purpose" during client visits and that purpose must be to capture personal information, interests, opinions. Then use that information to create highly-customized correspondence. Over time your customers will notice and most will respond back to you favorably.

SEND ONLY HIGHLY MEANINGFUL COMMUNICATIONS TO PROSPECTS AND CLIENTS

In another section of this book we established one of the worst ways to market your practice—that is, by making personal cold calls. This is often one of the primary methods fledgling accountants embrace first because it seems to be the least costly and appears to hold the lowest level of risk. Actually, any marketing action that you take that does not effectively prequalify clients in some meaningful way is a high-risk proposition for you.

One of the ways to lower your level of risk and raise your marketing effectiveness is to increase the level of meaning that is attached to your marketing communications. Remember: Your prospects and clients must become emotional shareholders of your consulting practice. Investigate very carefully the kind of communications that dynamically draw your potential clients into a greater, expanded relationship with you.

Part of the answer to the question, "What will make your marketing work better and most efficiently?" lies in using the power of repetition so that your message cuts through the clutter to be seen by your prospects. However, the aspect of your marketing that enriches and enthralls clients will always be more effective than others because meaningful marketing is more self-serving to the client. So to become a highly successful marketer of your accounting services, you must become the artist, the extraordinary storyteller, the magician and the lover who woos the hearts of your prospects every time.

Eliminate the junk mail and other meaningless marketing efforts. Throw out the cold prospecting letters. Give up on cold telemarketing efforts. Only use powerful messages that contain the most meaning for your target clients.

Here is a powerful way of applying this idea: Start with the marketing methods that you are already using. Immediately add a new dimension to your present marketing methods by including a direct-mail component that increases the value of all your messages. I have a client who is an accountant. She used to just ask her clients for referrals without sending them a self-serving meaningful message attached to the request. After taking my advice she began dealing with her clients more positively by sending them a big box and two smaller boxes of Godiva Chocolates with a special note that said:

> "I just wanted to say thank you for your business in the sweetest way I could think of... by the way I have enclosed two extra special boxes of chocolates in pre-paid self-mailing pouches with a little brag card. If you would be so kind, would you consider sending them to a couple of friends who might be interested in our services too... before the chocolates melt? Perhaps you could take a minute and add a phrase to the enclosed cards telling them the results that we obtained for you. Then you will help us by telling others how much you think of what we did for you. — Enjoy the chocolates!"

You can apply this idea in one of thousands of ways. I have encouraged clients to send travel magazine subscriptions to prospects who love to vacation. I encouraged one client to assign one employee the part-time task of building friendships with prospects by calling and finding ways to give interested prospects samples of their consulting experience in the form of valuable teleconferences and phone seminars. Another client spent time gathering the "hot" interests of customers in a database, and every quarter would send out articles and books related to their hottest interests. These are powerful applications of the idea of finding special ways to increase the meaning of all your communications to prospects and clients, as well as increase the probability that your prospects will respond to you in the most favorable and accelerated way possible.

–18–

DEVELOP DEEPER ONGOING RELATIONSHIPS WITH YOUR CLIENTS

So many business owners and managers view their relationships with clients as "guaranteed." They take clients for granted. They wait passively for clients to return, expecting them to come back for their next tax or accounting service. If you have ever fallen into this pattern of thinking about your clients, as we all have from time to time, I want you to commit to taking a different view. I want you to take the position that you have developed the most valuable investment to date in maintaining your relationship with each of your clients. The longer that you have been in business the more rewarding this approach will be for you. Make a new commitment to yourself to nurture client relationships by taking a higher level of initiative in sustaining them.

Never forget that you must continually earn the respect and commitment of clients during each encounter. Your clients look to you for all kinds of new product and service recommendations. Developing the perspective that your clients will continue to be clients for life requires you to continuously recreate your business by serving them in better ways. It is difficult to deepen client relationships without excellent empathetic service and a consistent and enduring word-of-mouth referral system in place. When your present clients are happy, they actively seek out friends and relatives and recommend them to you.

Your clients are an ongoing source of additional revenue and referrals. Your employees have to be fully committed to your clients. Your aim is to pull clients into your business family and make them feel proud to be a part of your community of clients.

You must ethically "program" your customers to recognize the superior benefits and advantages that they receive when they continue to pursue a relationship with your business. Making your business a part of their lives encourages clients to persuade their friends and relatives to do the same.

The steps you must take in order to build ultimate relationships with your clients are simple:

- Understand that you and your clients share mutual needs, and resources. Your clients need more than great accounting services; they need interaction, connection, answers that give them a better future vision. Clients will choose an accounting firm that they feel recognizes their unique needs, and they'll seek out and patronize the firm that offers more of what they feel they need. Make your business a total resource center for your specific kind of clients, one that helps them reach their goals in many different ways.
- Learn, understand, and become sensitively aware of your clients' goals, needs and resources. Talking with your clients about their personal desires and goals future-paces them toward greater awareness of their own concerns, and helps them to bond with you at a deeper level.
- Stimulate mutual interest with your clients on the phone and in person. Find points of sincere common interest as you chat with them. You must make each client feel that they will benefit greatly from building a relationship with you. Set a long-term plan that gives every staff member the people-skills to demonstrate and express their level of mutual concern towards each client. Your staff must be skilled at sharing the specific benefits your service gives. Then your clients will understand what to expect from the growing relationship they have with you in one-, three- and six-month intervals. Develop a ten-year plan for your clients that precisely describes your goal for specifically how your business will benefit them each year they are with you. It is your vision for how you will make each client's business and financial life systematically brighter in continually different ways. Clients are drawn to people and businesses offering important solutions.

The communication of common interests fosters progressive relationships with your clients. A healthy degree of mutual interest is always important in maintaining client relationships. If you embrace the attitudes and ideas I have presented in this session, by applying them to every client interaction and communication, then your clients will understand how much you appreciate them. Then both you and each of your clients will experience a sincere and lasting connection, but more importantly one that they will always remember.

–19–

IMPLEMENT THE SEVEN-STEP ACCOUNTANT-CLIENT RELATIONSHIP-BUILDING STRATEGY

As an entrepreneur and accountant you face tremendous challenges. Many successful accountants mention that in order to continue to be successful they have to remain focused on marketing activities. Many accountants find this difficult, yet challenging, because they must constantly work to pull their whole business together while simultaneously pushing it forward. Staff members, partners, clients, accounting subcontractors and everyone else must move together in step.

Your accounting business is an extension of you. It shares your personality and becomes a further reflection of you. Achieving success is tough because your productivity depends upon your ability to market your services, sell your clients, create and deliver the service experience while attempting to do all of it yourself. Often, the greatest difficulty lies in your ability to clearly see the value of the services you give. You must determine that it is only by creating and managing the right team-based efforts that your business system works better, faster, and cheaper for you.

No matter which steps you choose for your journey, having a powerful relationship-building strategy in place will create more certainty for your clients and for you. Over time, the environment of your business—the terrain, weather conditions, players and circumstances—change constantly. In the face of tumultuous change, the Accountant-Client Relationship-Building Strategy will serve you well. Here are your seven steps:

STEP ONE

You must develop, nurture and expand the loyalty of your staff towards your business and your clients. Even if you have a skeleton staff of two or three people you must analyze and increase the level of loyalty of your staff. Loyal staff members create consulting efficiency and a foundation for understanding the value of retaining clients. Without the support of a loyal staff, you cannot succeed.

STEP TWO

You must develop loyal clients. How can you attract clients who are likely to be loyal? Some segments of clients are inherently disloyal. When you communicate to each of your clients one-on-one it is important that you influence each client to become more faithful to your firm, you must condition clients to work with you. Ask them how you can do this. This process programs your staff and your clients to focus on loyalty. Let the butterflies flit off to bounce between your competitors, target the honeybees that loyally take your ideas and produce sweet honey-like results together with your firm.

STEP THREE

You must get to know your clients well. You must change as your clients change. Flexibility is important! Pick up the phone and connect with clients regularly. Conduct informal focus groups and in-depth interviews with existing clients so that they can tell you what they are thinking about, and systematically learn what is most important to them. Ask what services they value most. Move beyond the abstract into the specific details and issues that are most valued. Talk to experts regularly and gauge their impressions about which way the market is heading. Be one of the first accountants in your market to know about specific areas of change first. Be the fastest to respond.

STEP FOUR

Create appropriate pricing. Develop client-based pricing by focusing on the results that clients want to receive and basing your pricing on the results. If you sell cassette programs or books, create distinctive offers. For example, instead of trying to sell a book or cassette, inform clients that they can receive your materials for free if they hire you for one to two hours of consulting. You might say to seminar attendees, "If you buy my book, you can expect to pay $25; however, if you want the book free, just prepay for one half-hour of my telephone consulting time."

STEP FIVE

Continuously communicate with your clients. Stay connected and keep listening. The frequency of your regular attempts to stay in touch with clients is very important. If you are not reaching out at least once per month with a unique, highly personalized communication — a letter or special phone call — then you need to make more of an effort. Ads in trade journals leading people to your Web site for a continuous flow of valuable information are powerful. Build relationships by direct mail. One accountant mails small, inflatable desktop punching bags to clients with a message that read: "Stressed out? Call us; we understand and we can help." Using care lines or client service hotlines is another great way to give service and obtain feedback. Give your clients your toll-free number and encourage them to call for free books, recorded technical information, and other gems. Use telephone contacts to check to see that frontline users have gotten the results that your accounting firm was hired to achieve or to alert clients of new updates in the industry. One accountant simply uses the telephone to thank clients for their business after a job was completed — a simple step that most competitors forget.

STEP SIX

You must upgrade the skills of your staff continuously. First you must set performance standards for your staff. This is not easy to do. Create special checklists for each staff position to act as a self-evaluation with specific performance-goal descriptions telling staff members how they will know when they have performed with excellence. Coach and encourage your staff with warmth by imparting your confidence in them to perform well. Become a role model for your staff. Your staff must consist of mature people who are self-taught through experience.

STEP SEVEN

Pull your entire accounting business together continuously, keeping the business in step and in sync with itself and with clients' wishes. Continue to build commitment amidst your staff by taking small steps every day. You must revisit and reconstruct your vision every day and get your staff to talk about how they can expand your vision. This process will be most successful if you share highlights of your vision by telling enthralling stories of jobs well done that are based on actual client appraisals of your business. Give staff honest messages. Let them know that the world is full of surprises, which can impact the business. Remind them that together you can work to smooth out obstacles. Offer them openness and loyalty in return for their flexibility and loyalty. Most of all, you need to create a business- and marketing-plan vehicle that is well thought out.

Making your accounting practice better is a challenge. Marketing pervades your business at many levels. By using the Seven-Step Accountant-Client Relationship-Building Strategy you will see new ways to pull your accounting practice together into a well-integrated relationship-building system.

−20−

BUILD BETTER RELATIONSHIPS

While it's important to get new clients, you should never forget your existing ones. They are your true bread and butter. Nurture your relationship with them and you can build lasting connections. And remember, a happy client is more likely to refer you to others.

Here are six tips to help you build better relationships with your clients:

1. Host picnics or other open houses, and invite clients and prospects. This can be done during the holidays as a "thank you for business," or any time of the year to recognize your clients.
2. Remember important personal details like spouse's and children's names, birthdays, and anniversaries. Most people forget that something as simple as a "Happy Birthday" card or phone call can help build a long-lasting business relationship. If you remember to recognize such personal milestones, and your competitor doesn't, who do you think will get the next phone call when a business need arises?
3. Know your client's business. If you ever see important news stories or articles relating to their industry, make your client aware — clip any relevant pieces and mail.
4. If you know a client likes to golf, suggest one time you meet on the green to discuss business. In other words, always think of new ways to make your client value your flexibility and creativity.
5. Do lunch, breakfast, or tea. Treat your clients to something special.
6. Make office visits. Nothing beats a face-to-face meeting and a good, solid handshake.

FOLLOW-UP WITH YOUR CLIENTS

Professionals often fail to convey to their clients that the clients are important or that the client's views and opinions are important. To overcome this obstacle, professionals should have an initial consultation form that solicits the names of the client's spouse and children, his or her interests, and as much pertinent information as possible. This lets you know something about the client so you can make him or her feel important.

After the visit, you or your assistant should telephone to inquire how he or she is doing, did the techniques work well for them, were they please with their greater tax savings, are they implementing the tax-saving strategies, etc. Indicate that you are always available if they have any questions.

Sending Christmas and birthday cards or notes with a personal touch makes people feel important. It is vital not to drop clients once their problem is resolved.

Pay special attention to your waiting area. Often the magazines and publications offered are worn and out of date. Maintain a high tone by making available new publications on a rack or table. It would be even nicer if the receptionist kept some magazines at the desk, handing them to the client when she or he signed in.

The receptionist should be warm, inviting and friendly. He or she should know something about the client and be able to converse in a meaningful way. If the staff member they are waiting for is running late, the receptionist should announce, "Steve is running a little late. Do you have an errand you need to run or do you need to use the phone to call anyone?"

Do anything you can to make that client feel important.

Consider installing a few computer terminals that are tied to the Internet for waiting clients to work at. When one accountant retires his previous generation of computers, he keeps three in the waiting area for this purpose. Install a television; offer warm and cold beverages, possibly a bookshelf with books on a variety of topics. These are ways to make the individual feel important.

Perhaps another convenience could be the availability of a VCR with a selection of good G-rated or PG-rated movies. What is a $119 investment? Nothing.

You can also acknowledge personal events such as birthdays and holidays. It pays to acknowledge these events for family members as well, not just for the client. Cards are nice. What is even nicer is if the receptionist calls on the morning of your birthday to wish him or her a Happy Birthday. Or if the client has a little girl and the receptionist calls with the following message: "Your accountant, Jim Luden, couldn't call this morning, but he asked me to wish your daughter, Julie, a very Happy Birthday. He is sending some McDonald's certificates so she can take some of her friends to lunch."

What is this worth in terms of goodwill? Give something meaningful that reminds them of you, something that will ingratiate them to you for rendering noble service.

If you cannot allocate your staff's time, it is worth hiring a caller for a few hours or at Christmas time. Instead of sending Christmas cards, he or she will call your clients and say: "Jim Luden asked me to call and let you know that he wishes you and your family the happiest of Christmases (or Hanukkahs) and a very, very wonderful New Year. He hopes it will be a good year for you." What is that worth? It will cost you $5 an hour, maybe $95 total, to call all your clients.

-21-

GET TO KNOW YOUR CUSTOMERS BETTER

Once I spent the entire day with a client who taught me more than I taught him. I relearned an important lesson I had forgotten. The lesson was to get back in touch with the real, live pulse of your marketplace by staying involved with clients, especially as your business grows.

By handling two or three dozen client encounters per week to better comprehend what your customers' interests really are you discover what turns them on. You uncover their true interests and desires. You should take customer service calls once a day and re-read all the indicative customer complaints that are received.

I'm finding that business-people tend to be more inclined to not care about the market, but rather attempt to tell their market what they should want.

The tendency not to become intimately familiar with the desires and problems of your marketplace is suicidal, yet so commonplace.

Not only should you try to spend time with clients, personally investigate complaints, and read all the mail your firm receives, you should talk to a dozen or so of your former customers to see why they are or are not working with you now.

I've always advocated shopping your competition. People respond to ever-changing stimuli and unless you keep a close watch on the vital signs of your marketplace's, your business will die down on you very quickly.

Pivotal changes occur in the attitudes of consumers. They become risk averse, commitment averse, change averse, and action averse, and if you fail to acknowledge this change in motivation, your market could evaporate.

On the other hand, if you start monitoring your sales closely, actually start calling and chatting with past and present customers by actively listening to their felt needs, and shop both your company, as well as your competitor's, you'll gain a perspective advantage that will give you much deeper insights about the offers that your clients will best respond to. Then you translate those insights into all of your other marketing approaches in unique ways. You will carry the understanding that you gain in the presence of your clients into direct mail, and other advertising methods to create infinitely higher levels of overall marketing success.

–22–

THE SECRET OF MAKING CLIENTS LIKE YOU

Customer relationships are the number one asset you have. Sometimes we forget and take for granted the price we have paid to obtain our clients. We must do everything in our power to develop better, deeper, more sustaining and enduring client relationships. You can develop better customer relationships by:

1. Keeping in touch—whether by telephone, mail, e-mail, or in person—all customers want to feel they are special and that you take a special interest in catering to their needs.
2. Providing post-purchase reassurance. Each time a customer hires your service, call him or her a few days afterwards to see how things are going. This will allay any post-purchase dissonance. This provides a great opportunity to demonstrate that you are working for them and that you care. Making this simple effort will make you stand out from your competitors profoundly.
3. Give your clients the best deals and guarantees possible.
4. Preferential pricing—let your existing clients in on the best offers first. Give them the opportunity to buy your sale items before the public does.
5. Building rapport and trust. Be as honest as you can be with your customers. People do business with ethical people whom they can trust.

Keep an accurate and timely customer list. Updating and reusing your customer list is crucial. If you have a solid customer list, you've got a solid client base. Work those clients who have already used your service. If their initial experience was positive, chances are they will be enticed to return. This advice is the main message of this session.

You should run your business as you would expect it to be if you were the client. Constantly look for ways to improve the treatment of your customers, because they will respond to you through the most important vote of all, their sales dollars.

Taking it further, do not accept mediocrity in any phase of your accounting business, particularly in your customer relations and your sales efforts. Those two functions form the basis of every company and serve to separate the marginal companies from the more successful businesses.

A case in point: Why do so many people appreciate McDonald's? It is because of the efficiency, cleanliness, and manners of their employees. How long do rude or slow counter-people last at McDonald's? Consider also their product line. Every time you order, whether in Maine or California, you know what to expect. There are no surprises.

I believe anybody who has a moderate quantity of customers should immediately begin a perpetual communication with their customers to set the stage that they are a trusted friend and advisor.

The way to do this is to send a letter within five days from the time of your customer's first transaction with you:

1. Thank them
2. Resell the value of your company
3. Reassure them of the prudence of purchasing the your services

Such a letter essentially programs the customer to repurchase, revisit, and rethink in terms of dealing with you again. It is always a good idea to first test your messages because they will be different in every situation. Sometimes you might be thanking the client for a recent visit. At other times you may be sending a holiday card, or gift certificate for half a dozen pastries at Panera Bakery with a reminder to visit your office soon.

Consider making your customers an offer of additional services that they can purchase on a preferred basis, or an offer that they can try a new service at an advantageous price— later you can up-sell them to a better and more comprehensive service, if they need it.

The point is, you must continually reinforce the client's buying decisions. This simple action can prove extremely powerful because it builds your long-term and back-end sales. The lifetime value of such customers can be very large. You must contact your customer after that customer has made an initial contact, and have a program set up to reinforce their buying decisions.

Thank the customer and give him or her an opportunity to bump up to a more extensive aspect of your service. Also tell the customer in the letter that because you are concerned about him or her, because you care more than to just make a profit and leave, not to be surprised from time to time if you write to inform and alert him or her of new developments in your business, to keep in touch.

You may have figured the number of times a customer will repurchase from you on their own. But have you considered how the value of a customer increases if you actively solicit them again and again? The key to determining what a customer is ultimately worth to you is the extent of your back-end, or ancillary, sales.

Step one is to upsell or resell right at, or immediately after, the initial sale, preferably at the point of purchase. Then, if you can get them to add another item or service that is synergistic to the one they are buying, you can dramatically improve the profit. Experiment with add-on products or services. Offer a package of related items for a 40% discount if they buy it now.

Contact or visit a customer right after the sale to see how they like their purchase, and offer them a deal on a related product or service. One out of every three customers may take you up on it. Upgrade the sale by cutting $100-off of a superior version of what they are buying, if they upgrade now.

Secure the rights to high-profit or repeat-type products or services that are logically suited to your new customers' needs then follow up with calls, visits or mailings to sell those other products. Consider working with software licenses, bookkeeping supplies, exclusive office products, etc.

For example, if you sell a tax consultation, your return is the charge for consultation, nothing more. But, you can set up a relationship with a marketing consultant that allows you to offer your buyer a discount, with 20% of the profits going to you. Then set up a deal with a consultant for 20%... or an advertising agency... or a local business creative expert—there are a number of possibilities. If you sell something else to 50% of your accounting customers—you could add thousands of dollars in profit to every sale. You could do the same thing with products—software, ergonomic office furniture, etc.

Once you know how much extra income you can earn on the "back-end," you can dramatically expand or increase the amount of money you spend advertising your accounting service for hire.

You can justify spending a lot more time and money cultivating your customers—since they are no longer worth just "A" dollars, but rather they're worth "A" + "B" dollars.

If you do not want to sell other people's products or services, you can turn over your leads or prospects to other companies whose products or services are compatible, and take a flat fee per lead or a percentage, albeit less than if you did it yourself. This quickly increases the lifetime value of a one-time-only customer. If a customer is worth only $20 more, that's $20 more you can afford to spend to get other customers, which can build a pyramid of profit with an expanding customer base.

CREATE A SYSTEM FOR CONTACTING CLIENTS REGULARLY

Set up a regular monthly, quarterly, semiannual, or annual contact strategy, based on test marketing offers to your present clients.

Let's say you have a service your customers should hire you to perform two- to six-times a year. You can send out a letter every month or every quarter in which you acknowledge their importance as a preferred or valued customer. Tell them a bit about what is going on in their industry or in your business, and make them a preferential offer — a better price, or a special combination package not available to new customers.

Be the first to approach them about new services or equipment that you are willing to reserve for them, if they'll call you, come in, or send back the card. By "working" that customer and repeatedly communicating with him or her, you can stimulate many more reorders.

How many more clients will this strategy provide? Every situation is different, and you must test various approaches to find the ones that produce best, but by regularly working your customers, you can usually pull from 20% to 300% additional business. People are silently begging to be acknowledged, informed, given advance opportunities and led to action.

You can use a mail-gram or mock mail-gram, a cassette tape, a card, or a gift bearing an offer. The point is to follow up and test new versions of your approaches against your more standardized control approach.

When they order again, you go right back and work them with an acknowledging letter, maybe external to the package, with different material in the package, and sequential mailings at every month or quarter year. Try to induce your clients to buy more from you by trying different offers.

-23-

USE THE PRINCIPLES OF CREDIBLE INFLUENCE WITH YOUR CLIENTS

In his book, *Influence: The Psychology Of Persuasion*, Dr. Robert Cialdini outlines the most powerful ideas on applying principles of influence that have been explored to date. Here are the best principles and a few spin-off gems that I have tested in my practice with ever-increasing results:

USE YOUR AUTHORITY

Establish your position with each client early on in interactions by demonstrating your extensive knowledge of the industry you serve. A more important point is that you can often help to increase your ability to influence clients by admitting your weakness first. I once was involved with a seminar for *Money Magazine*. A mutual fund investment manager spoke as a panel member at the event. The thrust of his strategy was to disarm the audience. While the other competing panel members were busy talking about how great their short-term fund performance had been, this gentleman told the audience how many poor investment choices he had made in the past. By doing this he was admitting his weakness first. This smart strategist disarmed his audience from the beginning. The strategy worked well because the audience understood that most funds that have performed poorly in the past have a better chance of performing better in the future. He knew that his audience understood the performance factors of funds. As the panel discussion progressed, the genius investment manager had the audience in his pocket. The audience laughed with him and really connected because of his ability to admit his weakness up front. He put his new friends at ease and this increased the authority and influence of the words he used because he showed the audience the superior methods that he had developed from his mistakes.

Finding independent ways to put objective proof of your credentials in front of your clients will increase your authority to influence them. Nothing increases your ability to influence better than having other well-known experts praise and acknowledge you. Creating a tangible way to capture the praises of other experts takes some initiative. Jay Abraham, for example, attracts many well-known speakers and authors to his business seminars. It is not uncommon for camera crews and audio technicians to corner the most well-known personalities, capture dramatic opinions, and obtain endorsements from people such as Michael Basch, former VP of Marketing for Federal Express, simply by asking them what they liked about the seminar. The key to increasing your perceived level of authority in marketing your practice is to make independent proof of your tangible credentials available to more people.

USE GENUINE SCARCITY

Dr. Robert Cialdini executed an interesting study on the effects of using scarcity to dramatically influence the sale of beef. The study was conducted using the telephone sales staff of one of Dr. Cialdini's students, who owned an importing company and sold beef to retail food outlets. The company's clients were phoned and sold beef in one of three ways. One set of clients heard a standard sales presentation before being asked for their orders. Another set of clients heard the same sales presentation plus the information that the supply of beef was likely to be scarce in the upcoming months. A third group of clients received the standard sales presentation and the information about a scarce supply of beef, too; however, they also learned that the scarce-supply news was not generally available information — it had come, they were told, from certain exclusive contacts that the company had. Thus the clients who received this last sales presentation learned not only was the availability of the product limited, so also was the news concerning it — this is the "scarcity double-whammy."

Do you know how much more beef the second group sold by adding a basic scarcity message to the exact same sales presentation? The second group purchased 200 percent more beef than the first group. What was the sales and marketing result of the beef sales messages with the scarcity double whammy? Sales of the last group were 600 percent more than the clients in the first group, who only heard the standard sales message alone. Isn't that powerful?

As a accountant, you offer clients a unique set of advantages that are so exclusive that clients cannot obtain them from anyone else because the service you offer is customized and exclusive. You can elect to offer your clients an experience that is genuinely scarce and valuable, and you can do that just by reinventing and repositioning the way you market your business. You can share information about upcoming events that will impact clients profoundly in ways they may not know about yet. You can research and find exclusive information by delving deep into the intricacies of your niche field specialty. Most importantly, you can tell your clients that only your exclusive accounting team has invested time and resources in researching this little-known information about these certain events and has created a very exclusive plan to help them improve their business — creating your own "double whammy." By positioning your accounting service from the vantage point of scarcity, you will heighten client demand dramatically.

RECIPROCATION
Be the first to give the best service, information, and concessions. First give, then receive, and then give again. Most people do not wait for the exchange to adjust the balance of the power in business negotiations and relationships. As an accounting professional you will have much greater success in receiving information, if you first give information. This is an incredible principle. Try this experiment: Next time you are visiting a client ask yourself how you want to be treated by that client. Then, immediately start giving your client the very thing you want to receive. If you want your client to appreciate and understand you, begin your interaction by lavishly showing this client your appreciation and communicating how much you understand them. Then observe what you receive throughout the entire interaction. You will receive back from your client the same flow of energy that you are giving. If you want to appear to be more interesting to your client, then become more interested in the company and watch the client's interest in you come alive. This is another powerful yet very subtle principle.

LIKING
Liking involves building rapport and making friends to influence clients. Dale Carnegie discovered that one of the secrets to building better relationships with anyone was to tickle their ears by using the word that consistently sounded sweeter to them than

any other word. That word is their name. Here are three additional areas that increase the chances that a client will really like you:

- Find a series of similarities, things that you hold in common with your client.
- Uncover areas for giving genuine compliments.
- Continually discover new opportunities for cooperation.

CONSENSUS

Consensus is the process of demonstrating to your prospect or client the responses of many other people. Using this idea can be as simple as showing the past successes you earned for other clients through your services, such as telling clients the story of how you helped them achieve a certain result for others. Other applications of this principle would be to use a multitude of testimonials that are similar. The idea behind consensus is that you can demonstrate to your prospect your effectiveness by recounting other client's experiences that they can identify with.

One of the best ways to apply this idea is to incorporate it with the concept of "Social Proof." Seminars could be conducted, as can live Internet chat sessions or live phone/video conferences, with large groups of potential clients. Have clients become involved in these events to share how your accounting services have given incredible results. Have a few actual clients share the results you've given and challenges you have resolved for them. Existing clients can tell potential ones how you successfully and powerfully converted their problems into high-profit opportunities through your accounting expertise. Prospects will be in a state of mind to receive your presentation with much greater levels of acceptance because their peers will have helped you disarm them.

Use the principles of influence ethically to obtain results that help you and your clients receive the outcomes that are built upon excellence.

–24–

LISTEN INTENTLY AND
INTERACT WITH YOUR CLIENTS

During my consultations I have visited many different accounting firms in different areas of the country. I have analyzed the important skills that leading accountants actively and consistently use in interacting with their clients. As I have compared the different skills with the real results obtained by accountants using quite varied approaches. As I have observed a success pattern emerge, I noticed that some accountants listen to and engage their clients profoundly. While some conduct mostly "one-sided" conversations—either by not letting the clients get a word in edge-wise or not offering much advice at all. You will only be successful in the eyes of your clients by listening intently and responding appropriately to their needs. This is a highly competitive profession, and the firm with the most loyal clients survives the longest and achieves truly sustainable success.

LISTEN TO YOUR CLIENTS

To develop the kind of meaningful relationship with clients that is based on really knowing them, and empathizing with them, you must get to know them by opening your heart and mind, as well as ears. You must begin to listen for the most valuable advantages they want you to give them, because they will tell you precisely which advantages they want and which benefits they truly desire from you. When you identify the specific advantages and benefits they want, you've struck gold, because you can customize their experience with your accounting business to satisfy them at a much higher level.

I know one accountant who began studying the hidden needs of his clients. He discovered that most of his clients wanted his staff to service them later after hours. This led him to stay open until 12:00 midnight during the busy tax season. Then he began asking his clients what else he could do for them to give them better service. He learned that many clients arriving directly from work did not have a chance to eat dinner. In response he had pizzas and a full cooler of soft drinks delivered to his office every night so that he could offer food to his starving clients. His clients were very appreciative. Many clients switched to his accounting service, not just because of the food, but because it communicated his desire to care for his clients. He received favorable word-of-mouth and many non-clients who heard about his willingness to extend himself for clients switched to his firm. Many positive benefits accrued for this accountant because he consistently listened to his clients and made changes to provide them with better service. They felt that he was listening to them.

One of the keys to the success of the accountant in the previous example was that he took time during each client encounter to listen to client suggestions for improvement. He was sensitive enough to listen carefully to what his clients were actually telling him. He would probe his clients by asking them questions. However, his clients didn't tell him they were hungry. He was sensitive enough to observe his clients. It wasn't until he heard a few tummy's growling that he understood what he needed to do.

You must develop an acute sensitivity to the needs of your clients. When you steamroller a client, or if you step on a client's words by interrupting them as they speak, you risk losing them. If you use hard-selling tactics to push services on them, you jeopardize losing them. On the other hand, if you are too passive, you risk not giving clients the professional leadership they need. If you have staff members who are just starting in this business, they are probably very excited about connecting with your clients and sharing the things they believe will help them. Always remind new staff members to be sensitive to clients. Remind them to do a lot of listening when interacting with clients, to ask clients questions about their needs, wants, desires, and aspirations. They must demonstrate that they really care.

INTENT LISTENING: THE LOST AMERICAN ART

The only way you and your staff can give clients the services and products they desire most is by staying completely focused on developing client rapport and trust. Trust is necessary to build a successful base of loyal clients.

Listening to your clients only with your ears will severely limit what you hear. More than half of what we communicate as humans is nonverbal. So you must remember to watch your clients when communicating. You must look for congruity between a client's words and physical expression. For instance, if your clients say something, and their facial expression or body language contradicts their verbal message, then they are probably giving you better information with their actions than their words. At least you can tell that there seems to be a conflict between what a client is saying and the level of confidence that client is expressing physically. Looking for body language cues will help you listen and understand what clients are actually saying. Notice when they smile and frown. Look into their eyes and notice when their eyes get really wide with excitement. Try to read their happiness, sadness, excitement, apprehension, fear, and other emotions. Reading their body language while listening gives you a complete picture about what they are really saying and feeling. If their words and body language is incongruent, then your client is in conflict. You must also listen with your body and respond to them with your assuring nods and deep eye contact to show that you care and are open to them. If you and your staff do this carefully and sincerely, you will set yourself apart from the vast majority of service professionals who "talk at clients" without really engaging or listening.

Intent listening ensures that you will customize the best solutions using the appropriate products and services of your firm to solve each client's most pressing problems. Your staff must establish themselves as credible experts in the minds of each client. Remembering that experts always give their highest and best objective advice, thus positioning clients for a successful outcome.

An accountant was working with one of his newest clients. The client was an interesting person; he had traveled the world giving talks to businesses about the future of the Internet. The accountant asked him who had referred him to his practice. The man mentioned that his dear friend had referred him. Then the accountant astutely asked the man many questions about his speaking engagements, only to discover that he was having trouble getting paid for most of his engagements. The smart accountant had spent a good number of years in the accounts receivable department of several large organizations and understood the man's dilemma intimately. So the accountant sketched out three possible strategies that would help the man get paid for his services. In addition to the tax preparation services, the man also hired the accountant to create and implement a simple system for getting paid. The man was ecstatic about the capabilities of the accountant and over the course of the next year referred 20 clients to his firm.

The moral of this true story is that you and your staff must help people solve their most pressing problems and concerns. You must give clients answers that really work. Answers that match the whole picture of their lives, not just one small portion, so that you can make their situation brighter and better. That is why you must continue to train, go to classes and seminars, and stay up on all the newest professional information, and pass that advice along to your clients.

TIPS TO ENSURE THAT YOU'RE REALLY LISTENING TO YOUR CLIENTS

- Allow your client to finish incomplete thoughts by pausing until they have completed their thoughts verbally. If client seems to be "thinking aloud," give him or her lots of time to finish their ideas. When they finish, don't jump in with your words too fast. Clients may need more time to think and say a little more. Be patient and really listen.
- When your clients ask you a pointed question, answer the question succinctly. Get to the point quickly, but politely.
- Listen for your client's reaction to your questions or comments by focusing your attention on the verbal and nonverbal ways that your client communicates.
- Never interrupt the client when she or he is speaking, but always let the client interrupt you any time they want. Stop thinking about your thoughts when your client interrupts you and engage your mind in the listening process immediately. Catch everything that your clients say to you. Use your ears and eyes.
- Express genuine interest in everything the client communicates. Always tune one ear and two eyes into the subtle messages that your clients give you.
- When you talk about your services with your client, watch him or her to ensure that what you are saying is interesting. Change the pitch of your voice to engage your client's attention, and continue to smile as you speak. If you are losing a client's attention, or if the client seems uninterested for any reason, change your approach. Ask your client a question or two about the problem he or she wants to resolve, and then draw the product or service into the discussion. Never disagree with your client.
- Your first 10 to 15 seconds with a new client will set the tone for the quality and length of your relationship. There

is an emotional-response that people use to size-up others quickly. Use it to your advantage.

- Take notes during your first few minutes of a consultation with a new client to communicate that you are really intent on learning about them.
- If your communication with your client is going nowhere, they may not feel comfortable enough to disclose what they really want. Try this approach: Ask about the kind of desirable service experiences they expect to receive from you now and in the future. Then take careful notes so that you can later customize each client experience.

–25–

DEVELOP INCREDIBLE PEOPLE SKILLS AND MODEL THEM TO YOUR STAFF

You already understand the importance of building the right kind of atmosphere at your office that fosters a climate of connection with clients. I am certain that you understand the importance of selecting employees with the right, consistently-positive attitudes, who have learned how to help you attract the right mix of clients, or you wouldn't have gotten to this point in your career. Now your aim is to challenge yourself and your staff to take your clients' experience with your business to a new level of excellence. Now it's time to creatively enhance the positive people-chemistry that expands the energy and magic that grows between you, your staff members and your clients.

Does your business resonate and pulsate with the energy that comes from you and your staff working tightly together to give excellent service to your clients? It must come not only through your service and but also through every source of communication, each moment of eye contact, each client meeting that says to each client "you are special and important." It takes more than a "quick hello" to welcome a client into your office. It requires charisma, warmth and charm, and the ability to reach out to your clients. Every staff member must embrace this philosophy.

If your business is lacking this extra feeling of "charisma," or has lost it along the way, you can reverse it by displaying a newer and higher level of passion for clients. Often you can transfer a strong feeling of caring to your clients, indirectly, by genuinely nurturing your staff because it will bubble down emotionally to the client. So lavish your staff everyday with tangible representations of your warmth, care, appreciation and compassion for them. The little extra-special things you give to your staff mean a whole lot more than you realize. Here are some first steps that you can take to do this:

- Always smile genuinely. Project warmth in your smile as you make eye contact. It will be difficult for your clients not to smile back once you make contact with someone who genuinely shares their smile with you. Your smile can change your clients' and employee's mood and improve their day.

- Give at least five meaningful compliments a day to each staff member. Start each day this way. Take time to really focus on others by getting out of yourself. Demonstrate a genuine interest in them. Nurture your staff members and then nurture your clients in the presence of staff, and watch it begin to rub-off on them. Your staff will begin nurturing your clients with you. Your appreciation for your clients is transferable. It can be learned. When you give compliments, they somehow are returned to you. If you compliment people on their behavior, they will tend to think you are being more sincere — e.g. "I appreciate the expertise that you demonstrated on that project," or "You're always right on time."

- Learn your clients' names and use them often. While you are greeting new clients, listen carefully so that you hear their name the first time. If you don't catch it the first time, ask them to repeat it. They usually say it slower the second time. Once you know their name, use it often. It is the sweetest word they will hear. When you are greeting clients use their name. For example: "Kim, you must have been on vacation recently. You have such a wonderful tan." Use people's names genuinely and often. I suggest using each client's name at least seven or eight times throughout a visit.

- Reach out and touch everyone. Literally, many studies have been conducted in service industries, and the evidence is overwhelming. When you touch clients (and staff) in non-intrusive ways — give a pat on the shoulder, a finger's touch to the elbow, etc. — clients tend to feel that they receive more caring and helpful service. When you touch others non-intrusively, you create a warm bond that people cannot explain. Try an experiment with your best three clients, shake their hands; give their shoulder a pat; touch an elbow; venture to hug a client if you feel comfortable and if they seem open. Watch how your clients respond to you by the end of their visit to your business.

But avoid being false, obtrusive or offensive in your approach.

- Eye contact is engaging. Look deeply into your client's eyes when they talk to you. Show them with your facial expressions and your eyes that what they are saying is important and interesting to you. Generate an interest in them.
- Generate a strong sense of humor. Rent funny videos. Read books that make you laugh heartily. Tell non-offending jokes. Get silly sometimes. Laughter is contagious!
- Never argue with your client. Never disagree with a client, because you can never win. Arguments will always shut your client down. The slightest tension that clients experience can drive them away from you for good. So even if your clients are wrong, remind yourself that you are not fighting a war or on your high-school debate team. This person is your business, your client, and your responsibility. If a client is upset, ask them by name what you can do to make their experience better for them.

–26–

USE SAVVY TELEPHONE SKILLS FOR INCOMING CALLS

Do you know how many businesses lose clients all over the United States because someone in the office is too busy to respond to the ringing phone on time? The answer is too many. If you are like most of the business owners and managers I consult with, you are probably an overachiever. When your receptionist is away I'll bet you answer the telephone with your most positive "thank you so much for calling" voice.

One of the problems that I identify time and time again is that some accounting and bookkeeping professionals would prefer to let the phone ring than to seem overly anxious to a client. I think some people are afraid to appear desperate for business. I tell them that it's okay to be hungry and eager. You are investing time and money in advertising, and when a client responds to your efforts in any way, it is time for celebration because it means your advertising is effective.

Think about all of your advertising efforts—television, newspaper, local magazines, yellow pages, radio ads, direct mail, gift certificates and accounting-business promotions — that result in clients taking some action to schedule an appointment. You cannot afford any bottlenecks or hindrances to client responses in any aspect of your business system. Your investment in advertising is required to attract that client. Remember that every client represents five or ten potential clients — this equals hundreds and hundreds of dollars that you may be losing when the one client per week is unintentionally ignored. The same holds true if a client can't find your physical location.

Your telephone is your lifeline to success. Your phone gives clients immediate access to you. When a client calls you for the first time, they often make an immediate judgment on the level of professionalism, caring, and empathy that your business projects. Sometimes they instantly decide that they want to work with you based on their phone call to you. The telephone is one of your most valuable resources. Smart accounting service marketers use the phone to their best advantage. Let me show you how.

TIPS FOR DEVELOPING ACCOUNTING SERVICES TELEPHONE SMARTS

- When answering the phone, make sure that your staff sounds warm, inviting, and friendly. Take the "I'm so glad you called" attitude, not the "what do you want" stance.
- A smile can be projected on the phone. People can hear it. Looking in the mirror when talking with client's on the phone will remind you to smile.
- Pump up your energy when on the phone. If your day has been hectic or frustrating, don't take it into your next phone call or appointment. Instead, project your voice as if you are about to speak publicly or are about to sing. Take a deep breath, stand up tall, and speak slightly slower than you would in a face-to-face conversation.
- Experiment with the volume, pitch, and rate of your voice. Try different vocal inflections. Change your volume when you are excited. Use higher pitches when you want to take your energy higher and lower pitches to sound more down-to-earth. Talk in a "loud whisper" to share a secret. Vary your inflection to move your clients emotionally.
- Speak to your clients on the phone as if they were standing in front of you. Picture someone actually in front of you. Don't eat or drink while on the phone. Avoid doing other tasks while talking to a client because they will detect that you are not giving them your full attention.
- Always identify and greet the caller and yourself when you pick up the phone. Let's say, Suzy, a receptionist, answers the main number and the caller asks for Shawna. When the call is transferred to Shawna's desk she should answer "Good afternoon (morning or evening), this is Shawna.," and not use "hello." This would is too informal.
- If you are initiating a phone call, remember to state your name and the purpose of your call at the beginning of your conversation. Always ask if you have called at a convenient time. Of course, always try to call at convenient times by avoiding early morning, dinnertime, or late night calls. You caller will appreciate your sensitivity to their needs.
- Conclude business phone conversations in a timely manner. Clearly communicate your office policy to your

staff to chat with friends and family at home, not at the office. At the office, keep your phone calls fairly brief and to the point.

- Always thank the caller at the conclusion of the call. Say, "Thank you for calling, Sally." Always add the caller's name. If you do not know who is on the phone, politely ask their name after identifying yourself. Use clients' names often.

- When taking messages for others, capture all of the important details—whom the call is for, the callers full name, the caller's phone number, the best time to return the call and, when appropriate, leave a message.

- If you have to leave a message on voicemail, speak slowly and clearly. Give your full name, your business name, your phone number, and a brief message and consider repeating your phone number one last time.

- Every time you are on the telephone at your office, remember that you hold in your hand perhaps the most valuable resource you own for bringing in new clients. Handle it wisely. Respect it and increase your business with it. Make every moment and opportunity count.

–27–

EXPAND YOUR FIRM'S
HIDDEN GROWTH OPPORTUNITIES

If I asked you to spend some time creating a list of all of the assets that comprised your accounting business, you would probably list mostly tangible assets. I bet I would be hard-pressed to find a lot of the intangible assets on your list. If you were to systematically reinvest in them they would have a very high potential for increasing the value of your business. The realizable potential of these intangible assets is often difficult to see objectively within one's own business.

Your business has many valuable, but dormant, intangible assets inside of it right now that you may have not yet to taken advantage of. The reason for this may be that you simply have not taken time to think about creating a simple plan for catalyzing your use of these intangible assets.

When you begin to understand the value of the intangible assets of your business you will discover how much more infinitely profitable your business will become.

Right now I want you to do the following:

1. Make an list all of the tangible and intangible assets that your firm possesses. Think about your location, your inventory, your equipment, and everything else, including your services and any "extras" that come to mind. As you make your list try to determine how much actual value your assets add to your business.
2. Now make a list of all of your tangible and intangible liabilities: All your debt, your weak areas, and anything else that is keeping your business from expanding. If your clients cannot find parking at your building, include that on your list. Try to list as many elements as possible.
3. Brainstorm as many ways as possible to improve your most pressing intangible liabilities. Sometimes just by

thinking about creative ways to reverse your tangible and intangible liabilities you can develop many exceptionally positive ways to improve your business.

4. If any of the items from the below list of Highly Valuable Intangible Assets does not appear on your above asset list, then consider adding them. Read through the explanations below and create your own system for optimizing each high-potential intangible asset. Apply your own ideas for new intangible asset management systems to your business:

LIST OF HIGHLY VALUABLE INTANGIBLE ASSETS
- Your list of inactive clients
- Successful advertisements and promotions
- Your most important customers

YOUR LIST OF INACTIVE CLIENTS

Some clients may cease hiring you because your firm unknowingly stops offering them an profound reason to continue the relationship. Maybe a staff member that they really liked is no longer working for you. Perhaps you have hired new staff members, and some of your clients feel that you no longer provide the same level of service that you once did. Sometimes I find that accounting firms implement a program to improve the quality of their service, and things go great for a while until, at some point, they lose the momentum that attracted new clients. This happens for many different reasons.

How many inactive clients do you have right now? Asking the question another way, "How many clients have you lost over the course of the last year?" If you are not sure how many clients may have left your practice, then you must research your records immediately. If you know how many clients you tend to lose per year, then in addition you must know exactly why each one has left. You will find that each former client's reason for leaving will be as unique as they are.

Ask yourself this question: "Are my inactive clients no longer with me because I no longer offer them the level of benefit they want?"

There are many reasons that clients stop using your service. Sometimes they somehow got out of the habit of using your business. They may have experience an interruption in their lives, such as, an illness or perhaps a vacation has thrown them off of their course. Another reason is that perhaps they had an unresolved problem or conflict with one of your staff members. Maybe a mistake was made on a filing or your receptionist was unknowingly rude to a client, thus driving your client away.

The great news is that no matter what made your clients become inactive can easily be reversed. Every business has client attrition—a percentage of clients who stop doing business with you. Maybe you are not sure of your attrition rate. The best way to reverse the leaks in your business system that are making your clients disappear is to simply call up your inactive clients and humbly ask them if anything has gone wrong. All that you have to do is take control of the leak by contacting your clients. It is difficult to do, but necessary. If the client mentions that something went terribly wrong, offer to correct the unintentional wrongdoing. If someone at your office was rude apologize to the client assuring them that will never happen again. Then ask the former client for a second chance. Consider offering them a free service to remedy their problem. Statistically, clients that have experienced problems and a successful recovery/remedy, become more loyal than clients who never have trouble. I think that the reason for this is that when you go through the process recovering a client, you actually give them very personalized attention that centers intensely on solving their problem. Clients tend to respond well to that.

Decreasing your rate of client loss can be that simple. All it requires is a little caring and extra effort.

YOUR MOST SUCCESSFUL ADVERTISEMENTS AND PROMOTIONS

Look back at the most successful promotions that you have run in the past and consider whether there has been a sufficient enough waiting period for the promotion to work again. Look at your advertising history and compare it to your overall sales before, during, and after you ran each advertisement. Once you have identified two or three highly successful advertisements or promotions, try to figure out what made them so successful. *Then consider how you can expand on that success by running them again, or more frequently.*

Here is an interesting idea that comes from outside the profession of accounting, but the underlying concept is very pertinent to your business:

One of my clients has a modeling agency/school and full service hair and beauty salon in California. She found that after several special events, that included special entertainment and hors d'ouvres, her salon sales tended to double. She ran the events every six months, one in spring and one at Christmas time. She decided to analyze what made the events so successful, and determined that her primary point of effectiveness was in inviting other appearance- and health-conscious professionals to attend. They were cosmetic dentists, massage therapists, health club owners, cosmetologists, and many other community opinion leaders. They were given free food and drinks, entertainment, modeling and fashion shows, and cosmetic demonstrations. The response of the influential guests always resulted in favorable word-of-mouth. My client decided to add two more annual fashion show events to her salon calendar. Each event was coordinated with one prestigious non-profit association in her market. She donated a large portion of the proceeds to the association. The level of publicity that her agency obtained through the events was incredible. Her tie-in with the local associations gave her special access to the media.

Once my client recognized that she wasn't limited to holding her special event only at Christmastime, she began developing other kinds special events that she could run year-round.

Simply by considering ways to increase the execution of her most powerful marketing method—by doing it more often—her modeling school attendance tripled.

Go through your records to determine your top three to five marketing methods. Find the methods that have given you the best results—the best responses and clients—and consider executing them more often. If you have been running print ads and they have been highly successful for you, consider running the ads more often or testing the same ad in different kinds of publications. If you have been successful sending out direct mailing, perhaps sending postcards to new businesses and residents, then consider sending out higher quantities, more frequently. Take the marketing that you know you can obtain a predictable result with because of your past successes and increase your use of it.

YOUR MOST IMPORTANT CUSTOMERS

Accounting and bookkeeping business owners who take a good, hard look at their base of clients will discover several unique observations. The first observation is usually apparent—that 20% of your customers will tend generate 80% of your business. These are your best customers, so focus on them. Second, about 80% of your problems will come from 20% of your worst customers. Did you every think about developing a strategy for dealing with them? You must manage them in some way in order to reduce your costs and compensate for lost productivity. Third, 20% of your costs will come from 80% of your clients. Try to lower the costs incurred on these clients. Remember, you must identify these groups of clients and develop strategies to deal with each of them.

I am certain you have already worked to identify your best customers. Your best clients are found in the top 20% of your base. You must get to know these clients well and cater to them in unique ways. Important clients may be more willing to purchase customized products and services. You must take the time to determine what unmet needs they have for your newest services so that you can offer them to your best clients first. Perhaps you will discover a whole new set of needs that your best clients have for purchasing other company's products through you.

One of my clients is a successful accountant. She came to me because she felt unmotivated, listless, and tired. She told me that she was frustrated and ready to quit her practice because she felt no sense of fulfillment. I asked her some questions about why she thought she was struggling with the issue of staying in her own business because her business seemed to have been highly successful financially. She told me that she was sick of sitting at her desk doing the same tasks, talking to the same folks year after year. I asked her what she thought needed to happen to turn things around. She said having more time to do the hobbies that she loved — hiking and mountain biking — would do it. I told her that in one hour's worth of consulting I could turn her business and life around completely. I don't think that she believed me. Here's the advice that I shared with her:

> Go into a quiet room. Take with you a list of all of your clients sorted by their relative value to your business. In other words, sort your list by putting your big money clients at the top and graduate the list down to your least valuable clients, those who spend the least with you. Now, go through every name on the list. Codify each client's name by using the following criteria:
>
> A Clients who are very profitable, with little to heavy workload.
> B Clients who are somewhat to moderately profitable with little to moderate workload.

C   Clients who are less profitable with more work than they necessitate.

D   Clients who have low profitability who are more work-intensive, or are low-yield/high maintenance.

She did it. At our next meeting she had completed this awkward assignment. She asked me what the purpose of the assignment was, because I told her that I would keep her in suspense until she completed it. I could tell that her patience was waning. Then I explained that the purpose of her assignment was to reevaluate her clients so she could give herself the things that she wanted most in life. When I asked how much it would mean to have her life back, so that she could do more of the things that she loved and less of the things that she now hated to do. When she responded she said, "I would like that very much," I said, "Good, then you're ready for Part Two of your assignment." Here's what I told her to do:

With all of your C and D clients, raise your fees significantly. This will cause many of them to seek other accounting services, however a certain percentage of them will stay with you. Have your junior consulting staff service the ones that remain. Get them out of your hair.

With all of your A and B clients, raise your fees moderately. Communicate with these groups of clients by sending special letters, invitations and cards telling them that they are your best clients. Thank them for being your best clients. Create special events for them, special services and other exciting offers to increase their business with you.

She did it. I know that it took a lot of courage for her to take my advice. But the result was that she cut her workload by around 45% and increased her total aggregate profits by 118%. That was a cutting-edge feat. She met her goal of having more time for her hobbies. Of course she ran a much leaner business, one that served less clients, but that was okay with her because she got her life back.

-28-

CONVERT YOUR MOST RECENT CLIENTS INTO LONG-TERM CLIENTS

Short-term client relationships are much more expensive for your accounting practice to manage than long-term relationships. There are huge penalties, some visible and many hidden, for accountants who churn clients. Accountants who keep clients over decades derive exceptional value. Excellent accountant marketing is about creating, nurturing, and maintaining highly successful long-term relationships with your clients. And of course the best starting place is with your most impressionable clients — your recent ones.

Those who have freshly hired you are more likely to have been smitten by Cupid's flaming arrow because they have seen the results of the magic your services have worked for them. Your opportunity is to spend time communicating with these clients to help remind them of the extraordinary service value that you gave them within the ordinary confines of their businesses. Your marketing actions must reveal an inspiring vision for what the future still holds for them by continuing to work with you.

In the long term, your clients often pay a premium price for investing in your service. As time passes they know that they could go back out into the market and obtain a lower cost for accounting service. However, there is a value, an advantage, and a quality about working with you in which they have confidence. Your aim is to find out what every client sees in you. Why do clients first hire you? Once you know that, you can craft a customized plan to give them more of the qualities they like about you and the services that they love. This is a simple but exceptionally effective approach. This is so much more refreshing than asking what problems you need to fix continuously. Don't you agree? And this approach works so well because it will teach you more about the exceptional things clients see in you and your business.

By openly communicating and ascertaining the reasons why your new clients have employed your services, a new world of insights will appear. This information can be used to re-invent and improve your marketing program in a short time. In addition, here are some ideas that will help you to hold onto your most recent clients for a long time:

- Try to influence your client to fully implement your accounting services so that the client is more dependent upon you. New arrangements, training and setup can create more cost and time penalties for switching to other accounting service providers.
- Remember the more fear, uncertainty and doubt your clients feel about replacing your accounting service with a competitor, the less likely they will be to do it. So work hard to give a continual flow of credible independent proof sources to all of your clients that you know more and give better service than any of your competitors.
- Create a recent client system that is so totally enthralling and captivating that your client feels swept up into it.

ONE OF MY CLIENTS CAME UP WITH THIS SIMPLE MARKETING STRATEGY

During consulting sessions she tries to uncover as many of her clients' heartfelt needs as possible. She records personal needs, business needs, and special interests and puts them all into her database. Over time, as she systematically builds more trust and confidence, she finds unique ways to meet more of the needs on her lists in the most nurturing ways she can think of. She does this in addition to performing all of the regular programs that she was contracted to perform. Sometimes she hand-delivers special baked goods to clients to tell them that she was just thinking about them. At other times clients receive gift certificates from her for dinners to their favorite restaurants.

One day her approaches to create an enthralling client system took a unique turn. She planned an event to surprise her best client by giving her a flight to a secret family reunion. This gave the accountant so much joy that she started researching and delving more deeply into the lives of her clients. She tells me that her new goal is to plan special family gatherings for clients by secretly enlisting their spouses to help plan the surprise events. She wants to plan birthday getaways for overworked clients. Right now she is planning to send a massage therapist to the office of a stressed-out and under-nurtured client as a special surprise. She always creates the unique relationships with her newest clients and she gives so much that could never be replaced by any another accountant at any price. She values her clients deeply and most of them would never consider replacing her.

Remember that one of your biggest opportunities to grow your business is by finding unique ways to convert your newest clients into your most loyal ones.

−29−

USE THE ACCOUNTING SERVICES MATRIX TO OFFER MORE SERVICES TO YOUR CLIENTS

C arefully track the specific kinds of services that each of your clients has hired you to perform. Put together your accounting services matrix so that you can clearly track which services your clients regularly use and which services they have yet to try.

CHECK YOUR ACCOUNTING SERVICE PENETRATION RATE

Let's say that you have four clients and you offer five different areas of service. That means you have 20 possible transactions that can take place if all of your clients hire you to perform all the services you offer.

As you begin to use the Accounting Services Matrix — to track how many services all your clients have experienced out of all possible services — an important pattern emerges.

In the Accounting Services Matrix shown here, Client One has only tried two out of five services. This means that Client One's penetration rate is 40 percent.

ACCOUNTING SERVICES MATRIX

	SERVICE ONE	SERVICE TWO	SERVICE THREE	SERVICE FOUR	SERVICE FIVE
CLIENT ONE	TRIED	TRIED	NOT TRIED	NOT TRIED	NOT TRIED
CLIENT TWO	TRIED	TRIED	TRIED	NOT TRIED	NOT TRIED
CLIENT THREE	NOT TRIED	NOT TRIED	TRIED	NOT TRIED	NOT TRIED
CLIENT FOUR	TRIED	NOT TRIED	NOT TRIED	NOT TRIED	NOT TRIED

Your overall penetration rate, the rate of all of your clients, on the Accounting Services Matrix here, is 7 out of 20, meaning that your clients only use 35% of the services you offer. Penetration rates below 80% mean you need to get cracking to improve your marketing. All it usually takes is customizing letters to each client explaining some of the other services they have yet to try.

Looking at the Accounting Services Matrix here, there are 13 remaining services that your clients have never tried; this immediately indicates powerful service opportunities that are lying dormant for your clients and for you. Just by systematically attempting to coax your client into trying them will automatically increase your business. Perhaps you can use a sampling strategy, or mail letters with customized special offers to induce your clients to try new services that they otherwise may never have thought about.

Use the Accounting Services Matrix to look for new opportunities to market services that have never been tried; clients who are open to trying them will automatically lead you to your highest probability additional sales first. Now you know instantly which clients are the best candidates to approach first with highly leveraged offers. Your aim is to track the overall penetration rate of your service effort every month to set specific new goals for each client — then each meeting with each client will have a new purpose.

-30-

DEVELOP A PROFITABLE BACK-END OF SALEABLE PRODUCTS AND SERVICES

Nothing would be more embarrassing to you than waking up one morning and realizing that for years you have been consistently missing one exceptionally good opportunity to market your business every day. What if you discovered that there have been opportunities to increase your business profits sitting right there under your nose, but because you could not see them you had simply been missing them.

Every time a client walks out of your office and you don't find a new way to give them more of the advantage they have hired you for, you lose just a little more. Let's look at your accounting business from a different perspective, one that will be very lucrative for you. By doing so you will discover many excellent opportunities that you may have been forfeiting without even realizing it.

One opportunity that you may never have thought about emanates from what we call the "back-end" of your business. The back-end is where many of the high-profit opportunities exist. Most back-end opportunities yield higher residual value with excellent profit margins. This is the case because after you acquire a client any additional costs associated with further marketing efforts to that client decreases significantly, compared to the cost of acquiring a new client. That is why I share with entrepreneurs that expanding their businesses by engaging more of the preexisting back-end opportunities that are available to them is one of the smartest initial changes that they must be make to their businesses.

You must develop a "back-end" of services because they offer you windfall opportunities. Consider adding one or more small groups of new of products/services that give your clients something different than you have previously offered to them. Consider offering them something valuable. Your aim is to offer your current, future, and past customers, a full compliment of back-end enhancement services—giving your clients increasing advantages.

Your present clients trust you. They return to you for the results they have come to depend upon you to receive. So it is easy for you to introduce them to additional products and services that give them greater value over time. It is important for you to recognize that even inactive clients are prime prospects for the additional products and services that you will sell as part of your back-end business. You see, when you develop a strong back-end business, what you are doing is introducing your current, future, and former clients to new ways your firm can improve their lives and businesses. It is just that simple.

THE STORY OF AN ACCOUNTANT WHO SUCCESSFULLY USES A BACK-END STRATEGY

I know an accounting professional who added a marketing consulting service to his business. He decided to start a marketing research and planning division to his existing accounting business. He hired a friend who was beginning his career as a marketing consultant. His arrangement was that his friend would provide marketing services to his present accounting clients, most of which were medium-sized businesses. The marketing services they offered ranged from collateral material creation to market research. The accountant retained 35% of the gross marketing consulting fee as a referral fee, which was derived from converting his present accounting clients into the marketing clients his friend serviced. The remaining 65% were given to his marketing specialist. This arrangement worked out so well the accountant developed similar relationships with several other professionals. Eventually he licensed his practice to three other junior accountants, splitting his client list into thirds and receives a fee of 40% of the gross accounting fees that his three sub-accountants bill out. Now he has more time to do exactly what he wants. He services only a few high-paying corporate clients. He now earns more income than he previously did when he handled all of the work by himself, and now carries no more than 30% of his previous workload. This is an example of a successful automatic back-end business that is leveraged by diversifying and referrals.

Identify your own set of unique opportunities to create a back-end of products to offer your clients.

Answer this key question: What other products or services, or combination of products and services could I offer my existing clients that would be a logical extension or a complement to the benefits they gain from coming to me in the first place?

Once you have successfully identified the specific back-end products and services that you will incorporate into your program, then conduct a little test. Pick out an appropriate product, service, or a combination of the two, and discover what happens when you offer them to a client in a nonthreatening way. Maybe you will decide to offer the back-end services to them by phone, by letter, by Internet; e-mail or on your web site, or you may make your offer to them at point of purchase in your office. You can start in simple and subtle ways. If clients excitedly embrace your offer, then I want you to try it again with more clients and see what happens. Start small and simple, and your business will continue to grow.

If your clients respect you, and I have confidence they do, they will be delighted and appreciative of the interest you've shown by offering them more back-end products and services. A large number of your clients will purchase them from you and you will meet your goal to increase your business because a lucrative back-end alone is enough to dramatically grow your business to new proportions.

CREATE A BACK-END OF TECHNICAL SUPPORT SERVICES
Accountants play important integrating roles before, during, and after client interactions. Take a moment to use your creative imagination to play a quick game. Imagine yourself not only as an accountant but also as a great orchestra conductor who has become a fabulous accountant:

As an accountant, you use your skills like the conductor of a great orchestra. You are an artist and a technician. As conductor, you must know how the music sounds before you ever hear it played. Just by glancing at the plan — the music —you must know the score. You must bring creative teams together — people of all skill levels who must study the piece. At times you must encourage your creative team to join in harmony. At other times you must remind them of their cues and when to join in again. You are the conductor. In one hand you hold the directing baton and in the other hand the plan, the master musical score. You love your craft. You welcome the unexpected. You see life's humor. You embrace life's joys as you see them manifested through your beautiful music. You mount the challenges that arise during rehearsals, smooth them out before the final performance arrives. Although you enjoy the journey through the rehearsal halls, like all excellent, well-respected conductors, your experience of greater joy comes through the radiant music that arises from your orchestra. You await the sweet atmosphere that the pleasing sounds create. You experience all of the invigorating sounds that you sense which are like parades of harmony inspiring you to reach new heights of fulfillment. Your client has entrusted himself to you, you have performed exceedingly, and your performance was unmatched. This is the payoff that catapults you to experience the true joy of accomplishment — helping your team conquer the next most challenging piece of music.

As you read the above paragraph, what images did it conjure in your mind? Often times the success of your practice is all a matter of the way you think of the service you give and how you approach marketing it.

Accountants are somewhat like grand orchestra leaders in that they are trying to implement programs that help clients pull their businesses together, but the opportunities that lie in the most basic areas are often forgotten. Just like the great orchestra leader, your musicians must have enough technical skill to effectively play their instruments.

One of the best and easiest opportunities that you have is in providing special skills to your clients as a follow-up to your regular service. You can sell add-on services in the form of in-house technical training to enhance your clients' businesses.

Try to find several specialized, highly-needed, weak skill areas during each intervention.

Once you find one to three weak areas where the skill sets of your client's employees are lacking, suggest that your client allow you to perform a "no-cost" skills test of their people to measure general productivity. You may already have several other skills providers in mind who you can use to provide additional services to your existing clients outside of the area of accounting advice.

After the results are in you might suggest:
- In-house productivity seminars that you subcontract.
- Teleconferencing seminars.
- A technical telephone hotline for the client's employees to contact you or other experts for questions or special instructions.
- The creation of special training manuals and other systems to smooth out workflows.

One accountant created a whole back-end business simply by hiring other accountants to follow-up by providing technical skills training. The accountant became so successful in his sub-field that he created teleconferencing seminars that the employees of his clients' were able to attend. All he did was talk to a teleconferencing company to set up class times, and sold the classes to his clients—who paid $300 per month for employees to attend three one-hour classes by phone. He then hired accountants to call into the conference from their homes to lead the classes. Most of his classes had 6 students. He built up the business to 15 classes and earns a gross of approximately $27,000 per month, just by adding a back-end technical training service to his existing business.

Could you have sold five or six of your present clients some kind of extra technical services that would make their employees more productive? Could you have done that by networking to find trainers to help you give the service? Could you build a back-end of technical support that raises the all-around value of your service significantly? The answer is, "Yes," you can build a profitable back-end business any time you want to.

Another accountant, specializing in international trade consulting, created a back-end profit center for his business instantly. He raised his consulting rates, raised the prices on the "already high-priced" manuals which he sold at seminars, then he added a toll-free number for technical help. Any client who invested in a basic consulting package or who purchased his basic trade manual could call him for a year with any technical questions about how to apply his ideas. His business profits doubled because of the perceived increase in value that he offered through his back-end technical support program.

-31-

PROMOTE THE PRODUCTS AND SERVICES OF NON-COMPETITIVE OUTSIDE BUSINESSES

After you have done business with a client the first time you have established a bond, an affinity, trust and a level of respect. I want you consider expanding your relationships with existing clients in a more concentrated and profitable way. I suggest that one of the easiest and best ways of expanding your business is by making creative arrangements to offer the products/services of other businesses and professionals directly to your clients. Some accounting professionals simply license the use of their mailing lists for this purpose. Others formally market the products and services of other businesses and professionals. Even if the number of clients in your customer base remains the same, you can expand your business profits by promoting the products and services of other businesses and professionals to your clients.

Your client-base is valuable because you have invested a lot of resources in gathering this special group of loyal clients. Therefore, your clients are like their own mini-market—a market that you have created with your own sweat and blood. This market has a high value that can be transferred to other noncompetitive businesses' products and services. Other business owners recognize this value because they can use your "market" to reach hundreds qualified prospects overnight with information about their products. They may even be more than willing to provide you with a significant percent of the profit on anything that you sell, in addition to a fee for the exposure.

The new products and services offers that you allow your clients to be exposed to do not necessarily have to directly relate to the primary services of your business. This requires advanced strategic thinking and a creative open mind, but the rewards for developing a diversified program can be tremendous.

In order to promote the products and services of other businesses to your clients, you must do two things:

1. You must have your clients listed in an organized format—a database is preferable. This means that you must have their name, address, city, state, zip, phone number, and interests in your file. I strongly suggest that you use a database on computer or contact management computer program, such as Filemaker or Excel to organize your client list, if you haven't already done that.
2. You must also identify and organize your clients' areas of interest because client-base consists of people with special interests who will be more receptive to certain offers for specific kinds of products and services than others. Your aim is to identify client interests and use that information responsibly. You can store this information on your computer database and then view subgroups of clients with similar interests.

After you have completed these two tasks, ask yourself this question: *"What other products and services do my clients tend to buy before, during, and after they hire me to perform my service?"*

In other words, there are obvious products and services that your customers need and desire before they hire you. There may be certain things that enhance your services. And there are additional products and services that are appropriate for clients after they have received your service. There are products and services that have little connection to your accounting business, however, your clients may need them or simply think that they are fun. You must use your best judgement regarding client's potential impression of the tone, nature and character of your involvement with the additional products and services that you select to offer to your present clients.

ADD A REMINDER SERVICE TO YOUR BUSINESS

You may notice that your clients are consistently late in filing their quarterly taxes. Perhaps you could hire an outside "reminder service" to help remind your clients not only about the taxes, but birthdays, special occasions and other important life events. You could simply sell this to your clients for a flat annual fee, keeping a portion of it as your profit, paying the remainder to the service provider. Then turn the work over to a local reminder service with their payment. The service would send the client a form of "remembered events" to fill out. The service would begin immediately. You would be doing your clients tremendous service by helping them maintain their priorities.

EVERYONE WANTS INTERNET ACCESS

Another idea that could work well for high-volume accountants would be to create a partnership with a small local Internet access provider. Create a special web site for your business that can only be accessed through you if your clients will use your dial-up Internet access service. Have the local Internet Access provider customize an Internet navigator software to bring clients who buy your dial-up service to your private web site as the home page of the navigator. To maintain the integrity and exclusivity of your value-rich site it must only be available to clients paying you a small fee for dial-up access. Negotiate with the local Internet company to give you a group discount for signing up clusters of your clients. Charge your clients a reasonable normal local Internet access rate. Keep the profit and sell advertising space on the automatic homepage the browser is programmed to default to. You can hire a programmer to create a special portal at your web site. There clients may submit computer work files in Quicken, Quickbooks, Peachtree, and other formats in order for you to automate a portion of the delivery of your normal accounting services workload through the Internet.

THINK ABOUT THE CONCEPT

This concept here is valuable. It is to convert your clients—who normally purchase accounting or bookkeeping services from you—into purchasers of other things. Since they need these other things anyway, you may as well figure out a creative way to capture their business by fulfilling their needs in a unique way.

You can apply this idea in many ways and you are only limited by your imagination.

Analyze every opportunity to market more services and products to your clients by looking at what their behavior suggests about other things they need outside of the scope of your services. Start making a list of possible before, during, and after products and services that you can offer to clients by hiring other businesses and professionals to provide them without requiring additional effort from you.

–32–

HOW TO BUMP UP YOUR SALES

To meet your sales goals and grow your business to new proportions you simply must sell more services and products more often to more people. There is no other way around this. Whether you market face-to-face through a client interaction, or impersonally through your Internet web site you must continually strive to increase sales. In this chapter we are going to make several key distinctions that will help bump-up your sales continually.

Every time your clients benefit from your service in some way, they are developing a deeper relationship with you and your business. They are investing more in you, your staff and your business. Immediately after you perform a service for your clients they are usually in a positive emotional and psychological state. Perhaps they are relieved as they feel the protection that comes through the advice you have given. Perhaps they feel more secure knowing that their assets and tax situation will be safeguarded and overseen by you.

Many accounting professionals may not realize it, but the most critical time in your entire relationship with a client is immediately after the client has received your services. This moment is easier than any other to learn more about your clients, and discover the unmet needs they have for additional products and services that can be added to your offerings.

Once you have their confidence and have built their trust, it's easier to offer your clients another product or service which provides additional advantages.

It is critically important to develop an "after first purchase" marketing strategy. Unfortunately it is not seemingly obvious to most business people that there is significantly greater potential for profit after you have just provided service to a client. By understanding that the likelihood of increasing earnings at the time of, or just after your clients' first sale, your mainstream business can be dramatically improved by pursuing your customers for more orders immediately after the first sale. This is "reselling." You will also have opportunities to sell different kinds of products related to their main purchase at this critical time, too. This is "cross-selling."

Your aftermarket—consisting of all possible repeat sales and ancillary sales—is where the large profits exist. It is one of the vital keys to successful marketing. When a person buys from you once, it is much easier to influence him or her to buy again and again. It is much less expensive, too, because you do not have to spend as much money on advertising as you do on the front-end—in capturing the client initially. You must resell, up-sell, and cross-sell all of your customers.

- Reselling is simply selling them the same thing they bought before.
- Up-selling is influencing them to buy a better, more expensive, or more sophisticated service.
- Cross-selling is influencing them to buy something else that's related to the original service.

What additional products and services are you selling to your clients at the point of their initial purchase? What could you be selling? Consider how not selling at this critical time drags down the Lifetime Value of your average customer.

UP-SELL YOUR CLIENTS TO SUPERIOR SERVICES AND PRODUCTS

Up-selling is graduating your client to a superior and usually more expensive alternative service or product.

Your client may have felt content making a decision to hire your firm to perform a monthly payroll service for their business. While you perform the service, you ask them pertinent questions and you discover that the reason they want to have you perform their payroll is because you can do it for less money than the cost of their in-house staff. Your client likes the payroll service you offer. However, during the interview you also discover that the client's daughter has been responsible for running quarterly taxes for the business and that this task is zapping her energies and productivity. So you decide to recommend a larger, higher-quality, or enhanced version, of the accounting services you are confident will give them greater results. Suggest that the client consider hiring your accounting service, not for your standard payroll-package, but rather for your deluxe service. You recommend this because this service will free your client and family members from becoming overstressed, because you will be performing the tax preparation and giving the client five other services which will free them from doing most of the accounting tasks they dislike performing. Knowing that your accounting firm is set-up to do the services faster than they could, you mention that the deluxe package is at a 35% greater cost than the standard package, but will free their time up by more than 75%.

CROSS-SELLING: INTRODUCING ADDITIONAL VALUE-RICH SERVICES AND PRODUCTS

Cross-selling involves introducing your client to additional products or services that will add another dimension to the existing purchase by giving your client greater results.

Another client feels confident making a decision to hire your firm to perform a monthly payroll service. You discover that this client pays a lot in sales commissions each month. Perhaps they need a better way to track the sales performance of their sales staff. You're obligated to give your client greater outcomes and higher advantages. You have no choice but to recommend additional products and services that enhance your client's business. Perhaps you'll choose to offer them software products that will track the number of prospects called or visited and the conversion ratios of prospects to actual sales or clients. They do not have to purchase this additional product, but you do have an obligation to demonstrate the differences in performance and outcome they can expect to obtain and give them an incentive for considering using this product to obtain additional results. The client buys the software from you and is happy because you have exceeded their expectations.

Your clients will appreciate you for cross-selling accounting products and services to them because they will receive better results in much less time. When your clients choose superior or additional products and services their advantage becomes self-evident. When they choose them, with your help, they obtain a superior outcome and performance from your business. And when they receive greater results, they're happier.

THE KEY TO BUMP SELLING: OFFER YOUR CLIENTS BETTER ALTERNATIVES AND INCENTIVES

The concept of bump-selling involves using different combinations of cross-selling and up-selling continually. It is the philosophy of continuously adding more value to client transactions to graduate clients to the higher value-centers within your business. This means that you can graduate clients with low Lifetime Values, who tend to buy infrequently, or in small transaction amounts, into better clients.

Your aim in any transaction using up-selling or cross-selling is always to offer your clients better alternatives. Offer them alternatives for services that perform better and which are in their best interest, not yours. Your clients have this sixth sense and they know when you are not sincere about creating a greater advantage for them. When you are not legitimately concerned about your clients' interest first, they will refuse to try your extra products and services because they will think you are just trying to sell them something in order to make more money.

Another key element that makes bump-selling more appealing is when you add a financial incentive to your offer to your customers. If they choose service "A" but you realize that service "B" is far more beneficial and valuable for them, you can offer it to them at such an advantageous price that they would be crazy not to consider selecting the superior alternative.

Remember, the reason you are up-selling or cross-selling products is because doing so benefits your clients, and gives them a greater value. It also adds considerably to your business profit. Have fun finding new ways to bump sell.

NEW DISCOVERIES IN ADD-ON SELLING TO YOUR CLIENT BASE

Let's say that you service 100 clients per week. Of the 100 people who hire you in a given week, assume that the average purchase is about $100. What would happen if you gave your staff a simple phrase they could say to your clients—right when the person is ready to pay for the service and is happiest about what you have done for them—that would persuade one out of every two customers to add an extra 20% to their transaction with you?

If you could successfully induce half of your customers to add $20 more to their purchase each time they buy from you—you've just added a significant extra revenue per sale.

If your business sells to 100 people a week, by using a simple little phrase, you could probably add $500 in profit to your cash flow every week—selling more to one out of four clients. Multiply that by 4.3 weeks in a month and you've just produced $2,150 in found profit that you never would have had before per month. Do this every month for a year, and you will have added $25,800 in extra revenue, just like that!

If you're curious about the magic phrase, let me now explain it. All you have to do to add 40% to 1500% more profit to every sale your business makes is to ask each customer, as they're finalizing their purchase, if they'd like to take advantage of an unpublicized, special offer, only available to customers buying a minimum of $100 (or any other dollar figure you want) worth of your services.

Put together an appealing "package" of easy to execute services or value-added products to be offered at the point of purchase. This package must be perceived by the customer to be extremely valuable, advantageous and desirable—but in reality, your cost must be very low. Let me give you a few examples:

If you are consulting with someone on their tax return, and you offer to include a $100 special organizing cabinet for just $58, which actually costs you only $20 and one out of every two clients buys it—you would add $38 profit to every other sale— that's like adding $19 extra profit for every client who walks through your door. If 100 clients visit you each week and you add $19 profit per client—you would be taking in $1,900 a week in absolute pure profit to your bank account. Multiplying that times four days a week equals $7600 per month. Even if you cut these estimates in half twice to remain conservative, you would still make a minimum extra profit of just under $2,000 per month, just for asking your clients if they're interested in keeping their personal finance records organized.

If you owned a restaurant and you offer your customers free dessert and coffee if their check is $10 or more, how many people might order a more expensive meal? You'd be surprised. This same principle applies to your accounting business.

You may be saying that this is too easy. Perhaps you think these ideas are too obvious and that everybody operates using the same knowledge, but everybody doesn't! People are surprisingly conservative—they are myopic—they suffer from tunnel vision and do not know how to experiment, test, and try different, unfamiliar things. Not one in 20 accounting businesses incorporates any of the techniques I have just outlined. Stated differently, that means you have an advantage in over 95 out of 100 businesses.

Another method you can use to boost your profits is telemarketing. What would happen, for example, if somebody from a company you are familiar with, whom you liked and trusted and had a good relationship with, called you up and offered you a proposition on either a service, or a package—a combination of products or services—which was only being made available to an exclusive group of customers, and not normally available? Chances are, if it were something you were excited about, you would probably agree to purchase it.

So try taking the initiative to call your customers. Educate them about the products and services you have over the phone. Put a special package together and call your preferred customers. Offer your customers a product or service that you do not normally provide as a special offer. Clients who are waiting for information on their finances will usually consider a phone call from their accountant to be important. When offering news about tax refunds or an opinion of their financial position, why not mention a special service to them that will enhance their financial future and their experience with your firm?

Calling clients behind a special mailing can also be used to strengthen your mailing efforts. Have your sales staff divide up your customers by those they have the best relationships with individually and follow up by telephone. A client of mine made an extra $40,000 dollars a few years back when he first started using telephone follow-ups to intensify and enhance the results of his mailings.

-33-

POWER UP THE SELLING SKILLS OF YOUR STAFF

M ost accounting professionals shy away when I suggest that they need to play the role of "sales person" in order to succeed in reaching their business goals. The reality is that without excellent leadership ability, people skills, and selling skills, you're in trouble. Most of your staff members are probably selling constantly without ever realizing it. They do it when they try to sell a friend on the idea of going to their favorite restaurant for lunch, or using persuasive selling approaches in other situations. Selling is a very easy and natural process. Remember, you are selling solutions that satisfy client needs and *you are selling the feelings associated with the benefits that you are providing.*

Let's look at each step in the Accounting Selling Skills Process and see how you can use a successful process to satisfy client needs at a much higher level.

"QUALIFY" YOUR CLIENTS BY ASKING QUESTIONS TO UNCOVER THEIR MOST PRESSING PROBLEMS AND UNIQUE NEEDS

When you begin to qualify clients you try to understand the needs and challenges which motivate them the most. When you match their needs to the specific advantages and associated feelings that your services give, then you are taking the first steps toward successfully selling. Please notice that I didn't say to match their needs directly to the service that you provide—rather clients accept what you offer because of the feeling that the service advantage gives them. Your clients would be more receptive to a service that offers them the feeling of freedom, than one that offers them nothing. Therefore, it becomes essential to qualify your clients to determine which advantages are most important to them. They you can recommend certain services based on the emotional and logical advantages that the services give clients, not merely the generic services themselves.

To qualify your clients you simply ask them questions. There are two kinds of questions you can ask. You can ask questions that open clients up to elaborate more on their needs and challenges. We call these "Open-Probe Questions." You can also ask what are called, "Closed-Probe Questions." These are questions that tend to limit client responses to a set of alternatives.

OPEN PROBE QUESTIONS: BEGIN WITH WHO, WHAT, WHEN, WHERE, WHY, HOW, IF AND TELL ME.

- When did you feel that you began losing control of your receivables?
- What challenges do you have with accounting programs?
- How long does it usually take you to complete your own tax preparation?
- Tell me, about any other problem areas you have noticed?
- When have you been the most frustrated with your bookkeeping?
- Etc.

CLOSED PROBE QUESTIONS: BEGIN WITH IS, ARE, DO, DOES, WHICH, WOULD, SHOULD, CAN, HAVE, HAS AND HAD.

- Would you be interested in a way to solve the problem of neglecting your receivables?
- Do you like this particular bookkeeping method?
- Would you prefer an alternative action plan for reducing costs by 30% in one or two days?
- Have you devised a tax-reduction plan that gives you ample legal write-offs and significant tax relief? Would you like to?
- Etc.

USE OPEN-PROBE QUESTIONS TO UNCOVER NEW CLIENT NEEDS AND CHALLENGES:

Accountant: *How do you handle your billing?*

Client: *We don't do it consistently enough... we're looking for a better system for executing it.*

USE CLOSED-PROBES TO CONFIRM THAT YOU HAVE ACCURATELY IDENTIFIED A CLIENT NEED.

Accountant: *Are you looking for a way to make sure it gets handled consistently without taking up the time of your employees?*

Client: *Absolutely!*

Each challenge is an opportunity to solve an underlying problem by providing the appropriate products and/or services.

After you have uncovered a sufficient number of client needs, confirmed the needs and summarize all of the needs you client has accepted during the meeting. Now it is time to gain your client's commitment to engage your services to satisfy all of their needs.

USE CLOSED PROBES TO GAIN THEIR COMMITMENT TO TAKE ACTION

Gaining your clients' commitment is as easy as asking a simple question. Use your closed-probe questions to confirm the clients' needs, for example:

> Accountant: *Would you like to conduct a three-month trial of our bill-paying service for your personal finances and your small business?*

Attempt to gain the client's commitment to use your service to solve each problem that your client has presented. Never skip over a problem, or you will simply not be giving your clients the level of attention they deserve.

Putting all of your clients through this entire process during each visit makes them feel as though you are taking time to care about them on a very personal level. This also becomes the format of your entire selling system. Use this selling system consistently, you will sell more service to more clients, and you will reap the benefits in the form of higher revenues per transaction.

EXTRA VALUE-ADDED IDEA: TRY FUTURE PACING WHEN CLIENTS ARE WITH YOU

One of the best ways to influence your clients to try a new service is to use future pacing. Future pacing is simply describing to the client how a new service will change or improve some aspect of their life as he or she partakes of it at some point in the future. The best way to future pace your clients is to describe the advantages the service will deliver directly to them. Don't over-promise. The key is to be realistic and always over-deliver. The most basic future-pacing technique involves describing what the client will experience when they first start using the service and how their lives will change as they move forward in time.

Here is an example of how you might use future pacing to influence a client to try one of your accounting or bookkeeping services:

- You'll find that once you start using our bill-paying service, you'll have more time to do the things you love to do — because you'll have more time on your hands.
- Our bill paying service will help you remake your financial situation. Your account information will be updated more frequently, and you will receive reports as often as you like. This means that you will have infinitely more control over your financial situation than you have had in the past. You'll be in better position to make wiser decisions.
- Your future financial vision will expand and grow because you will have more time to focus on earning profits, instead of just balancing your books.
- You will have an abiding sense of well-being because our advisors will work with you to steady your biggest areas of financial instability first. Once those areas of challenge are stabilized, your outlook will shift to the areas where you can make the largest long-term gains to enhance your financial stamina one-hundred-fold.

–34–

YOUR CLIENTS WANT TO BE LED...
LEAD THEM

Your clients are silently begging for you and your staff to lead them. Did you realize that most people are eager to be told what to do, how to do it, and why to do it in areas where they lack expertise? Your clients expect to be led by you. If you don't lead them they may feel disappointed.

The flip side to this is that even though people will resist being manipulated at all costs, most are very eager to be educated, informed and instructed about things they're not knowledgeable about. Everyone wants expertise, because expertise leads to knowledge and knowledge is power, and when power is applied to our tasks, we get the results we desire. Your clients want the power to enhance their physical appearance, because doing so gives them greater certainty and confidence which spills over into other aspects of their lives.

Your first goal in leading your clients is to look out for what's best for them. You have to give them recommendations and advice about how to obtain the final outcomes that they are seeking from you and your accounting business.

When you lead your clients to obtain greater results, and you provide them with well thought-out reasons for obtaining the services that will given them results, they will tend to take the action you recommend. They will appreciate your efforts and hire your services more eagerly than ever. They will seek your services more frequently. Your clients will learn to value you for leading them sensitively. Because you are always giving balanced and realistic recommendations by showing the advantages and disadvantages of each service clients know they can trust you.

The moment you become aware that your clients want to be led, your vision of what's possible for your business will start to change. Your marketing, advertising, selling, and promotion strategies will begin to shift. This will occur because you will make sure that your communication with each client leads him or her progressively to a higher level of certainty. This means that you will always give your prospective customers and present clients your best-reasoned advice, fresh new ideas, education, new late-breaking facts, news about products and processes, valuable information, valuable advice that no other accounting and bookkeeping business in your local market gives them. Then, word-of-mouth marketing will become almost automatic. This will occur because word will spread that you help clients make money, save money, and obtain much better advice than from any other accountant.

You may decide to create information sheets or booklets that accompany each service or groups of services you provide. If so, fill the publications with tips that increase the performance of the products or services that you have been hired to obtain. Use educational tools to state the case by telling the client why they need to consider using the services.

I know one accounting professional who distributes a five-minute educational audiocassette to her customers describing the services they just received. It includes an overview of the others services she offers describing what they can do throughout the year to keep more of the money they earn. Her clients appreciate the extra information and love having the ability to review it again at a later time. They get tremendous value out of the information, and love the cassette format. By doing this, she puts her clients on the road to obtaining greater value, and added enrichment to their lives. The cassette program becomes one more "pillar of influence" in their lives so that she can help them make the changes they so desperately want and need. She is leading her clients by using a powerful educational tool.

When you take a leadership position in all that you do to promote your business, you are committing to investing extra time giving prospective clients elaborate explanations, education, and direction. Put a new sense of leadership into all of your marketing methods. For example, create print ads and/or mail brochures that describe pressing problems and solutions that clients are experiencing. Explain which service choices are best suited to solve their problems by presenting information clients can use to make more money and save more costs. Then simply lead you clients to the appropriate services.

—35—

MAKE ALL OF YOUR MARKETING APPROACHES RESPONSE-ORIENTED

Once you take initiative in leading your clients, it is your responsibility to show your clients the specific actions they must take, in order to receive the greater advantages and results you have promised them. You must make all of your ads action-oriented by telling potential clients the precise next step they must take to get the results or offer you have promised. You must have an action objective for every marketing effort you make. This means that you must suggest that recipients of your marketing approaches take a very specific action that will move them closer toward developing a relationship with you. You should do this by offering to give them the benefits they desire most from you in a way that contains little or no risk for them. Each individual page of your web site must have a clear action-oriented objective, maybe to submit their e-mail address to you. Each mailing piece you send out must have an action objective, perhaps to have prospects call you for a free consultation. In addition to having an action objective for marketing efforts developed for non-clients, you must also have a very specific action-based objective visits and interactions of your present clients.

You must be fully committed to putting clear action-based incentives, motivation, and direction into every aspect of your business promotion.

Your role as marketer will not be effective unless you lead people to take a specific action. People will rarely take action if they don't feel comfortably and authoritatively led. Your role as marketer and leader unite firmly together.

In all of your marketing approaches, suggest that clients take action every time you communicate with them. Whether you are creating a print ad, a letter that includes a gift certificate, or a cooperative promotion with another business who shares the same clients that you do, include a specific call to action. If you want them to call for an appointment, tell them to call you, and give them a special incentive to do so. If you want them to bring a 30%-off certificate into your business, tell them to do so, and put an expiration date on it to create an incentive to act soon. You can put an expiration date on the promotion—"Return this Gift Certificate for a Free Tax-Burden Reduction Consultation by March 5th."

POSSIBLE ACTIONS THAT YOU MAY WANT TO SUGGEST IN YOUR PROGRAM:

- Walk-in for tax, bookkeeping service
- Walk-in for expenses slashing/profit-increasing consultation
- Call-in for an appointment to file a tax return
- Reminder to come in for their next appointment
- Mail in a card saying they are interested in highly-customized services
- Refer you to their friends, relatives or colleagues

YOU CAN CREATE SPECIAL OFFERS AND INCENTIVES FOR NEW PROSPECTS TO BECOME YOUR CLIENT:

- If you bring a friend you will both receive 30% off of the regular cost of your tax preparation
- First-time small business clients receive a free evaluation and consultation on how to keep books, files state tax returns, and will also receive a free filing system to keep their records in perfect condition for tax season

Briefly describe your offer, your services and other information that you want to convey to your clients. Use some short sentences to spur action, such as: "Come in now and save! Call now!" Short sentences like these work well in promotion.

TEST THE FOLLOWING ACTION-YIELDING WORDS IN YOUR PROMOTIONS:

- Call now
- Come in today
- Space is available
- Seating is limited
- For a short time only
- Be the first

Motivate your clients to take action by using the action words in a compelling offer. Your offer must have meaning and propose a valuable solution to your clients challenges. Often your best point of leverage will be to promise to try to help clients save a significant amount of money and time on taxes, in their business, or on personal expenses, through your analysis.

Tell clients exactly what taking action will do for them. Whether you mail a tax organizer booklet, send out postcards, or mail a eight-page letter to your clients you must spur them to take action. The action they take must be to contact you to receive more information on your offer and ultimately become a transacting client. If your marketing efforts until now have not contained words that motivate potential clients to take action, then by adding a bold tag line next to your phone number that gives clients a reason to call, you will certainly increase your response rate.

–36–

CREATE LONG-TERM BUYING PROGRAMS FOR YOUR CLIENTS

Some months bringing in more clients seems like a painful struggle and some months it seems so very easy. So many accounting professionals struggle needlessly, allowing their businesses to barely survive sometimes for months at a time during slow seasons. You do not have to let this happen to you. One way to level out the hills and valleys is by taking a long-term view of your client relationships. By creating a long-term buying program, you ensure that your clients are obtaining the highest possible value that they can receive from your business.

Long-term buying programs involve special strategies to help your clients gain greater benefits, results, and advantages from the services and products that you offer. They influence clients to think about your relationship over a longer period of time. Your first step is to help your clients develop a long-term strategy by making the services you offer them immediately perform better for them.

Your biggest challenge in crafting a long-term buying program is to take a long-range view of your client relationships. It is always imperative to remember that your business offers a much higher-level of long-run benefits than the short-run, generic accounting services you sell. You do not just sell generic service, such as "tax preparation," "accounting" or "payroll services," but rather the more desirable benefits that the generic services bring. Benefits such as the *security* or *freedom* of knowing you are providing a tax strategy to help clients forever avoid the problem of overpaying taxes. The more valuable specific benefits that you provide include elements such as *greater freedom, certainty, security and the power to make better, wiser financial decisions with infinitely more confidence.* For example, your services may give clients greater security by showing them how to keep more of their money, how to get out of debt, or find new sources of business or personal income. If so, these special and unique advantages should become the basis of your long-term program. The bottom line is that because your accounting service is solving specific long-term human financial-related problems, you owe it to yourself and your clients to formulate a progressive long-term program that your clients will accept.

Knowing the specific long-term benefits that your accounting clients want most puts you miles ahead of your competition. I say this because 95% of competing accounting and bookkeeping professionals do not understand this simple distinction. And if your competition does understand it, they probably have not taken the initiative to act on it by articulating the specific benefits to their clients on a consistent basis. So just by taking consistent action to communicate your long-term buying program, you are already light-years ahead of everyone else in your market. Knowing that you are ahead before you even get started should motivate you to begin by expanding on the benefits and advantages of your firm and formalizing them by crafting a long-term client-buying program.

One way that I will lead you to increase the value of your business will be by converting the obvious and hidden benefits you give to your clients into tangible value for them. You may not be consciously aware of many of the benefits that you have already been giving to your clients. If this is the case, as I suspect it is, then you are undervaluing—perhaps under pricing—your services. When you fully understand the long-term benefits given to your clients, then you will be focused on creating additional value for them by adding extra service and other unique touches. Then it becomes easier for your clients to value your services at a much higher level and perhaps be willing to pay you more for your services while being motivated to use them more often.

Once you recognize the specific long-run benefits your business gives your clients, you can begin to create new programs and strategies centered around your clients. You must develop better advisory services, customize more personal financial decision-making tools and other programs for your clients. Clients will have more effective ways to become free of the routine bookkeeping tasks of their small businesses. You will give better solutions than your competitors to clients who find themselves in overwhelming tax/debt situations. You will give your clients more long-range options to select from.

One of my clients took my advice after finding her hidden benefit and created what I call a "lifetime financial security approach" to her accounting business. Her program was so successful that she restructured her marketing approaches around this new long-run concept. The reason that she decided to change her business approach was because she had been a tax accountant for years and was tired of the seasonal feast or famine fluctuations that she had been experiencing. She simply knew that her business had to change in order to improve. She observed a wealthy friend, who lost his high-ranking job, and then spent five years on the unemployment roles, only to lose his savings due to several bad business decisions he made. She noticed that for years her friend longed to experience the security he once had when he had been employed. This inspired her to use her knowledge to help others make sounder and wiser financial decisions. So she began converting her regular clients into enrollees for her "lifetime financial security" program. They paid her a monthly fee, signed a three-year agreement, and received a long list of highly-customized services that guaranteed the improvement of their financial picture, giving them greater security. Within a year and a half she hired others to help her perform her lifetime financial security counseling, and she was clearing over a half-million dollars in gross revenue. This occurred because she recognized that a large number of potential clients also wanted to find a way to increase the feeling of security they were missing. Once she adapted this key benefit of helping clients find greater security into her business as a long-term program, she transformed her business from one that offered generic accounting services into one that improved the lives of clients in an exceptionally unique way.

I want you to take some time to look at your business from a fresh perspective as you consider the example. You can take your business to any level you want by using this concept. Converting your clients into long-term buyers. Buyers not of your generic products or services, but people who are loyal to the outstanding advantages that you give. Ones that improve their business and lives profoundly.

Make a list of all the accounting, bookkeeping, and a financial services that you now provide and the hidden advantages and benefits that each one offers to your clients. Now consider how you can rearrange all of these advantages into a program that will allow you to increase the value you give to your clients. It's a reverse thinking challenge. I am asking you to lead with a though process that puts the self-serving advantages that your clients receive from you first. It's like leading with a bold promise. By explaining the advantages that each of your services gives first you will communicate better and hook your clients faster.

One idea is to bundle together some of your services and offer 3-month, 6-month, or yearly packages of the bundled services. You can explain to clients that the advantage is that they receive totally customized service at an incredible savings. Clients can buy your services by time periods with the incentive that you will give them additional services or unlimited access to your advice. This ensures that they will not make decisions throughout the year that will hit them in the wallet next tax season.

Another idea is that you add some unique services to your mix of present accounting services, such as a web site, which gives your clients special tools to self-analyze their entire financial picture quickly. Maybe you will decide to make bonus financial software available to your clients in exchange for a small yearly membership fee.

PERSUADE CLIENTS WITH APPROPRIATE PRICING INCENTIVES

Pricing inducements are a simple, but often overlooked, way for you to persuade your existing clients to try new services. They work especially well when you combine them with a long-term buying program.

You can test all different kinds of inducements to persuade your customers to hire you more often and to attract brand new clients to your door. If you have never tested the influence that different "pricing incentives" have to motivate clients to take action, then you have been missing out on potentially huge revenues.

A lot of your clients will appreciate being offered an incentive for coming back and purchasing more often. It is so simple. I know of restaurants that have created frequent dinner points, coffee houses that use frequent patronage cards for free cups of coffee, record clubs that use similar incentives, such as six CDs for $.06. If all of these other businesses use incentives to persuade clients to buy, why can't your accounting or bookkeeping business do the same? Do these incentives work? They work exceptionally well.

Ask yourself this key question: How many ways can I use pricing inducements to persuade my clients to hire my business more often?

One accounting professional, who decided to expand his business into the financial services area, sells investments to his clients under a separate business that he has a stake in. When he started converting his accounting clients into investment clients many of them asked him why they should use his financial services. He understood the necessity of giving them an incentive to work with him, so he decided to build a long-term buying incentive into his business by taking part of the commissions he received by selling securities and giving a portion back to his clients in the form of more securities. He did this as a reward every six months. The result was that he developed a unique approach that made his services appear different to clients. His clients tend to be much more loyal than those of any competitors. In addition, he also gave extra service, information updates and he created an e-zine—an e-mail magazine that gave extra valuable information. The total "impression package" that he marketed to clients was one of extra attention, service, freedom, and added value in the form of tangible securities.

You should use the idea of creating long-term buying programs in multiple ways to create extra value. I am certain that many of your own "spin-off" ideas are now apparent to you that may not have been before reading this chapter. Your next aim must be to test these and many other ideas to target finding your best alternative long-term buying program.

Here are more suggestions for developing a successful long-term buying program in your business:

- Offer a price incentive to clients for buying three months worth of accounting or financial services or any other combination of your services or products for a monthly fee. Charge this fee each month to their credit card.
- Sell membership packages that give certain exclusive clients access to your advisory services for specific periods of time.
- Give clients who buy $250 worth of "start-up, small-business advice" an extra $100 credit towards first year tax preparation for paying up front.
- Provide clients with a special incentive for buying three or six months' worth of services for one flat up front payment for a cost-savings.

Spark up your creativity and get excited about the possibilities that are before you in developing a long-term buying program.

There are all kinds of new opportunities and spin-off ideas that can be tested using a long-term buying program in your business.

–37–

HOW TO INCREASE THE PROBABILITY THAT CLIENTS WILL HIRE YOU AGAIN

Your primary objective after the client has hired you to perform service is to make certain the client is inclined to use your firm again. I have created a list of activities that most accountants would acknowledge as good client relations on any service engagement, but which most accounting professionals would admit are often overlooked. Please read this list with exceptional caution. There is a profound difference between simply acknowledging the tactics listed below and having an organized plan of action to ensure their execution.

Listed below are powerful ideas for creating mini-systems aimed at dramatically improving your client-relations approaches:

I. GO THE EXTRA MILE ON YOUR CURRENT CONSULTING ENGAGEMENTS.

- Increase the quality of your presentations by adding information summaries and bullet points. Spice up the graphics on your presentations to make them look exquisite. Provide presentations to all clients using multiple media and in more than one format — reports on paper and electronically (i.e. portable document files/ Adobe Acrobat files— pdf).
- Increase the quality of your documentation; provide more documentation, extra explanations, and more accessibility to value-added information.
- Improve your turnaround time and your service completion time on specific portions of your service. Remember: the most difficult aspect of any project is finishing the last 15% of it. Push harder at the end of each project to crank out the last, most sluggish portion faster. Put on one or two additional staff members toward the end of every project (I call them "push catalysts").

2. DRAMATICALLY INCREASE THE AMOUNT OF CLIENT CONTACT.

- Call clients on the phone regularly. Double check everything and never assume that clients are content. Use an extra staff member to call clients, ascertaining that no task falls through the cracks. This increases clients' awareness that they are receiving first-class attention.
- Every opportunity should be taken to visit clients. Send special part-time or full-time staff to client offices to double-check on the client. I know one accountant who sends a representative to different clients once per week, gives the staff pastries, and lets the small business owners know that their accountant was thinking about them.
- Invite clients to the office of your firm.
- Have special get-togethers and fun social events. Have an intimate cocktail party for groups of select clients. Schedule business meetings near mealtime. One popular accountant schedules business lunches at the client's place of business and surprises them with a fancy catered lunch. Administrative staff is invited to partake. They all love the accountant's gregarious efforts and remember him favorably when he calls or walks in.
- Make special occasions to introduce your clients to the partners and staff of your firm. Give your clients the feeling that they are being introduced to a happy family of people who love and respect them.

3. BUILD A STRONG BUSINESS RELATIONSHIP.

- Help your clients develop new and better contacts.
- Conduct special seminars for client staff. If you know that there are special skill areas that would boost the productivity of your client, consider conducting free mini-seminars during the lunch hour as a bonus. You could also hold seminars using teleconferencing or video conferencing technologies.
- Volunteer to attend special internal client meetings to give your advice on the issues that are raised and how to increase collaboration and overall productivity.
- Offer a session of consulting service on non-project issues. You may decide to offer your advice in some specific areas that add extra value and an objective evaluation. Promise to spend two hours to a half-day making an evaluation on the issues and always give your client your best-reasoned

advice.

- Continually send your clients useful articles that relate to the issues they have hired you to work on. Continue to do this even after your primary issue-related consulting session is finished. Sending articles that you have written and published boosts your credibility.
- If possible, become a source of referrals for your clients.

4. BUILD STRONG PERSONAL RELATIONSHIPS WITH YOUR CLIENTS.

- Share outside social activities with your best clients regularly. Send them articles, books and high-quality self-improvement programs related to their favorite interests and personal hobbies.
- Actively learn about and remember special personal events, such as birthdays, personal and family anniversaries, etc. Make it a special point to celebrate regularly the personal events that are most precious to the lives of your clients.
- Obtain tickets to scarce events that your clients would love to attend. Attending plays, ballets, sporting events, music concerts, jazz dinner theaters, and other cultural events tends to make people feel special. Add this special dimension of giving to your to-do lists and watch your relationships with clients grow deeper.
- Consider providing your clients with your home telephone number and your personal e-mail address.
- Welcome your large clients to use your firm's facilities for certain projects. If your facilities hold larger numbers of people than your client's facilities, offer to let them use your auditorium for a special event.

The level of nurturing and client care that you and your staff give must be preeminent. You must positively change the mental and emotional state of your clients every time you contact them. You must develop new ways to pump more advantage-rich experiences into the lives of clients in every way possible. Your clients are not just clients; they are people with feelings, emotions and vital interests. Cater to these aspects of your client on a multitude of different dimensions and they will retain your services to a significantly larger degree.

−38−

ACTIVELY PURSUE THE NEXT ENGAGEMENT DURING EACH BUSINESS-TO-BUSINESS CONSULTATION

As an accountant you are the hunter. Your prey is to capture new opportunities and to continually expand your relationships with your clients. Just like the hunter you are always striving to improve the skills of your craft. Instead of a bow and arrow your two primary tools are:

Tool One:　Digging out intelligence on new client needs
Tool Two:　Assembling opportunities to make the client aware of how you can satisfy the new need

Here are the best tactics we have discovered to assist you in your hunt for finding and pursuing the next consulting engagement:

I. CREATE OPPORTUNITIES TO TANGIBLY DEMONSTRATE YOUR COMPETENCE AND ABILITY TO TAKE INITIATIVE:
- Volunteer services of partnering consultants to provide fresh areas of expertise your client has not yet been exposed to. Create teams with other consultants as subcontractors and allow them to jump-start new projects toward the end of your time with your client. Take on new consulting partners in your business if you work alone. If you do not work alone, have partners that you bring in on field assignments or farm work out to; create a broad-spectrum network of competent partners.

2. DIG OUT NEW INTELLIGENCE ON NEW NEEDS:
- Get invited to special strategic meetings that the client conducts regularly.
- Arrange to meet with other executives, partners, and/or spouse of the client to get a fuller picture of their needs.
- Spend more time with the client's staff at all levels.

3. ASSEMBLE CONCRETE EVIDENCE OF NEW NEEDS:

- Most accountants conduct an initial needs and situational analysis at the beginning of a consulting intervention. Try adding additional analyses. I suggest conducting a mini-study half way through to give the client an update on your progress and to share with them how their needs may have changed. Toward the end of your consultation, conduct a new need analysis that shifts the core focus of the need areas into several new areas that will translate into additional benefits for the client and more billable work for you.
- If possible, conduct additional interviews toward the middle and end of your project to uncover new needs areas.

4. MAKING THE CLIENT AWARE OF NEW NEEDS:

- Bring problem areas to the attention of the client early on in the process. Find ways to alert the client of possible threats to his or her well-being.
- Provide clearly documented evidence of needs and associated problems to the client in multiple forms. Use graphs, charts, descriptions, and documented letters from different managers or clients to really make the problem areas stand out.
- Compare the primary statistics of your clients' problem areas to those of other clients, which will drive home, their understanding of the most likely consequences their need poses.
- Share tangible results and proof of the work you have performed for others in similar need and problem areas.

5. LET THE GAME COME TO YOU. ASK FOR THE NEW ENGAGEMENT AT THE RIGHT TIME:

- Point out opportunities to solve problems early and often in the process of your consultation.
- Never use "hard-sell" tactics. If you have done all of the above the new engagement will practically sell itself.
- Present your proposal only when you think it will be accepted. Do not wait until your engagement is over to present it. This will probably be too late.

Even after all of your efforts to continue to obtain more new business from existing clients, you will still not convince every one to re-hire you. Pay close attention to your patterns of success. Look ahead. Use your past experiences to help you predict those clients who tend to rehire you and the reasons why they do. Keep your eyes open and take consistent action to move each client into a deeper relationship with you.

–39–

PROPERLY RE-INVEST IN MARKETING TO OBTAIN BETTER CLIENTS OVER TIME

Profits from loyal accounting clients increase over time. At the beginning of your relationship your cost to acquire a client might range from $50 to $1,000, depending upon your industry and specialty.

First, you have to know how much you must be willing to invest in your marketing program to acquire a client. So many accountants invest too little of their resources and find that their marketing results are poor. Let's calculate the cost of acquiring your client. I will use a direct marketing example—mailing to your house list of hot prospects. Perhaps you have spoken at several association meetings and obtained names of people interested in your services. Maybe you have been networking and have gathered the business cards of interested potential clients. You now have in your possession a list of hot prospects—individuals or businesses that have an interest in your services. Let's say that you have a hot list of 1,000 clients in your database.

How much are these potential clients worth to you? How much should you invest in additional marketing to influence them to hire your accounting service? Well, the answer is found by determining the value of those clients to your business.

One rule of thumb is that you should be willing to invest the dollar amount equal to at least your first transaction with them. How much is your average first transaction typically worth in dollars? How much does a first-time client pay you on average for one consulting session? Let's say this amount is $400 for the first transaction with you. Okay?

Now keeping that in mind think about how much your client is worth to you as an estimate over their lifetime of doing business with you? If your average accounting transaction is worth $400 and your client hires you six times per year (on average) and stays with you for about three years (on average), then the lifetime value of your client is $7,200 ($400 x 6 x 3 = $7,200). If you already have 1,000 clients, then your client base has a lifetime value of $7.2 million. Now you can see the power of delegating work to teams of employees and farming out more services to outside professionals.

If you know that you must be willing to invest $400 per client to capture one, then how can you use that knowledge to automatically guide your marketing decisions? It is easy! Using direct mail you can send valuable information to each prospect on your list of 1,000 clients. In the first two mailings to the whole list you can offer something of exceptional value for free in return for their response. You can offer a CD, a video, a book you have written, a cassette program that you have created, in exchange for their response to call you, write you, or e-mail you. If your first two mailings cost you 55¢ per mailing, then you have just spent $1,100 on the mailing. If you get a 5% response, (that is, 50 people), you have only invested $22 per client. You have $378 left to invest to obtain each client. Do you see how to measure the value of your clients to guide your marketing investment?

Now you have a decision to make. You can mail again to the list of 1,000 clients to see if any more of them are going to call you in response to your free offer. This is a great idea. Let's say you do that and pick up another 2% of the remaining list. Now you have 70 very interested people. You have still only spent $23.18 per interested client to get those 70 people to respond to your offer. That is 2950 mail-outs at 55¢ apiece divided by 70 prospects obtained. Right? This means that you still need to invest $376.82 per final client so you have still invested way too little in your marketing program. Got it? Good!

Now we have invested in marketing to capture 70 really hot prospects for your accounting service from the original 1,000 names on your house list. Following our logic, if you call up your 69 hot prospects, or visit them in sales calls, or offer them an initial needs analysis, or mail them a book per week from the hottest author in your industry, or send them some very valuable information, then you will convert some of them into clients. Let's say you are confident that you can convert 50% of them into clients—which would be about 35 people. Calculating the value of your time and continuing efforts to capture these 35 clients you should be willing to spend about $188 on the 70 clients to make 35 of them convert. How you do that is completely up to your creative abilities, time and other talents. Just remember according to lifetime value calculations, your 35 new clients will bring about $252,000 worth of new business to you. Continue investing in your client base until you have invested the proper amount in each of your clients. Chances are that you may have been investing too little until now.

Your goal in marketing accounting services is to invest the appropriate amount in obtaining clients, as I have just explained. Most accountants have a tendency to invest too little in their marketing. Then one day, they awaken to fully understand the value their clients possess.

Now you know what 99% of the business world does not understand about the power of using marketing to invest in clients. And you now know what it really takes for an accountant to use marketing successfully to capture prospects systematically.

INVESTING TIME AND MONEY IN MARKETING

Allocate time to marketing. Work with different associations, different groups, different ads and different mailings. Sometimes you will have a hundred responses; other times you will have twenty. It is a cumulative process. Always experiment to find the approach, the articulation, the headline, and the unique selling proposition that draws and converts the most responses.

Keep in mind that receiving the "most responses" does not always mean the "most clients." You have to analyze the results of each marketing effort. And it is not a one-shot deal, it is a perpetual function.

Professionals have to look at time and financial investment in marketing as any businessperson would. Seed your strategy with capital—whatever you can afford. Thereafter, reinvest a significant percentage of the new business that comes in. In other words, if you know that thirty days after presenting a seminar you normally receive 10% of the people as clients and if the average seminar draws a hundred people, that means ten new clients per seminar. If you charge $70 for first-time clients, the lecture is worth $700 in new business to you. And most will return many times. Commit the whole $700 that came in from that seminar towards the next promotion.

Or, to use another example, if every time you mail out 1,000 newsletters, postcards or letters, and ten new clients respond within 45 days, assuming their worth is $200 each in the first month, that indicates the mailing is worth $2,000 in business. Reinvest that $2,000, or a percentage of every month's additional revenue, in marketing the next promotional mailing.

You need a commitment to reinvest on a regular, structured

basis or your marketing efforts may fall through. In order to maintain its effect, it must be a perpetual program, which you are committed to forever, or until you achieve the level of client saturation of the practice that you are looking for.

-40-

PUNCH-UP THE SPEED AND QUALITY
OF YOUR SERVICES

Some accounting and bookkeeping marketers don't think about the importance of speed and service quality. These are very important marketing tools because they can separate you from your competition and generate more word-of-mouth for you. You can use this as the primary basis of your competitive point-of-difference. Help shape the expectations of your clients by sharing what your turnaround times are for each project. Give each client a description of the service quality that you will give them to help them set their expectations regarding your standards for doing business. Mention your high-level standards for all projects regarding speed and quality through all of your advertising to make it clear to all clients what they should expect from you. Consider including mention of the reason why you are faster and have higher-quality service than competitors in your unique selling proposition.

Your clients would love to have the opportunity to receive fast answers to their most pressing questions. If your service is twice as fast as your average competitor that alone will make you appear different. If the quality of your work is two-times better than your competitors—perhaps you can prove that your clients experience half of the number audits of competitors—that alone will set you apart. If you poll your clients you will discover their specific determining dimensions for high-quality service. For some it means more pampering and attention, which takes a little more time. So you must try to find a balance by working with clients until they are satisfied.

Because your aim is to completely "wow" your clients every time by enhancing the quality of your services you need to constantly monitor and improve five key areas of your business:

Reliability: Performing your accounting service dependably and accurately

Tangibles: Making certain that the appearance of your physical facilities, personnel, and communication materials are impeccable

Responsiveness: The desire of your staff to help clients and provide prompt service

Assurance: The knowledge and courtesy of employees and their ability to convey trust.

Empathy: The caring, customized, individualized attention you and your staff provides to clients.

TEN WAYS TO INCREASE THE PERCEIVED QUALITY OF YOUR ACCOUNTING PRACTICE

There are special qualities that position top-performing accountants ahead of all competitors. These little-known qualities stimulate word-of-mouth more than all the paid advertising of a lifetime in business. Marketing your accounting practice begins with the ability to describe the critical dimensions of your service in a way that builds trust and coaxes your clients to want more of the edifying services that you offer.

I have created a special list of the 10 dimensions of service that all accountants should articulate and exude during every interaction with their clients. I have included sample articulations, which will give you spin-off ideas for applying the concepts to your business. You may want to apply these ideas to your business by printing your approaches to them in your brochures. They can be articulated verbally by communicating what can be expected of you. Imagery may be used to take your clients forward in time to help raise their level of expectations by denominating what they will experience—giving a detailed preview—to help establish realistic expectations when using your service from beginning to end. This is a very powerful way to communicate to new clients not only what specific services you give, but also as proof that you render your services with excellence. Using the list that follows as a checklist to create your own list of selling and marketing advantages will instantly position you above competitors. Here are the dimensions and some sample applications for communicating the high service value that you give to clients:

DIMENSION ONE
RELIABILITY — INVOLVES CONSISTENCY OF PERFORMANCE AND DEPENDABILITY.

HOW TO USE THIS IDEA:
- Keep accurate billing and work logs.
- Keep records correctly.
- Perform the accounting service at the designated time.
- Make a tickler file of "client promises" and come through on all promises to all clients.

ARTICULATION:

"Joan (potential client), when we say that our accounting practice strives to give complete reliability, this is what you can expect from us: We will perform the service right the very first time we do it or you do not have to pay for it; it means we honor our promises to do the following for you:
- "To give you total accuracy in billing;
- "To keep records using a special time-tracking computer program so that you are only billed for the hours we actually work for you and never more;
- "We perform the service at the designated time that we say we will and never later."

DIMENSION TWO
RESPONSIVENESS — CONCERNS THE WILLINGNESS OR READINESS OF YOUR EMPLOYEES TO PROVIDE SERVICE.

HOW TO USE THIS IDEA:
- Call clients back quickly.
- Take actions when your window of opportunity dictates, i.e., mailing a transaction slip immediately when the client requires it.
- Give prompt service—when the client wants the service.

ARTICULATION:

"Joan, whenever you or any of your people call our offices, your phone call will be taken immediately. If I or my staff are unavailable, the secretary will take a message and I or a critical care staff member will call you back within 20 minutes."

"Your final report will be created within three days of your last in-house interview and a complete plan will be shipped overnight to you."

DIMENSION THREE
COMPETENCE — POSSESSION OF THE REQUIRED SKILLS AND
KNOWLEDGE TO PERFORM THE SERVICE.

HOW TO USE THIS IDEA:
- Increase the knowledge and skill of your whole staff to serve the client with excellence. This means creating a total marketing and learning organization.
- Give your front-line assistants continuous "people and communications" training.
- Continuously analyze the capabilities of yourself and your accounting business objectively to improve the quality of the intangible assets you offer.

ARTICULATION:
"We have hired the best staff with excellent levels of competence and education. To give you an idea of the competence level of my staff, I want you to know that our newest staff member has a minimum of seven years of active hands-on experience in working with clients. Our average employee has spent 10 years in this field and we have invested over $10,000 in professional educational development per year in each employee.

"We have a very exclusive research team consisting of three highly-trained and tenured MBAs. They will be assigned to your business for three weeks to help you scour your industry for the best possible opportunities to franchise (fill in the need of your client) your business. They will have a franchise buyers list of over 100 qualified buying partners in the first week alone."

DIMENSION FOUR
ACCESS — INVOLVES APPROACHABILITY AND EASE OF CONTACT.

HOW TO USE THIS IDEA:
- Use technology to increase speed and productivity and not unintentionally block access to your company services. Telephone audio text prompts can make small companies look like big businesses and also make them as non-customer driven as their larger counterparts.
- Reduce the waiting time for appointments to receive

service.
- Give unconventional hours of operation — i.e. 24-hour on-call service.

ARTICULATION:

"If my office and staff are exceptionally busy, your greatest waiting time for an appointment will be no more than 12 hours from the time you call us."

"To obtain information about the work that has been done on your account, you can read an updated report on our secured server Web page. You can get information any time you need it — 24-hours a day."

DIMENSION FIVE
COURTESY — INVOLVES POLITENESS, RESPECT, CONSIDERATION, AND FRIENDLINESS OF CONTACT PERSONNEL.

HOW TO USE THIS IDEA:
- Train staff to have common courtesy and consideration for client's property (no muddy shoes during visits).
- Clean appearance of public contact staff.
- Well-spoken staff members who know how to maintain the esteem of clients.

ARTICULATION:

"My staff will always take your request with the utmost respect for you and your time. In everything we will always try hard to consider your resources before we take any action on your behalf."

"We always try to be friendly and give you a reinforcing and pleasant experience. Our philosophy is to nurture our clients during every aspect of the consulting encounter."

DIMENSION SIX
COMMUNICATION — MEANS KEEPING CUSTOMERS INFORMED IN A LANGUAGE THEY UNDERSTAND AND LISTENING TO THEM. THIS MAY MEAN ADJUSTING YOUR LANGUAGE FOR DIFFERENT CLIENTS.

HOW TO USE THIS IDEA:
- Take time to explain the service itself.
- Explain how much the service will cost.
- When writing a final report include a cost breakdown showing your fee for sourcing additional future services for them.

ARTICULATION:

"I will explain the most pertinent aspects of our service to you so that you can choose the aspects that are best for you."

"I will explain how much each service component will cost and help you to compare the costs so that we can work together to choose the best alternatives for you."

"We will spend time discussing the trade-offs between services."

DIMENSION SEVEN
CREDIBILITY — INVOLVES TRUSTWORTHINESS, BELIEVABILITY, AND HONESTY. IT INVOLVES HAVING THE CLIENTS' BEST INTEREST AT HEART.

HOW TO USE THIS IDEA:
- Expand the reputational capital of your name and your company name.
- Enhance the personal integrity characteristics of your staff.
- Reduce the amount of "hard sell" involved in your client interactions.

ARTICULATION:

"You may notice that my aim is to build trust. I do not believe in hard sales tactics because we want you to work within your comfort zone. I hope that you will make a decision to work with me when you feel most comfortable."

"Our company has a reputation for working hard to please clients."

"Most of my staff hold the same philosophy and characteristics. Keeping our promises is most important to all of us."

DIMENSION EIGHT
SECURITY — THE FREEDOM FROM DANGER, RISK, OR DOUBT.

HOW TO USE THIS IDEA:
- Increase the financial security of the client.
- Explain the steps you take to reduce the client's risk.
- Outline ways you protect client's confidentiality so that your dealings remain private.

ARTICULATION:

"In order to increase your sense of well-being and to protect you financially, your accounting retainer fee is held in escrow by a private outside escrow firm. We have absolutely no access to these funds. With your retainer safely in place, we will then begin your accounting service. After our first 25 hours of billable work is completed, and you have had a chance to evaluate the level of results we will derive for you, a portion of the funds are released to us and we will continue the relationship. If you decide not to proceed, the entire retainer fee will be immediately refunded in full. You are totally protected with no risk."

DIMENSION NINE
UNDERSTANDING — KNOWING THE CLIENT IS ABOUT MAKING THE EFFORT TO COMPLETELY UNDERSTAND YOUR CLIENT'S NEEDS.

HOW TO USE THIS IDEA:
- Learn the specific, precise requirements of the client.
- Provide customized attention.
- Give regular, frequent, high-paying special recognition.

ARTICULATION:

"Part of our consulting process involves spending some time with you to look deeply at the need dimensions of your business. We will spend about five hours with your people. We will systematically look at every possible requirement that you have."

"Because you are one of our best clients we want to take out a full page advertisement in your leading industry trade journal telling your clients all the wonderful things you are accomplishing."

DIMENSION TEN
TANGIBLES — INCLUDE ALL THE PHYSICAL EVIDENCE OF THE ACCOUNTING SERVICE THAT YOU GIVE.

HOW TO USE THIS IDEA:
- Your appearance must be flawless, including the dress of your staff, the appearance of your office, and the reports

and materials you create.
- Virtually everything that you give your client tells a story about you.
- What other clients say about you forms your tangible reputational capital.

ARTICULATION:

"Virtually everything we do for you will be impeccable. The work we do, the reports we generate, and the advice we give you will be the very best we know how to create. If something ever seems the least bit off, tell us and we will make it right immediately. But we don't think that will ever happen based on the track record that we have in this industry. We want you to know that you are receiving the very best service possible at all points along the accounting continuum."

BOOK'EM FASTER... BOOK'EM SMARTER

To make more money everyday, you must see more clients. Use a booking strategy that keeps clients rolling through your business smoothly. If you usually make appointments on the hour, as most service professionals do, try making a simple change. If you make appointments every half-hour or 45 minutes, you can increase the number of clients you see and you will boost your income dramatically. By tightening your system, you will make use of every minute.

If you schedule clients using this method, you can increase your sales dramatically in only a few days. To help with the process, hire assistants to perform initial client interviews and perform other tasks for you at critical moments. Contact colleges and universities in your area to see if they would be willing to help you by referring interns to your office as paid student assistants during peak times.

MAKE EVERYTHING YOU DO REFLECT EXCELLENT SERVICE
- Prepare a written document that details the principles of your customer service program. Perhaps you will hang it on your waiting area wall so clients will know that your dedication to them is your core goal.
- Make sure your employees share the vision of how important customer service is to your success. Tell them exactly what kind of performance you expect from them, and reward them for delivering it.
- Make every aspect of your service extra special for each

client. When a client walks in for the first time, make sure they are greeted and ensure that every professional they connect with introduces themselves, remembers and uses their name, and makes them feel that they are important. Make exceptional client service your competitive edge.

- When you interview your clients (before performing any service), make sure that you ask them what their biggest challenges are. Really listen. This means doing less talking and more listening. Allow your clients to share their challenges. Let them know that you are really listening by making eye contact and nodding when you understand. Focus your energies on them. Throughout the entire experience use their name, too, as you make eye contact with them.

- Create tangible value for your clients throughout their entire service experience. Try my Experiential Marketing Test (EMT). Walk through your office and pretend that you are visiting it for the very first time. Pretend that you are a new client. Walk through each aspect of your business thinking about what your clients' experience is when they come in for service. Walk in the paths they walk. Stand where they stand. Sit where they sit. Carefully observe everything your client experiences from their vantage point. Take careful notes as you walk through your office. At each stage, ask yourself how many of your clients' experiences involve their five senses. Ask yourself the following questions as you experience each stage through your client's eyes.

  - What do my clients see?
  - What do they hear?
  - What do they feel?
  - What do they taste?
  - What smells do they experience?

As you walk through your office, notice which of their senses has not been positively impacted by your service strategy. If you determine that there is a missing sense from your client's perspective, for example, "if they typically taste nothing" at your office, consider adding gourmet coffees, and pastries. The sense of smell is very important. Many hotel marketers add the scent of apples and cinnamon to their lobbies and restrooms to instantly give the impression of feeling at home. The more positive sensations, that your clients experience at your office, the better they will perceive their total service experience. If your office is not clean, or if it is cluttered, clients will tend to be less satisfied with the total experience. Try my EMT test and let me know what

-41-

INCREASE YOUR CAPACITY TO SERVE YOUR CLIENTS WITH EXCELLENCE

Another very important aspect of marketing your accounting services involves communicating to clients that your knowledge and talent are being customized to their particular situation. Once your marketing efforts have been successful, your focus must shift to the second stage of marketing, which involves investments of time and resources to increase your capabilities to serve clients with increasing excellence. Some of your non-billable marketing budget should be dedicated to tasks that systematically lead to uncovering new client needs, or areas where the client is dissatisfied with their current situation, and to provide new documentation and evidence to persuade the client to proceed in new areas.

Here are some of the most practical, simple, and easy-to-apply ideas. I am continually shocked and amazed to discover that more accountants do not execute all of the steps listed below as an all-encompassing system of business marketing improvement. We have included ideas for corporate clients, as well as individuals. Use these vital steps to increase the level of excellence and professionalism associated with your accounting services:

1. MAXIMIZING YOUR KNOWLEDGE OF EACH CLIENT'S INDUSTRY

- Compile a list of every industry magazine, trade journal, and newsletter and read them thoroughly. Go to a university business library and study Industry Trade Summaries of each client industry.
- Attend industry trade meetings with your biggest clients. Attend key seminars at conventions and trade shows.
- Conduct proprietary studies and in-depth interviews with industry experts and authors of significant articles who have published in trade journals. Try to get a grasp of the key leading indicators of the state of the industry. Dig out the trends related to your area of accounting expertise.

2. SYSTEMATICALLY INCREASE YOUR WORKING KNOWLEDGE OF YOUR CLIENT'S BUSINESS

- Methodically study all client-collateral material. Read the company's brochures, annual reports, publicity releases, and other available documents.
- Request to see the strategic plan of every client.
- Volunteer to critique internal studies that have been conducted in specific areas.

3. INCREASE YOUR KNOWLEDGE OF YOUR CLIENT'S ORGANIZATION

- Always ask for a copy of the client's organizational chart. Early on in the consultation use the organizational chart to look for spin-off consulting opportunities across other departments and in other organizational areas. One accountant uses organizational charts in a unique way. He points to other key departments and asks the client how other departments interface with theirs; then proceeds to take down the names of the people responsible for those areas and enlists his current contact to help approach those people. If the contact thinks the accountant will be able to help in other areas, then the consultant requests a referral. He networks other business internally and usually multiplies his billable workload by 300 percent per consultation using this simple idea.
- Ask your primary contact who he or she deals with the most. List all of the additional information that arises from these internal relationships.
- Obtain full details about the power structure of the organization. Make certain you know the internal rules. I call this "tacit knowledge." It is often difficult to ascertain how to work the system. It often requires that you read between the lines.
- Arrange to interview other key executives to see if they help confirm or refute your initial impressions. Meet executives who are seniors and juniors to your main contact. Study the whole staff and look for the problems, challenges, threats, and opportunities for improvement. Carefully record all of your impressions.

4. INCREASE YOUR KNOWLEDGE OF YOUR CLIENT

- Find out what the client is most unhappy about. Look at the areas of the business that cause the most pain for the client. Target those areas first during your consultation.

- Find out how the department or business is evaluated. If there are no evaluation measures or guidelines in place, suggest that you be hired to develop and implement them. When consulting with small businesses, find out what procedures and standard practices have been formally put into place or what the company's best practices have been that relate to your area of expertise, and propose that they hire you to improve them. For example, most small businesses have very unclear superior/subordinate relationships. It is common for one employee to be unclear about whom they should report to. Knowing intimate details of the business, management styles, and how it is conducted is vital.

With all of this client knowledge to back you, you will have a much greater consulting capacity. You will be much freer to objectively explore new situations, see important patterns, and generate infinitely more astute recommendations.

-42-

MAKE WORKING WITH YOUR FIRM MORE PLEASURABLE

Everything about your accounting business—all of the interior design attributes, level of cleanliness, employee attitudes, and your ability to create a desirable, fun atmosphere—everything that your business exudes creates a continual and lasting impression. That impression is multiplied either negatively or positively through word-of-mouth referrals. I can't tell you how many business owners create an atmosphere that is a complete turn-off without ever realizing it. Sometimes the atmosphere created is oppressive. Sometimes it is sterile. Sometimes it is intimidating. Often it is anything but pleasant, or desirable, or comfortable.

As a marketer, your goal is simple: You want to do everything in your power to make working with your firm fun, easy, appealing, and so desirable that your clients hate to leave your office. You want them to feel excited to come back again. This means that you do not want to seem condescending in any way. You don't want to make any visit to your establishment awkward or intimidating in the slightest way for anybody or for any reason. You want to have everyone who works for you, everything you do, and everything you stand for, to become pleasant, enjoyable, and comforting for your clients.

Have you ever visited a business and been put off by how difficult they made it for you to do business with them? Maybe you had a bad experience at a doctor's office or a restaurant. Perhaps you had to wait too long in the waiting area for your scheduled appointment. I am sure that at least once in your personal experience you ran across a worker who was rude or unsympathetic when you came in to visit that establishment. I am sure you have had at least one service professional who did not respect or value you. My point is that these experiences were a huge turnoff. You either expressed your upset at the business people face-to-face or fumed at home, but you were unhappy for some significant reason. You may have told yourself or others that you would never go back to that specific business again. You may have even thought, "There has got to be another firm out there who wants my business."

You must value your clients. You have a tremendous opportunity to contribute to your client, to enrich their lives, to protect them, to connect with them, to impact them at many levels, and you have got to demonstrate and show appreciation in every aspect of your business.

This means that when a client calls your business establishment on the phone, the person who answers is appreciative that they have called. She goes out of her way to help, nurture, guide, direct, and connect the client to the solution, or the outcome, or the answer, or the information I am searching for.

This means when I go to your office, I feel good, I feel welcome, I feel comfortable, I feel valued. This means that when I experience your accounting services, the people delivering them personify the benefits that you offer.

Clients must become an extension of that same feeling of the benefit that they came to experience with you. As a client of yours, I want to feel your appreciation each time you greet me. Everyone in your office must become a nurturist, making it easier for clients to understand and use more of your services and gain a greater advantage. Your whole staff must be concerned that clients obtain the maximum result, benefit and satisfaction of performance outcome that is possible.

After a client visits your business, you show them that you are continually there for them by calling them. Asking them if they have any questions, or if they if they are happy with the results you obtained, giving them tips for maintaining those results longer. As a courtesy, make certain that clients know you will be there for them long after the service has been paid for, giving your assurance that they're not regarded as just a check or credit card to process at the bank. You demonstrate that you will view their relationship as ongoing, and you value them more as dear friends whom you respect and enjoy. That's when they'll know how much you really appreciate them.

When you move your business into this kind of position, your business is virtually assured because people will be thinking of your accounting business in the most desirable and powerful way. Your clients will send their friends and colleagues to you because it is such a pleasurable experience.

–43–

CREATE A PREEMPTIVE MARKETING ADVANTAGE

Preemptive marketing is the single most powerful technique anyone could ever use. Few firms use it. The first person in a field who uses it has an incredible advantage over all other competitors. Simply take the time to explain to your customer or prospect the processes that are inherent to your business.

The classic example, going back to about 1919, is Schlitz beer, which used to be the worst beer in the whole marketplace. It was number 10 or 15 on the list when a classic marketing strategist named, Claude Hopkins, was called in to try to salvage this number ten beer and lift them to success.

When he walked in, the first thing he did was learn how beer was made. He took a course in beer making, went through their facilities, and observed that Schlitz was domiciled right on the banks of one of the Great Lakes. And even though they were right there with this unlimited water source, they had dug five, 4,000-foot artesian wells right next to Lake Michigan because they wanted pure water.

It was revealed that there was a mother yeast cell which was discovered as a result of 2,500 different yeast experiments which had been done in an effort to find the quintessential beer that would create the proper taste. He was shown the special room where the experiments took place. Then he was also shown five different, three-foot-thick plate glass rooms where beer was condensed and redistilled and recondensed for purity. They concluded by showing him the "tasters" who tasted the beer, as well as where the bottles were cleaned and recleaned 12 times.

At the end, he was incredulous. He said, "My god, why don't you tell people the process that your beer goes through?"

And they said, "Well. That's indigenous to every beer; that's how beer is made."

And he said, "Yes, but the first person that tells the public about this will gain a preemptive advantage" He got them to number one in about six months by telling them the facts.

If you're preparing a preemptive approach, mention that you have seven tax specialists who carefully review the work of each of your staff accountants. Each of the seven specialists will check and double-check all entries, and run comparative statistics to confirm the accuracy of all of the work your firm performs. Then a final analysis is performed on the client's case to look for possible areas of business improvement. Special financial ratios are performed and a summary report is created that helps small businesses make better decisions; individuals are then able to budget and plan with a greater emphasis on their personal objectives.

The key to understanding the power of preemptive marketing is realizing that the first accounting firm in the market to relay information that isn't common knowledge, appears to be giving a profound revelation to potential clients. Obtaining a preemptive advantage is that simple. Therefore, you should use the media to systematically develop the image of a highly specialized expert. You will position you and your firm from a preemptive standpoint as the first to share with your market "inside information." This preemptive advantage will draw people in your market to you by giving them a very specific reason to hire your firm. You might be asking yourself right now how you will know specifically what information to relay to your market. That alone could become the topic of another entire book on the topic of applied marketing strategy. The answer to the question is actually very simple. You should relay information that your specific potential client desires greatly, knows little about and about which no other accounting firm in your market is known for providing. The good news is that you can often provide very basic, but different information that is highly valuable to your market and hit your mark. Again sometimes all that is required for success is to mention how your business system is different, perhaps by describing how it works to save the client more money, or protects the client against the chance of penalizing audits etc.—by describing how your firm responsibly handles important client issues. Just telling your clients what you can do for them, even if it seems mundane and common knowledge can often provide the basis for further preemptive elaboration in progressive marketing efforts over time. Never assume they are aware of all aspects of what you offer. You're might be the first to challenge them, and they may be pleasantly surprised.

People don't appreciate what you do for them unless you

articulate it very clearly and repetitively. That's why professionals must advertise consistently. When you advertise the right message and deliver it to your market, they will respond. However, once you reveal your preemptive point of distinctive difference— describing the specific ways you give clients a superior advantage—then the high quality clients tend to respond in greater numbers because they have a more compelling reason to want your services.

Preemptive marketing is a very delicate thing. If you sort through six hundred resumes before you pull out three hundred potential candidates before hiring one excellent accountant, how will your customers know about your impeccable standards for choosing excellent expert minds to consult with your clients unless you inform them of what you've done? People don't know what you will do for them unless you tell them in explicit terms. But you've got to do it very delicately. I believe everyone should always try to give more than anyone else does. It may be a longer warrantee period, perhaps something free when they buy from you, or something they are able to keep even if they want their money back. I think accountants should make irresistible offers. What you want to do is capture the client on the front end or influence someone new to try your service.

Consider this interesting story told by my friend Jay Abraham which illustrates this point:

> A couple visit an art museum in London, pay $5 for a catalog, walk through to the first aisle in the gallery, look around to see the masters and are extremely impressed. They know the Renoirs, Rembrandts and Gauguins. As they turn the bend, confronting them was this god-awful mural of acrylics and psychedelic day-glo. They search the catalog, but because the mural is improperly listed, they are unable to find a description of it. The couple is so appalled, they hasten away, and continue their tour through the rest of the gallery, admiring the other masterpieces and sculptures.
>
> As they reach the end of the gallery, lo and behold, they find the repugnant-looking piece enumerated at the end of the catalog, and in reading about it, they notice that it was only one of four pieces the artist had done. Two were in the Louvre in Paris, and one was in the Metropolitan Museum of Modern Art. It had taken the artist 22 years to paint this one. He was considered the master of the art. Two of his other paintings went for $4,600,000; one went for $3,200,000. This

one had just been acquired for $4,000,000.

The couple who initially was so repulsed ran back and admired the mural. They were now educated enough to appreciate its value. You must understand that the public doesn't always appreciate what it doesn't understand.

If I told people my shirt was the only one made of a certain material, that the dye was flown in from Greece, and that I had to have my tailor flown in from Italy to measure me—I could build a perception of value, by educating people. Don't perceive that people automatically understand anything about your product or service. You have got to educate them.

Human beings want information. If you give them information and you give them candor, even if it doesn't always make you money, it becomes implicit that you can be trusted, and people favor you. People want to know how they can enhance their circumstances. So you answer one key question for them: How do they benefit by doing business with you instead of with somebody else? If you can answer that, you're valuable.

—44—

WHY YOU MUST USE CLIENT-CONVERSION STRATEGIES

Once you have attracted readers to your ad/mailing or generated leads it is time to convert those people into loyal clients. Before a prospect sees or hears your appeal for their business it is always helpful to create a simple strategy that motivates more prospects to become involved clients. We call this process prospect-to-client conversion and your aim is to implement a plan that will increase your overall conversion rates. Below we present the best conversion motivators that have stood the test of time for successful marketers, adapt them in ways in which you feel comfortable:

STRONG GUARANTEES

The standard guarantee is to offer customers their money back or compensate them if they are not satisfied with your performance. A stronger guarantee is to let them try your product or service, and if satisfied, bill them only after thirty days have expired.

Stronger still is to have them pay only if your service validates the guarantee: They only have to pay your invoice after your service has made them, or saved them perhaps, two to five times the price of the service. Or, you could offer them one of my favorites: The "better-than-risk-free" guarantee.

Will clients take advantage of you when you offer a strong guarantee? A few will, but the money you lose on those customers is only a tiny fraction of the increased sales you will receive by offering the guarantee in the first place.

THE BETTER-THAN-RISK-FREE GUARANTEE

In addition to the usual money-back guarantee, offer the customer free bonuses along with your service. Ideally, these bonuses cost you very little, but have a high-perceived value. The better-than-risk-free offer is this: The customer is able to keep the bonuses even if dissatisfied with the service.

When you make your offer you can state it this way: These bonuses are worth more than $150, so even if you decide to ask for your money back, you will be $150 ahead just for trying my service.

This concept is a powerful extension of working the back-end. Its logic is this: You should be "client-mining" to break even on your initial promotion—or even lose a little—if you know you will make a profit on the back-end. The concept of lifetime value is at work here as well. If you know how much a new client is worth to you during their average life of service, then you will know how much you must invest up front to capture them in the first place.

CREATING MORE INCENTIVES

Charge Less For The Initial Purchase. This will bring in new customers — customers who were going elsewhere to fulfill their needs. Because these customers will receive such a good deal on their initial purchase, they will be bound to come back again. This becomes your back-end. Add extra incentives to buy. Add an extended warranty or guarantee. Include a free bonus if they hire you before a certain date.

Add A Special Bonus If They Pay In Full Rather Than In Monthly Installments. Your bonus could be free electronic tax filing so that clients' returns are received faster.

Give A Large Commission Or Incentive To Your Staff. If your staff brings in a new customer, give them the net profit on the initial sale. You can also have monthly contests for your staff, promoting competition. Provide incentives — like cash prizes, a dinner for two at a fancy restaurant or a weekend getaway vacation — to the top performing staff member.

The more expensive, abstract, complex and profound the purchasing decision you want someone to make, the more nurturing you have to be, and the more questions you have to answer. The more powerful a case you have to offer, the more credibility you will need to induce a client. Be aware that the client risk will increase. Often, it's not a simple one- or two-step process. It's a multi-step process. Many people sell items at a very modest price just to qualify people. Many people sell books or introductory quantities of a product just to secure a new client. That is just the first step. The subsequent step is converting them to a larger unit of purchase, or to the next product or service you offer.

BUNDLING YOUR SERVICES

Offer bundled services as an incentive. Bundling is absolutely one of the most effective marketing maneuvers for attracting new clients and selling more to existing clients. I have been enticed by the bundling concept myself. I know an accountant who sold securities. He created a course on investments, which he sold to his clients on his web site. The course had four manuals and four videos. The course could easily have been sold for $650 or more. Instead of spending a lot of marketing dollars to sell the course to cold prospects he decided to offer it in a bundle—for free—when a client purchased a subscription to his newsletter for $189. In addition, he would send out a one-hour monthly cassette tape describing the best investment strategies and tips that he had discovered to newsletter subscribers. The monthly cassette filled with valuable investment advice was a $170 yearly value.

It was a wonderful package. Just by creating a high-value bundle of products at a reasonable price he sold 1500% more subscriptions in the months that followed than he had in the three years before.

Instead of giving your clients dollars-off of services, or free services you could add more value to your present offers by giving one or two more services as a bundled offer. That way you could continue to sell your services at the same prices. In place of discounting price add more value to client service encounters by doing more for the client.

Moreover, by bundling your existing service, together with a value and benefit combination of features for a single, fixed price— you can own your market, provided you carefully and effectively inform and educate your prospect to properly perceive and desire the combined value you are offering. Look within your existing business for ways to package your products and services.

For example: consider bundling service agreements wherein you offer a monthly or quarterly service, 24-hour-a-day consulting hotline service, and annual tax preparation for one special price. By charging a flat fee, which you might automatically bill on a monthly or quarterly arrangement to the client's credit card, you make such an offer irresistible tot he client.

Well, you can let your imagination pretty much go wild. Use the ideas listed below. You can mix ideas, change the implementation of my suggestions by keeping the core concept intact.

Here are more idea stimulators. Adapt them at will:

1. The more synergy you can bring together in your bundle, the better.
2. By setting up clients on a monthly- or annual-service orientation, you position them favorably for perpetually renewing the arrangement every year—thus turning a one-shot sale into a perpetual one.
3. By reducing the cost to a modest and nonthreatening monthly or quarterly payment, you dramatically increase appeal.
4. By using simple, nonthreatening terms like, "billable quarterly to your credit card," you set up an appealing reason for the customer to furnish you with their credit card number to automatically charge every three months, without the hassle of normal corporate billing procedures.
5. By assembling a lot of different products or services together into one bundle, you can sell a lot of normally limited appeal or slow services. Even though you may discount the price on a given item or service, you aggregate more total profit per customer or per sale that even a 50% reduction in pricing could translate into a 300% increase in realized profit. Don't however, make the mistake of offering a product nobody wants within your package. That one unwanted item could turn them off to the rest of the package.
6. Don't forget, you have to first educate the marketplace before they can be expected to "see and seize" the value you are offering.
7. Bundling offers an enormous opportunity to tie up a lot of people, for a lot of purposes, for a long, long time and lock in a predictable and dependable stream of cash flow and profits you can build on. Give bundled service packages serious consideration as a marketing strategy.

One more point. Many clients consider bundling offers because they feel they give them tremendous value. Bundling should have tremendous appeal during any business slowdown that you may experience.

HOW TO HANDLE LEADS
Often, a campaign to generate sales leads is not successful

because staff members become discouraged in trying to follow up on leads that are unqualified. When staff members fail to follow up, then opportunities may be missed and prospects may view the company as uninterested. Staff must spend their valuable time selling to qualified prospects.

A good system is needed to provide your staff with prospects. It should include:

- A mechanism for audience response (web site offers, special email offers, direct mail, print ads, trade shows).
- A device for quick response to the audience (letter, brochure, sample).
- A follow-up phone call.
- A record of the inquiry noting its source and interest.

Toll-free numbers should be included for quick audience response. The follow-up phone call is a key to the success of the system. It shows the prospect that the company is concerned. Questions can be answered, and the next step can be decided.

When recording inquiries, categorize each one as a "hot lead" (buying within three months), a "warm lead" (buying within twelve months), "long-term potential" (not buying in the next twelve months but still a prospect), "no potential" (no need for the product or no authority to make the buying decision), and "unusable" (no longer in business). As always — test everything. Record the source of each inquiry and weed out promotions that are not producing qualified leads.

TECHNIQUES THAT HELP STIMULATE SALES

Here are some techniques that successful direct-marketing companies use to initiate orders or increase the size of their orders.

1. Offer credit terms. It is often the case that customers will buy more if they can buy on credit.
2. Introduce a trade-up offer. You might offer, for example, that for an additional $35, the customer can have a system that can also be used to better organize their personal financial records.
3. Increase the assortment. For example, a customer may hire you to perform a fiscal efficiency audit of their business once a year. You might point out the advantages of providing several extra services that help them create

new systems for greater efficiency, which includes not only an audit, but also business marketing consulting services, and new ideas for future monetization sources, etc. And if you can provide these extra services for only a little more than they are used to paying for the audit, then they may see the value of trying these extra services.

4. Offer special packages. This might include organization systems, time management systems, records storage boxes, etc.

5. Present a compatible item. After a bookkeeping service is sold, for instance, try to sell checking systems or payroll systems.

6. Offer an extension. Offer extended service contracts. If a new client pays for six months of your bookkeeping services, offer them an additional four months for the price of two, at the point of purchase.

7. Make selective price increases. You might try raising prices of your most valuable services.

8. Increase minimum-order requirements. If a portion of your clients hire you only on a yearly basis, convert them to quarterly clients by raising prices conservatively, and automatically offering more service.

9. Offer bulk discounts. Create an accounting services club-plan by offering your clients five years worth of annual tax-preparation service for a special price. Create a short consultation/check-up every six-months to keep them on track as part of the program.

10. Offer a premium on specific purchases. For some customers, a free gift will convince them to buy from you. For example, you could give the customer a free, expensive check-register organizer for hiring you to perform monthly bookkeeping services.

11. Introduce "unique bundle" offers. Computer marketers have increased sales by making "bundled" offers — e.g., offering a computer, a printer, software, and paper at a lower price than what the total cost of the separate items would be. You can bundle more services together at a reasonable price than your competitors. This can easily become your point of difference marketing strategy.

—45—

GIVE YOUR CLIENTS
WHAT THEY REALLY WANT

Accounting professionals have a myriad of challenges to face in marketing their services to new and existing clients. One of the most critical mental shifts that you must make in thinking about consulting services is to understand what you are really selling. You are never really selling accounting or consulting services per se. You aren't selling your time. It isn't about selling information or excellent advice. So then, what are you selling when you market your consulting services?

One of my clients runs a successful advertising agency. On the first day that I sat down with management at the agency's prestigious office building in downtown Orlando, I asked my client one question. I remember feeling awkward as I asked, "What does your customer really want from you?" I couldn't believe my ears when I heard the answer. One of the top people said, "Most of our clients want a 30-second blockbuster with the brand name as the finale." I was amazed to discover that their view of what their clients purchased from them had never progressed further than selling a print ad, a well-produced radio ad, or TV commercial. I then spent the next two-hours doing an experiential exercise to shift the thinking of the principals of the ad agency to understand that their clients wanted so much more. Their clients wanted payback. Payback might be the ability to create a stronger image and thus command higher prices. Payback might be a definable sales increase as the result of the ad. I tried to help them make a shift into that elusive "second-degree-out" dimension of what their clients really wanted, so they might develop deeper connections with their clients.

So the next time you're on a plane, flying first class to your next assignment, and your seat-mate asks you what you do as an accounting professional, what will you say? Will you list the services you perform as though you are reading down a dry service menu? Or will you talk about the results you are capable of giving your clients?

My father, who was a highly successful marketer for several manufacturers of engineering equipment, always told me two things when marketing anything. He says, always:

- Talk about the results you give.
- Ask for the order (which most marketers never do).

He has told me endless stories of how he has accomplished results. One of his favorite marketing formulas is the "Feel, Felt, Found Method," which ensures that you talk about results and gain client commitment.

The "Feel, Felt, Found Method" can be used to overcome objections, to add a touch of empathy, to add interest and credibility, and most importantly to talk about what you do that's different from anyone else. Here's how the "Feel, Felt, Found Method" works:

> Imagine that you are meeting with a potential client who voices a fear about hiring an accounting professional and displays the uncertainty of not knowing what an accountant can do for his or her company. In applying the "Feel, Felt, Found Method," you could say:
>
> "Well, Mr. Thompson, I understand the uncertainty you *feel* about hiring an accountant. I have a very special client in Winter Park named Mackenzie Cooper. Ms. Cooper also *felt* the same way because she never had the chance to experience the many ways an accountant could help with new cost-savings strategies. Then she hired us and *found* that she received incredible ideas, as well as a program of systematic budgeting which not only paid for itself, but could be used to triple her tax-savings."

Your clients would prefer not to hire an accountant. Their desire is to hire a superhuman who can give them the catalytic results that they are most hungry for. Your biggest marketing challenge is to erect huge pillars of "influence leverage" so that it is understood that what you do, as an accountant is totally different from anyone else. They must believe that you are capable of giving them the results they want.

First, it is necessary to determine what results your clients really value. This will enable you to focus on how you can prove to potential clients that they will receive more results and advantages by working with you. Here are some really convincing ideas for receiving the consulting results you talk about:

- Specify and denominate objective performance measures by letter of agreement that ensures that the company has an objective benchmark by which to hold you accountable.
- Tell your client they can pay you based on results. If you are a cost accountant, arrange that you be paid 20% of the money that you save the client. If you are tax consultant, make payment to you contingent upon an amount of tax savings by a certain date. You may not be able to guarantee actual results but you can always guarantee your performance.
- After you use the "Feel, Felt, Found Method," ask your client if they would like to contact the client that you previously mentioned (i.e. Ms. Cooper) to see that she had a more-than-positive experience with your business. Hand them letters from the client stating how much value was actually received from you.

If you are going to promise catalytic results, then you are going to have to make certain that you increase the skill level of your staff continuously.

−46−

POST-PURCHASE REASSURANCE

It doesn't do you any good to convert a prospect into a customer if they don't follow through with payment or do not pay on time.

Post-Purchase Reassurance is the simple process of reselling your accounting service and your company to the customer—reassuring the purchaser that he or she made a shrewd buy and an excellent decision.

By doing that for your customer:

1. You allay any "post-purchase dissonance" (buyer's remorse) that may be festering in the mind of your customer, his/her family or associates.
2. You dramatically reduce—and perhaps eliminate—the refunds, exchanges or costly service expenses that disenchantment may produce after a sale.
3. You make the customer more receptive to your next offer.
4. You develop a closer relationship with your customers and satisfy their cravings to be acknowledged.
5. You give yourself an opportunity to recommend a buying strategy that includes continuous repurchasing.
6. You have the chance to immediately "upsell" the customer to a more expensive service which is available to them at a preferential price, on exclusive terms, etc.—if they buy it within, let's say, thirty days of the original purchase. If you do it right, about 25% to 35% of all original customers will respond, and the added profit will be considerable.
7. You can solicit a customer's sales referral.
8. You can often turn the initial sale into a renewable annual contract by adding more products or services at a discount.
9. You can explain the use of the product so it will be used more often and reordered sooner."

A company once had a problem with clients returning a high percentage of the products they purchased. I instructed them to write up a strong statement extolling the virtues of the product, and include it in the order confirmation they sent them the day following the transaction. They found that broken trades (returned merchandise) fell off dramatically. Now they include a buck slip (1/4 page card) with the confirmation that congratulates them on their wise decision, tells them how great the product is, and how it will benefit them. This will work equally as well with your accounting services to resell the client on the idea of hiring you again, telling friends about your services, and to make an offer to come back in for more services soon.

–47–

TEST EVERY MARKETING APPROACH ON A SMALL SCALE FIRST BEFORE ROLLING OUT A LARGER CAMPAIGN

Testing every marketing approach gives you a simple way to always guarantee that your marketing and advertising dollars will never be whittled away and lost senselessly. I am referring to systematically testing each marketing element in your program. Each marketing method contains variables that influence the success of your results. Each variable must be logically fine-tuned using your experience in the market. Any unknown variables must be tested. If your marketing results are lower than you expect for a given marketing method, then go back to the drawing board by testing the variables in the program that you are still uncertain about. If you will do nothing more in all of your marketing efforts than try one approach against another you will always build upon success. Test one idea for a promotion against another. Test one way of doing something against another, such as, pricing, offers, guarantees, or ways of explaining something. When you measure and compare the results, you will usually discover that one method usually outpulls others, sometimes by a huge margin. I have often seen accounting professionals test newspaper ad headlines only to discover that one print-ad headline was superior to another by as much as 5 to 25 times. They discovered this by running the two versions of the print ad for the price of one using a technique called the a/b split, which I will explain below. Because my philosophy involves marketing the most unique aspect of your accounting business, I strongly recommend against copying the headlines, or mailing pieces of others. I know of a company that sells stock article columns and ads off the shelf. Even though this might give you some short-run results, this kind of strategy is easy to copy and provides no long-run competitive advantage.

You current marketing approaches could be under-performing. They may be delivering as little as 2% to 7% of their full potential.

This means that the ads, pricing points you use for services, benefits you communicate about your service, and other factors may be missing your market by just enough to allow you to think your efforts are successful. Yet, your ads may be under-performing just enough to keep you happy enough not to test new improvement methods. Yet you may be closer to obtaining exceptional response rates than you realize.

I have witnessed clients who have tested two different headlines, letter openings, seminar-presentation sales offers, guarantees, service prices, etc., and have seen increases of 500% to 2,500%. Until you test, question, compare, and analyze the different responses and performance levels that you obtain from different ways of promoting, describing, pricing, guaranteeing your accounting service, you are leaving tremendous potential on the table and walking away.

Because you are an optimizer, you must get the best possible yield from every step you take to promote your business. Your market will always tell you which elements they like best, by their responses and dollar votes. You can measure how many more clients call you, send in a bounce-back postage paid reply card, set appointments, and buy your services after specific promotions. You will measure your market's response or interest-level—by determining which of two headlines they prefer, which article they favor, which pricing point they are most likely to purchase at, by their acceptance of your marketing through their action-taking responses.

You can conduct some simple interviews by ask a small number of actual clients which ad, letter, headline, or commercial they would respond to. You will discover when you begin regular marketing tests that the various marketing approaches will pull extremely differently, as a result of making such small changes.

One of my clients recently discovered this when they changed the first sentence in a direct-mail letter to focus on the customer. After testing the opening sentence of the letter, 20 people in their target market were asked, by telephone, which introduction they liked best. My client used the one most clients had voted on and increased the response from one-half of one-percent to over forty-percent in one step. They mailed out 250 letters to potential clients, and 105 clients came in to visit.

TEST "FIRSTS" FIRST

No matter how you decide to promote your business, you can always test to obtain the highest result possible. I call this testing your way to success. Remember that every marketing or advertising method you use has a "first." You must always test "firsts." "Firsts" are the initial elements of any marketing effort that clients are exposed to before anything else. In a print ad your headline is your "first" element. In a mailing the first words of your letter or letter headline are crucial to the success of the entire campaign. If your staff is calling clients, the first words spoken will usually make or break the entire effort. Every marketing method has a testable "first."

This is where the idea of running an "a/b split print ad" comes in. If you are running print ads in local newspapers or magazines, your headline is the first thing your client sees. Right? Why not test two different headlines? Normally, the publication that you advertise with will actually let you run two ads that are identical in every respect, except for the headline (or the price offer or the guarantee), running one in every other print-run of the publication. This is an a/b split. You may be trying to get clients to come in for a special service at a special price by asking them to bring in a copy of the ad. If you want to test the pulling power of two different headlines run an a/b split of the ad with two different headlines. The ad that attracts more people is your winning ad. Remember: Everything else in the ad must be exactly the same except the one element you are testing, or your testing effort will tell you nothing.

Every marketing effort you undertake must be tested in the same way. If you call clients on the phone, the first few things that are said to them are the most important. So test two different telephone greetings and keep everything else that you say pretty much the same. Switch the approaches back and forth to test "Approach A" versus "Approach B" on every other phone call. If "Approach A" receives 25 positive responses in the form of booked appointments and "Approach B" receives 7 appointments, then you'll know which approach is most effective. Will you spend more time using "Approach A" next time? I hope so. You should test your flyers, brochures, phone calls, letters, cross-promotions, print ads, and all other way of marketing your business that you like. Remember that testing always gives you control by converting marketing from a loser's game into a winner's game.

HOW TO TEST YOUR MARKETING EFFORTS

Test only one variable within an ad or marketing effort at a time. This is the scientific principle of control. It means isolating a variable so you are sure of the source of different results. If you are testing a guarantee, do not change the headline. If you are comparing one price against another, don't change any other variable. This gives you the control you need to determine which version of the one marketing variable you are testing is creating more pulling power.

When testing two different approaches, you must design your test to give you specific results keyed to each approach. You must know which ad each and every prospect is responding to.

You can do this in different ways:

- If you have a web site, perhaps you will buy banner ads on the web sites of local businesses. If you do this then you will want to test two different headlines on the same banner ad. Your web master can make sure that every other page on the site your banner ad appears on loads a different headline. Therefore you will know which headline influenced more people to click on the banner to visit your site.
- Test your offers—create a differently-coded offer for each version of your print ad. Make certain the print ad requires clients to clip the ad and bring it in to you.
- Tell prospects to specify a department number when they call or write—there doesn't have to be an actual department, it just helps you track which ads are successful.
- Include a code on the mailing label that is returned with the inquiry on a "postage prepaid" postcard—the code identifies the source of the label or the version of the ad you mailed.
- Use different telephone numbers for respondents—each offer is accompanied by a similar, but distinct, phone number. Your local phone company can install an extra phone line for under $10 a month with a report of how many calls came through on each of two different phone lines.
- Make different package tests and bundles of specific services, and note which bonuses or prices people ask for.
- Have the caller ask for a specific person—the name can be fictitious. Each of two ads, postcard mailings or email efforts can mention two different people so that you are able to see which effort pulls more responses.

The obvious key is that you must be able to attribute each response to one of the approaches you are testing.

Keep meticulous track of each response and its results: Simple inquiry, sale, amount of sale, and previous customer. Keep track of every piece of information you need in your marketing. And be sure to differentiate in your record-keeping between responses (prospects) and actual sales.

Then when you have all the results tabulated by method A or method B, compare the two approaches and select the better one. Then test again, using your winner in competition with a new contestant.

MORE DETAILS ABOUT USING A/B SPLITS...

A/B splits allow you to test two approaches with one marketing effort. Whether you are running newspaper, magazine, newsletter or any print ad, you can use A/B splits. If you are testing Internet banner ads, A/B splits work very well.

The best example I can give you is to look at how the print media creates publication ads. Magazine and newspaper presses print on metal cylinders, onto which each page is etched twice. Each complete turn of the cylinder produces two copies of a single page. When a savvy marketer wants to use an a/b split-run test, he furnishes two different ads of the same size. The "A ad" is etched on one side of the cylinder; the "B ad" on the other side. Each complete turn of the printing cylinder prints two separate ads. Your ad is then distributed to demographically similar audiences. And because the ads occupy the same position within the publication, each ad is fairly tested under similar conditions. A/B testing keeps you from wasting thousands of dollars on losing ads. In this manner, you can also spend far less money pretesting ads in inexpensive, smaller circulation, regional editions.

Never test with large ads or huge mailings or expensive efforts if you can test on a small scale first. Before you spend a lot of money on a space ad in a magazine or newspaper, rent a list of subscribers to the publication you plan to advertise in and do an inexpensive mail test of the ad you plan to run. Say, for example, that a full-page ad in your local chamber of commerce magazine costs $2,000. Rather than run two ads for $4,000, you can pre-test by mailing using a brochure that looks that same as the ads to 500 or 1,000 names of people who read this magazine, for the amount of only $225-$450. This way, you can find out if your ad will work before you make a big expenditure.

The purpose of testing is to develop maximum performance from every marketing effort. Yet, it is amazing how few companies ever test any aspect of their marketing and compare it to something else. They bet their destiny on arbitrary, subjective decisions and conjecture.

No one has the ability, or the power, to predetermine what the marketplace wants and what the best price, package, or approach will be. Rather, you have the obligation, and the power, to put every important marketing question to a vote by the only people whose ballots count—prospects and customers.

How do we put a marketing question to a vote? By testing one sales thrust against another. One price against another. One ad concept against another. One headline against another. One TV or radio commercial against another. One follow-up or upselling overture against another.

When you test one approach against another, and carefully analyze and tabulate the results, you will find that one approach almost always outpulls all the others by a tremendous margin. You'll be amazed at how many more sales— or how much larger an average order—you can obtain from a similar effort.

For example, if each of your field salespeople averages 15 calls a day, doesn't it make sense to find the one sales pitch or package that will let them close twice as many sales and increase their average order to 40% to 200%, with the same amount of effort?

Remember, salaried staff costs you the same fixed amount whether they bring in $300 a day or $3,000 a day through their efforts.

Starting tomorrow, have your staff try different approaches— different client hot-button focuses, different packages or bundles of service combinations, different specially-priced offers, different upgrades, or different follow-up offers. Each day, review the specific performance of each test approach, and then analyze the data. If a specific new twist on your basic sales approach outpulls the old approach by 20% or 70%, doesn't it make sense for every salesperson to start using this new approach? Test every sales variable. If you do, you can easily achieve immediate increases in sales and profits. Good data can help you improve your sales efforts.

Make specific offers and analyze the number of responses, traffic, prospects, and resulting sales for each specific ad. Then compute the cost-per-prospect, cost-per-sale, average sale-per-prospect, average conversion-per-prospect, and the average profit-per-sale against your control ad or sales pitch. This reveals the obvious winner, the new control that you will keep running until a better control beats it.

Testing applies not merely to outside sales efforts, but to every aspect of your marketing. Test your prices. Every situation is unique, so test several different prices. You'll be amazed at the differences in order size and overall profit one price will produce over another.

−48−

THE VALUE OF DIRECT MARKETING TO YOUR ACCOUNTING BUSINESS

Direct marketing involves running ads more interactively. New technology, such as toll-free telephone numbers, the Internet, email, interactive CD-ROM, and fax-on-demand is taking direct-response marketing to entirely new levels. Direct response technologies are doing this by increasing access to information and providing a way for clients to interact with marketers one-on-one.

The concept of Direct Marketing, which I will also call direct-reponse advertising, is simple. It is designed to evoke an immediate response or action—a visit, a call, or a purchase from the viewer or reader. Direct-response advertising tells a complete story. It presents factual, specific reasons why your company, product, or service is superior to others. It differs from the conjecture of institutional advertising.

Direct-response advertising can be a one-to-one interaction in print, over the Internet, on the telephone. This process helps marketers make a complete case for the company, product, or service. It overcomes objections. It gives you, as a marketer, the ability to answer many questions and explains performance results. It backs the promise with a risk-free guarantee.

Direct-response advertising compels readers, viewers, or listeners to take action, to visit your establishment, web site, call you or send in money. Used effectively, direct-response advertising compels tons of super-qualified prospects to connect with you and your accounting business in different ways.

You can analyze the profitability and performance of direct-response advertising because it produces returns you can track and compute.

Institutional advertising produces no such results. If you are running institutional ads, change them to direct-response ads. Give your prospects information that's important to them, not to you. Give them facts and performance capabilities of your service. Tell them about your guarantee. Give the prospect reasons why your services are superior.

Direct-response advertising is more effective than institutional advertising because the prospect doesn't care one iota about your business or your motivations. The prospect only cares about what benefit your product or service renders. How will your product save effort, time and money? How will your product improve the prospect's life?

Tell the reader, viewer, or listener precisely what action to take. Tell them how to get to your business, what to look for, and who to ask for. Tell them who to call. Remind them of your risk-free service guarantee. Most importantly tell them what results they can expect from using your service. Give your prospects the answers to these kinds of questions and you'll dominate your market. By switching from institutional to direct-response advertising, you should improve your effectiveness many times over.

Most people think of mail order or direct mail when they hear the term "direct response" or "direct marketing." Direct-response marketing, or simple direct response, includes, but is not limited to, direct mail. As a matter of fact, it encompasses everything from direct mail to newspaper and magazines ads to telemarketing, to radio and advertising.

All types of businesses and professions use direct response. It is used to sell everything from auctions at the "Ebay" web site to Quicken Software—and everything in between. You can use it to prospect for new clients, to influence existing clients to visit more often. It can be used to get customers to come to your business, seminar, luncheon or any place you direct them.

Direct response brings immeasurable results—all at a fraction of the cost of traditional marketing methods.

USE DIRECT-RESPONSE MEDIA LAYERING TO INCREASE YOUR RESULTS

One of the largest areas of opportunity is in using the Internet in combination with several other targeted marketing methods. I call this "direct response media layering" and it can increase your marketing results by 30% to 2,000% depending upon your diligence and perseverance in using it.

Simply stated you could easily layer your direct response media efforts by sending a single message or offer, through multiple media, in the form of a requested action you want potential clients to take.

You should use media layering to accomplish at least two goals:

1. To generate a flow of new clients into your business—I call this lead generation—and lead conversion—converting a predictable percentage of those leads into transacting clients.
2. To reconnect with your existing clients at deeper levels so they will use your services regularly.

I know an accountant who took my idea of media layering and generated a 200% increase in the number of new clients that she generated every month. Here are the steps that she took to accomplish this:

MEDIA LAYERING STEP ONE:

She created a brief message and offer to her primary target market. Her target market was small businesses and home-based businesses. She knew that there were a large number of small start-ups in her city.

Her message was simple: "I am an accountant who owns a small business, too, so I understand your needs better than any other accountant in town."

Her offer was also simple: "For $25 a month I will do your bookkeeping, and during tax time I'll do your taxes free."

In case you are wondering how she fulfilled on this promise, she hired a college student, an expert in computer programming, to customize software that she had licensed from a small software firm. Since the needs of her clients were fairly simple, the software was configured to automate most of the monthly bookkeeping services for clients; and also electronically generate end-of-the-year standardized tax returns for her.

When a client would sign up for her service she would send them the software and coach them on how to use it for 15-minutes by telephone. The program was set to automatically dial up to her server by modem and download the client's monthly data to her computer. The process was almost 90% self-sustaining.

MEDIA LAYERING STEP TWO:

She obtained 15 clients to pilot-test the program to work the bugs out of it. This took one month.

MEDIA LAYERING STEP THREE:

She selected the top three media opportunities that she felt would reach her target market successfully. She selected the following marketing methods:

1. The Internet — using her web site and e-mail.
2. Direct mail – using full-color postcards, a newsletter she published to home-based businesses, and letters explaining how simple her program was.
3. Direct-response ads that she took out in local small business magazines and newsletters.

She used all three of these media as layers in her overall strategy as a predictable direct response client generator. Using these media she spent the first three months informing the local small business market about how her service was different and how it would benefit them.

After the first three months she ran testimonial-based layered ads showing how actual small business clients received a tremendous advantage from her services. For example; her magazine ad would tell the story of how her services saved a small business client 25% through systemized cost analysis. The ad used an offer that read. "to find out how Joe Davis's accountant saved him $1250 per month, call for a free information kit." When people would respond to the ad, they received a mailing that would tell the complete story of how her accounting program got results for Joe's business. Word of mouth soon took over.

MEDIA LAYERING STEP FOUR:

With her automated computer bookkeeping and tax service fully tested and ready to roll, she purchased a monthly mailing list of start-up businesses from a local business journal in her city. Each month the journal supplied her with a list of 2,500 to 2,700 contacts for a fee. She mailed postcards with her offer to businesses and received about 150 new clients per month. She also ran an ad in a local Chamber of Commerce newsletter once per month. The mailings and ads invited small business owners to her web site to learn more about having her do their taxes for free. While they were at the site she showed them a step-by-step demonstration of how easy her program was to use. On her web site, she explained how small business owners would save time and lots of money because of the high-tech service that she had innovated for them. She also sent postcards offering that clients call her to receive a free demo of her software and to obtain information about how her service would clearly save them time, money and headaches.

MEDIA LAYERING STEP FIVE

She replicated this successful marketing strategy each month faithfully. She continued to use media layering strategies to attract more new clients. Each month she doubled her client base. In one month she obtained 153 clients. In three months she had 441 customers, and in six months she had 891 clients. At that point she had to grow or level off because her ability to perform these services was maxed out.

Her initial development costs were about $3,800 to license and customize the software. Her monthly mailing costs were $700. Her monthly ad cost her $100. After one-month she grossed $3,750. By six-months her gross income was a little over $22,000 per month, and it was clearly time to grow her staff from two extra workers to about five or so.

As this example shows, it is clear that by using direct response marketing and the concept of media layering, you will increase the effectiveness of your marketing efforts.

DIRECT-RESPONSE MARKETING ADDS GREATER VALUE...

Direct response forces you to look at your total marketing effort—each part orchestrated in harmony with the whole. I honestly do not believe you will ever find a safer, lower-risk, higher-profit method of increasing your business than direct-response marketing. You can add at least one facet of direct-response marketing to your present operation. Direct- response marketing is worthwhile for many reasons:

1. It augments whatever you're already doing in your operation.
2. It's an affordable way to target specific segments of your customer base.
3. It's an indispensable tool for reaching people or businesses outside of your general market area whom you wouldn't normally be able to access.
4. It's an alluring way to upsell your products or services.
5. It's a low-cost way to obtain new business that might otherwise be exorbitantly expensive.
6. It's a powerful way to leverage modest amounts of increased sales into large profits, because the cost to obtain sales is so low.
7. It's a productive way to constantly communicate with your audience, enabling you to cement professional relationships while making a profit in the process.

It's also a great payroll-balancing vehicle. Whenever your employees have time on their hands, you can use direct response—targeted at your active customers and prospects to keep the dynamics of personnel in balance.

I know a consultant who sends out a postcard every month to her customers offering a advantageous price on services if they book service on one of the three slowest days of the year. Consequently she is booked up on her slower days and her employees (who would be there anyway) are kept busy.

When your business enters a slack period you still have a continual payroll, and your employees may not have much work. Direct response allows you to launch an immediate campaign to stimulate business activity. You can announce a sale or make a special offer. You can usually introduce something spontaneous, thereby keeping your staff busy. An active, direct response program will reduce the unprofitable lulls in business activity. Every business needs to employ these tactics aggressively to keep sales up.

—49—

AD STRATEGIES FOR ACCOUNTING PROFESSIONALS

A professional accountant runs a business, just like a shopkeeper or a software consultant. As in any business the bottom line will show a profit only if enough clients come through the door. You know that the way to procure these clients is through advertising. Effective advertising does not have to be crass and commercial, but it must be used to get your name out to the public. If your name is not familiar to people, they will not come to you. Your fixed costs will literally eat up your business.

Advertising can be effective in bringing new clients to you. If you expose your name to sufficiently large numbers of people, some of them are bound to need your services. But what kind of ad should you run? I recommend "reader ads," which not only place your name before your audience, but also provide information about the sub-specialty that you have expertise in.

Run a series of informative, educational ads with headlines such as:

> **HOW TO GET THE MOST DEDUCTIONS
> FROM THIS YEAR'S TAX RETURN**

Continue in a series of ads that provide a short course on the chosen topic in three, four, five or ten paragraphs. Using an on-going series of such ads establishes you as a source of reliable information on a variety of subjects in your field.

One of my clients is a financial planner. He uses headlines to grab the reader, such as:

- How To Become Financially Independent In The Next Three Years, Then Double Your Net Worth Every Five Years
- How To Out-Perform The Money Market

- How To Out-Perform The Stock Market
- How To Increase The Return On Your Investments
- Manage Your Money For High Yields

Write a corresponding special, a more elaborate report for those who call or come in. Offer free counseling if the prospect wants to know more. Send them your special report plus a review of your practice, your philosophy and the kind of work you specialize in, as well as a couple of case studies. Case studies let the professional showcase his or her innovativeness and success. You can use the ad to lead people to your web site. I suggest using the computer program called Adobe Acrobat® to create an electronic report that your web site visitors can download, making your distribution costs zero.

At the end of the ad, offer additional information in order to develop a prospect list. Write a booklet such as "A Guide to Healthy Finances." Write a tax-savings pamphlet. Write a plan for reducing estate taxes for families and their children. Offer a copy free to those who call or visit your office. If they call or write in, send them details about your practice, the kind of work you do and your philosophy.

Try different versions of the offer geared to different applications. For instance, create a special report on women: "How Single Women Can Avoid Over-Paying Federal Income Taxes." At the end of this brief educational ad series, conclude with a specific offer. For example:

> "I have prepared two special reports entitled, "101 Tax Personal Deductions You May Not Know About That You're Entitled To" and "100 Tax Deductions Your Business Is Entitled To That You May Not Know About." A copy of each will be sent to you upon request. If I can be of help to you in answering any questions you might have after reading the reports, call me. I'll also include information about the work we do, the clients we help, and the solutions we prepare for businesses or for individuals."

Always tie your ads to a specific offer. Then test which approach or version pulled the most responses.

After sending out the reports, your office should follow up. Your staff caller might say:

"Mr. Jackson, this is Kova Jones, Accountant Brown's assistant. He asked me to call and see if you received the report he sent and if you have any questions about it. Though his schedule is very heavy at the present time, he would be pleased to answer any inquiry you might have. He suggested that if you currently do not have an accountant you feel comfortable with, perhaps you might like to come in for a visit. We'd like you to know that he is available."

The aim is to create a charming, nonthreatening conversation. You need to follow up constantly on the prospects you locate. Their names are on your mailing list. Follow-up at three, four or five month intervals. Send further information with another follow-up letter saying, "We thought you might be interested in this special new service. Anytime you need the accountant's help or counsel, or you want to visit, we will be pleased to schedule you." Your staff must always be cordial, empathetic, responsive, and accommodating.

–50–

DYNAMIC HEADLINES POWER EVERYTHING FROM LETTERS TO INTERNET MARKETING

Whether you are marketing with letters, postcards, email, your web site, print ads, TV or radio commercials, your first marketing job is to capture your potential client with a headline.

Take time to watch the channel your local television news appears on one-half hour before the start of the news program. Take special note of the commercials your news anchor creates to entice you to watch the news program. It's the typical "news at 11:00" approach. Notice what words they use to get you to watch. This is the headline of the commercial. Often they have only about 5 to 7 seconds to capture your attention. You might hear words like "All New," or "Protect Your Child from the Latest Deadly Predator." My point is that when you see or hear words that powerfully entice you to respond to a marketing effort, notice what words make it work so well.

Just for the sake of clarity, I will call any "first words" written, spoken, heard or understood during a marketing effort to be the headline of the effort.

The idea here is that the initial approach is important and can greatly influence your marketing efforts. The first words in a sales letter or postcard are the headline of that mailing. The first words spoken during a client encounter is the headline of that encounter. The headline on the homepage of your web site is the most important part of the site. So if it simply just says, "Joe's Accounting Services" you have probably lost your client because the headline is not self-serving to the client. The first aspect of any marketing effort tends to set the pace in a particular direction.

How important is a headline to the success of your marketing effort? Consider this: Nearly six times as many people read the headline as the body of an ad. Unless your headline effectively sells your service, you are blowing the majority of your advertising money. The sole purpose of a headline is to offer the reader a reward for reading the body copy. The wrong headline, or no headline, can result in the failure of the ad to accomplish its primary goal to lead the reader into wanting to learn more.

To give you an idea of how important this is and to show you how it's done, I'm presenting some of my best headlines that grab your reader's attention:

- "Reduce Your Debt And Tax Burden Simultaneously"
- "Announcing Our Free Tax Service"
- "Discover Amazing New Ways To Cut Costs And Overhead"
- "Become Financially Independent In The Next Three Years, Then Double Your Net Worth Every Five Years"
- "Conservatively And Sensibly Invest In Capital Gains: Manage Your Money For High Yields Now"

A headline that offers topical news is often very successful. If your product or service is newsworthy put that special news announcement right at the top of your ad.

Incorporate eye-catching words into your headline, like ANNOUNCING, AMAZING, INTRODUCING, NOW and SUDDENLY. If you are promoting a product to one particular group, include a red flag in your headline that will single out these prospects. And remember this: specifics out-pull generalities.

Personalize a headline by singling out the city, state or group to which it is directed. Avoid humor and double entendre in headlines; they waste space and are non-productive 95-percent of the time.

Never run an ad without a headline. Test to see which headline is best. How many times have you scanned an ad in a newspaper or magazine and not had the slightest idea what it was all about, or whom the information was intended for? Ads, mailing pieces, web sites, email messages, or commercials all need a headline. A headline is an ad for the ad. Its purpose should be to reach only those who are most qualified to be a prospect for your proposition.

Without exception, humorous or abstract ads are wasteful. If you run ads in general interest publications, or TV and radio commercials, and your service is tax preparation, you should not use headlines or opening statements like, "Uncle Sam got you down?" Instead fashion a headline or opening that states the purpose of the ad and qualifies the reader.

Here's an example of the kind of headline I am talking about:

> **IF YOU'VE BEEN PAYING MORE IN FEDERAL TAXES THAN YOU SHOULD, CONTACT US ABOUT OUR TAX-BURDEN REDUCTION SERVICE**

Address your target audience in the headline with teaser copy or the opening line. If you want to reach people planning their retirement, for instance, call out to them by saying:

> **IF PLANNING YOUR RETIREMENT, YOU PROBABLY HAVE QUESTIONS ABOUT HOW YOUR PRESENT DECISIONS WILL IMPACT YOUR FUTURE TAX POSITION**

Whatever you sell, and whomever you want to reach with your story or message, be specific. Connect your message directly to your prospective customers, and tell them what you are offering.

Here are the key points for crafting effective headlines:

1. Attract the attention of your target audience in your headline or opening remarks.
2. State your proposition or offer.
3. Use the rest of the ad to develop, support, and present your offer and your reasons why the prospect should embrace it.
4. Finally, tell the prospect how to act.

From now on, always craft your message by communicating only to the people who are your primary prospects. And never again be content with humorous, nonspecific, or abstract headlines or ads.

MORE KEY IDEAS ABOUT HEADLINES

The headline is the most important element in most advertisements. It is the telegram, which decides whether the reader goes on to read the copy.

A change of headline can make a difference of ten to one in sales. I never write fewer than sixteen headlines for a single advertisement, and I observe certain guidelines in writing them.

My guidelines for headlines are as follows:

1. The headline is, of course, the "ticket on the meat". Use it to include the readers who are prospects for the kind of product you are advertising. Conversely, do not say anything in your headline that is likely to exclude any readers who might be prospects for your product.
2. Every headline should appeal to the reader's self-interest. It should promise a compelling benefit.
3. Always try to inject news into your headlines, because the consumer is always on the lookout for new products, new ways to use an old product, or new improvements to an old product. The two most powerful words you can use in a headline are "free" and "new." Use them often in your headlines.
4. Other words and phrases, which work wonders, are:
   - How To
   - Suddenly
   - Now
   - Announcing
   - Introducing
   - It's Here
   - Just Arrived
   - Important Development
   - Improvement
   - Amazing
   - Sensational
   - Remarkable
   - Revolutionary
   - Startling
   - Miracle
   - Magic
   - Offer
   - Quick
   - Easy
   - Wanted
   - Challenge
   - Advice To
   - The Truth About
   - Compare
   - Bargain
   - Hurry
   - Last Chance

Do not turn up your nose at these cliches. Some may be worn, but they work. That is why you see them turn up so often in the headlines of print and Internet advertisers and others who can measure the results of their advertisements.

Headlines can be strengthened by the inclusion of emotional words like:

- Love
- Fear
- Proud
- Friend

5. Five times as many people read the headline as read the body copy, so it is important that these glancers should at least be told what service is being advertised. That is why you should always include the brand name in your headlines.

6. Include your selling promise in your headline. This requires long headlines. When the New York University School of Retailing ran headline tests with the cooperation of a big department store, they found that headlines of ten words or longer, containing news and information, consistently sold more merchandise than short headlines. Headlines containing six to twelve words pull more coupon returns than short headlines, and there is no significant difference between the readership of twelve-word headlines and the readership of three-word headlines. One of my favorite headlines contained eighteen words: "At Sixty Miles an Hour the Loudest Noise in the New Rolls-Royce Comes From the Electric Clock."

7. People are most likely to read your body copy if your headline arouses their curiosity: so you should end your headline with a lure to read on.

8 Some copywriters write tricky headlines—puns, literary allusions, and other obscurities. This is considered in bad taste. In the average newspaper your headline has to compete for attention with 350 others. Research has shown that readers travel so fast through this jungle of information that they rarely stop to decipher the meaning of obscure headlines. Your headline must connect what you want to say, and it must connect it in plain language. Do not play games with the reader.

9. Research also shows that it is dangerous to use negatives in headlines. If, for example, you write, "our salt contains no arsenic," many readers will miss the negative and go away with the impression that you wrote, "our salt contains arsenic."

10. Avoid blind headlines—the kind which means nothing unless you read the body copy beneath them; most people do not read the copy that follows the headline.

MORE INSIGHTS ABOUT HEADLINES

- The purpose of the headline is to select people you can interest. You wish to talk to someone in a crowd. So the first thing you say is, "Hey there, Bill Jones" to get the right person's attention.

- Headlines on ads are like headlines on news items. Nobody reads a whole newspaper. One is interested in financial news, one in political, one in society, one In cookery, one in sports, etc. There are whole pages in any newspaper, which we never scan at all. Yet other people may turn directly to those pages.

- We pick out what we wish to read by headlines, and we don't want those headlines misleading. The writing of headlines is one of the greatest journalistic arts. They either conceal or reveal an interest.

- People do not read ads for amusement. They do not read ads which, at a glance, seem to offer nothing interesting.

- People are hurried. The average person skips three-fourths of the reading matter that they pay for. They are not going to read your business talk unless you make it worth their while and let the headline show it.

MORE HEADLINE GUIDELINES

1. Try to incorporate some self-interest into every headline you write. Make your headline suggest to the reader that here is something he or she wants. This rule is so fundamental that it would seem obvious. Yet the rule is violated every day by scores of writers,

2. If you have news, such as a new product, or a new use for an old product, be sure that news is included in your headline in a big way.

3. Avoid headlines that merely provoke curiosity. Curiosity combined with news or self-interest is an excellent aid to the pulling power of your headline, but curiosity by itself is seldom enough. This fundamental rule is violated more often than any other. Every issue of every magazine and newspaper contains headlines that attempt to sell the reader through curiosity alone.

4. Avoid, when possible, headlines that paint the gloomy or negative side of the picture. Take the cheerful, positive angle.

5. Suggest in your headline that there is a quick way for the client to receive something the reader wants.

–51–

YOUR ADVERTISING IS ONLY ONE-ON-ONE SELLING MULTIPLIED

Marketing your accounting services successfully is easy if you realize that advertising is nothing more than one-on-one selling multiplied. Your marketing methods should contain the same success elements as when you talk to clients one-on-one in your business. Your aim is to identify the largest success factors in your personal encounters and take those factors into all of your other marketing efforts. Think about the most successful encounters with your clients to date. Have you precisely identified what has made the client interactions so successful?

When you identify the strategies that have made your best one-on-one communications work well with your present clients, you are ready to apply them in web marketing, direct mail, and the other marketing methods.

I want you to focus on your market and the specific sales approaches that will work best for you. I want you to persuade your market to respond to you quickly by creating an appeal as if each individual client will be reading your ad, letter, or other media effort.

If you are sending a letter to newcomers in your area, your letter must contain a quick, but complete presentation of your main point of difference. Your one-on-one personal communication with clients contains certain nuances. You must magnify those nuances effectively as a pointed as a laser beam through each of your marketing methods. It is very simple. You have a tremendous advantage because you already know which words, ideas, communications and attitudes work well with your existing clients one-on-one. All you have to do is apply and translate your best individual approaches to your larger marketing campaigns and promotions.

Because advertising is merely one-on-one selling multiplied, and you're one of the most experienced people in your business, you are best able to write the most appropriate advertisements.

Ones that will be most appealing. You can do this better than anyone because you know first-hand what offers, words and tempting advantages tend to enthrall and tickle the ears of prospects. In order to optimize your knowledge and experience about what will work best in your future marketing efforts, try this exercise:

- Tape record or take good notes on all the conversations you have with your prospects and customers. In some states, this requires permission by all parties involved. Do this dozens of times so that you will have a good selection of sales presentations to work with.
- Transcribe the tape recordings. Then number each selling point that you make in your conversations.
- Give each point a priority number on a scale of 1 to 10, with 10 being highest based on favorable client responses.
- Cut out each selling point with a pair of scissors and divide them into three groups. The first group consists of those selling points which describe the benefits of your service. The second group consists of interesting facts about your service. And the third group consists of those points that don't really say anything about your service or help to advance your presentation.
- Throw the third group away and arrange the other two in rank order from 1 to 10. With 1 as the most compelling for your clients and 10 as the least compelling.
- Next throw out all points with a rank of five or greater.
- Now, forget that you are writing an ad or sales letter. Instead, concentrate on writing a memo. A long memo to a friend—don't try to be clever.
- As you write, concentrate on selling compelling advantages that are self-serving to the client, just as you did in your conversations with your prospects and customers!

Take your ideas one step at a time as you refine them. Show your finished ideas to trusted colleagues and friends whose opinions you respect to obtain feedback. Ask some of your best customers what they think of your ideas for advertisements. Then test your marketing ideas on a small scale in the real setting to see whether you persuade enough people to warrant investing in the actual advertisement. If you are running a direct mail program consisting of letters and a quick brochure about your newest services, then send out 100 or so as a test to determine if you are getting enough responses to continue. If your test generates less business than it costs, consider trying another list, more compelling offer, less risk, or a greater value/price incentive. Keep changing your selling approaches until your efforts pull profitably.

Here are some quick tips on creating advertising copy that gets response:

- Remember, your ad will be read by only one person at a time. Do not write to the masses—write to one person.
- Read your copy aloud so you can see where it doesn't flow and where it needs smoothing out.
- Edit your copy. Take out unnecessary repetition. Use short sentences. Write short paragraphs, and use everyday English. Use some one-word sentences. Use one-sentence paragraphs. And use a generous supply of headings and subheadings that make your copy look interesting and easy to read!

Good advertising is simply one-one-one salespersonship multiplied. Use one-to-one communication strategies in your ads to create highly self-serving, compelling advantages for your clients and you will multiply your effectiveness multi-fold.

–52–

CREATIVELY TARGET YOUR HIGH-PROBABILITY CLIENTS

In your all of your efforts to market focus intensely on reaching people who have the highest probability of doing business with you. In your ads, promotions, communications and presentations focus on create a message strategy that targets prospects who will be most responsive to the reasons and explanations that you give them about why you are different.

As a well-sought-after interactive marketing expert, I receive many promotions and advertising samples to critique. The primary error that business owners frequently make is in attempting to be all things to all people, instead of targeting the intended recipient. Focusing on your clients' needs and aspirations creates unity between your marketing and the people in your target market. However, not all clients with a need for your services will have a high-probability of becoming clients. This is why you must learn what makes a high-probability client a hot client. Some clients choose accounting service professionals for convenience—because their offices are close by or they extend extra service with a house-call. Some clients will choose to work with you because you have a personality that shines. Identifying what makes some prospects better, high-probability potential clients than others is an important step.

Start by profiling your present clientbase with the intention of determining what makes a prospect predisposed to respond to your marketing appeals. Simply ask your present clients what first made them respond by call or visiting your office. Find out why they are motivated to do business with you. You may find that there is a geographic component to your appeal.

I know an accountant who profiled his clients and determined that condo renters and apartment dwellers within a five-block radius of his office were higher-probability prospects. Guess what this astute accountant did? He rented a mailing list of every apartment dweller within ten-blocks of his office. He made a special offer to them in his direct mailing. He focused his letter intently on their special needs. In the months preceding tax season he continued to saturate his list of high-probability targets with new money-saving ideas and tips. This strategy made his business increase by 40-percent, while his advertising costs decreased by over 60-percent because he dropped the local "mass-media" ads that contained too much waste-coverage.

Your goal is very simple: Identify exactly who your prime target audience is and then communicate only to them. Do not try to be obscure, abstract, "artsy" or "fringy." Speak directly to your target market in your ads and letters.

When you run a print ad or send a letter, try asking a direct question as the main premise of the approach: "Are you paying too much in annual taxes?" Be straightforward, and send your message as if you are speaking to each individual in your market.

Your aim is to create immediate connection with the client who sees or hears your message. Pretend that your client is saying, "Communicate clearly, powerfully, and directly to me and no one else." Act as a lighthouse in the fog, signaling to the specific type of client your business has the precise answers for. It is as if your client is saying to you, "If you do not communicate only to me, I will not even recognize that your signal is for me and probably won't even perceive it. Then, I will steer my ship right past you."

Here is an example that will add more value to this explanation for you. I once worked with an accountant who had been sponsoring seminars. In the past, she printed brochures that advertised the advantages of attending the seminars, and she mailed the brochures to everyone in her geographic area, regardless of whether the recipients of the mailings had any interest in the seminar topic on not. I told, Nancy, the owner of the business, that this didn't make a lot of sense to me. I asked her why she was wasting 95% of her marketing effort. She was taken back by my forwardness; however, I explained that the people who were more likely to attend the seminars would be people who have an interest in the specific topics she was presenting, not just those who lived in her immediate area. Nancy agreed!

I created an effective marketing plan for Nancy. First, we compiled a list of target subscribers from two magazines. She was aware that a large percent of her clients read. The magazines happened to contain the largest number of subscribers in her area. We selected the subscribers list to contain names and addresses within a 25-mile radius of the local area where the seminar was to be held. Second, we obtained a list of everyone who had ever attended a local seminar on a similar topic within a two-year period. Third, we made an arrangement with local bookstores to promote the event to their customers. These collective efforts helped us concentrate our mailing on people who were more likely to be interested in the event. Fourth, we created a letter to accompany the brochure, which acknowledged that the recipient was a well-known attendee of business seminars, and that the event would be very exciting, as well as very beneficial for them to attend. The total thrust of the marketing effort was to focus only on the clients who had the highest probability of attending the seminar.

I reduced her marketing costs by 2/3 and her attendance at the seminar was double that of her last seminar. The point of the story is to show you the value of focusing intensely on your intended clients. Target them in precise ways and you can easily double or triple your success. Especially if you conduct layered marketing efforts, such as, performing multiple mailings and using targeted multi-media approaches to your niche market.

When you focus your marketing great things happen because you clarify your message. The people that you want to address simply have a better chance of getting the message with much less media waste.

–53–

FOUR STEPS TO WRITING PRINT ADS AND LETTERS THAT HAVE "DYNAMIC PULLING APPEAL"

It could easily take us a week to delve into all of the fundamentals that make print ads and letters successfully appeal to your clients in powerful ways. Here are the key steps you should take when writing an ad or letter to make the impact of your words more genuine and persuasive:

STEP ONE: THE HEADLINE OR LETTER OPENING - GRAB YOUR READERS' ATTENTION IMMEDIATELY

1. Your headline or letter opening—the headline at the top of your letter—should focus precisely on the kind of client you specialize in servicing, those in your target market. For example, if you want to reach successful business owners with your accounting services, consider putting a call-out to your market by using the words, "Successful business owners" in the headline.
2. Your headline and introduction (the first few words or sentences of the letter or advertisement) serves as a mini-ad within your ad or letter. The headline or introduction should tell your reader the essence of what you are saying in the body of the copy.
3. The headline should give your reader a significant self-serving benefit or promise. Write a headline about what your accounting firm is precisely offering.
4. Create an attention-getting headline to motivate the reader to continue reading more. Words that "pull" more in headlines include: *free, new, emergency, now, secret, easy, introducing, save, guarantee, how, why, today.* The hottest word of all is *YOU.* Think up 10 to 100 headlines, and then boil them down to just a few. Brainstorm with your buddies and check your ideas with them. This step is essential to the marketing success of your headline.

STEP TWO: STATE THE BENEFITS - REMEMBER THESE IDEAS WHEN WRITING BENEFITS IN ADS OR LETTERS:

1. Don't presume your reader understands the benefits your business offers. Clearly and simply explain the advantages that you give that make you different. If you can boil your "primary point of difference" down into one to three words, you have a clear understanding of your uniqueness.

2. Emphasize the benefits that your business offers instead of all the features. Your clients do not buy services or products, they buy advantages. State the features of your services as benefits in order to stimulate the readers' imagination in the direction of your point of difference. Instead of saying, "We offer bookkeeping services," say: "We offer stress-relieving, time-saving bookkeeping services."

3. Discuss buying points. Increase your readers' desire by spelling out specific needs that particular clients would like to have satisfied. Explain in simple, factual, and practical language how your service fills those needs.

STEP THREE: PRESENT A BETTER-THAN-RISK-FREE GUARANTEE

Offer a guarantee that compels and persuades people to try your services. A lot of accountants are afraid to give a satisfaction guarantee because they think that they might be taken advantage of. Try to avoid this way of thinking. More prospects will try your services because of a guarantee that is self-serving to them. I recommend you offer a "superior-than-risk-free guarantee" because it makes such a strong statement to your market. Creating a superior-than-risk-free guarantee takes a lot of confidence in your service, courage, and boldness. Often, the bolder your guarantee, the more easily you will persuade your market to try your services for the first time. Imagine for a moment the cost a potential client incurs to switch to your services from their current accountant. The potential client may tend to resist your offers because they think that the costs and risks to switch to your service are too high. Instead, you must use a superior-than-risk-free guarantee to reduce their perceived cost and risk.

Consider the power of this bold guarantee:

> **IF YOU ARE NOT COMPLETELY SATISFIED**
> **WITH OUR PERFORMANCE,**
> **THEN YOUR TAX SERVICE IS FREE!**

This guarantee gives your readers the feeling of control. It is also an indication of your confidence in giving satisfactory service. There are various guarantees you can offer. Create a strong risk-reducing guarantee, and use it in your ads and letters.

STEP FOUR: MAKE A SPECIFIC OFFER AND MOTIVATE POTENTIAL CLIENTS TO TAKE YOU UP ON IT

Your offer must be stated as simply and clearly as possible. You must strongly compel people to take one very specific action to receive the different, but dynamic, benefit you offer.

Create a strong sense of urgency by offering a special bonus or incentive to those who respond immediately. For example, you could say: "If you call before January 27th, we will give you five free hours of our small business start-up analysis and a free self-incorporation kit."

STEP FIVE: ADD A POSTSCRIPT TO YOUR PROMOTIONAL LETTERS AND/OR A CONCLUSION AT THE BOTTOM OF YOUR PRINT AD

Write a summary statement for the postscript—one that piques the interest of your readers who will often look at the postscript before reading the letter. You could say: "PS: Remember, our guarantee and outstanding service will enhance your success in business. Find out how by calling for a free consultation now."

You can use this same pattern of logic for any of your other advertising efforts by applying these ideas as a step-by-step template.

An accountant/financial planner could use this letter to reach prospective clients in his or her community:

WILLIAM DAVIS
CPA/FINANCIAL PLANNER
220 LOWELL STREET
PLEASANTVILLE, MA 01960
617-555-1234 PHONE

—Achieve Financial Independence In The Next Ten Years—
Discover Five Easy Ways To Overcome Cash Flow Problems
For The Rest Of Your Life!

Dear Mr. Jones:

The headline of this letter may sound audacious but frankly, it's true. As a practicing financial planner in this city for the last ten years, I have been able to show 500 of your neighbors and friends new techniques that have allowed them to structure a financial plan that has given them of all the passive income they need for retirement, for vacations, or for business investments. I have helped many people create a comfortable cushion of bank savings, for their children's education, or for the exciting luxuries they have dreamed about.

I achieve these goals without changing a person's lifestyle in the least; most often with dollars normally paid to the government through innovative tax-sheltering strategies. Most people have no real financial plan and don't understand they could easily create a total financial plan that provides plenty of passive income to maintain for all of their essential needs.

I've prepared a report entitled, "How to Achieve Total Financial Independence And Have More Tax-free Passive Income Long Before You Retire, Plus Have More Money for Extended Vacations and Adventure Travel." I'd be delighted to send you a copy or sit down with you and explain my techniques in person.

I am a professional who has successfully taken his own advice, I am financially free and I no longer require myself to work to generate income. I simply choose to help others because of the joy I receive from doing it. My practice is centrally and conveniently located at 220 Lowell Street. I keep fairly normal business hours and I am also available, on occasion, for evening and weekend consultations. If you do not have time for a personal consultation, I would be glad to show you a simple way to create your own financial plan. I have a form that is very easy to fill out which I will be glad to send you, as well.

Enclosed is a reply card. Send it back to me, and my assistant will send you the form and the FREE report. Then I will follow up and see whether you feel my services will be invaluable to you.

In the meantime, if you have questions or if I can be of any help, feel free to call me with no obligation.

Yours,

William Davis CPA

I directed one of my clients, an accountant/financial planner, to use a letter similar to the example above. The strategy we created became the platform of a highly successful marketing campaign for his accounting practice. I directed him to contact his local Chamber of Commerce to obtain a list of local business leaders.. My client obtained a list, which included about 375 contacts. About 60 of these people responded and most became steady clients. Because these clients are community-opinion leaders and are well known, they are in a better position than the average person to generate more referral business for my client. Their testimonial or endorsement also goes a long way in the community. Never hesitate to test mailing letters to VIPs in your community with very special offers.

–54–

DISCOVER YOUR CHIEF MARKETING AIM

For many accounting professionals, marketing their practices can be a frustrating and daunting task. During seminars, I am frequently asked to give three or four simple, definable steps, which will yield a maximum marketing outcome for a minimum investment of time and money. I have discovered that there is a way to be free from the confusion and frustration that often besets the best of us. I'd like to share them with you. Then you can experience more of the joy and fulfillment your business has to give you. There is no need for you to ever feel frustrated in marketing your business.

There are three primary activities highly successful accountants and bookkeepers have learned to execute consistently, and with tremendous rapidity, in order to obtain boundless, replicable, enduring marketing results. These three activities will help you focus on your high priority marketing areas when your business seems to be diminishing; they will also enhance your practice when it is at its most successful peak. The very hallmark strategies that I am about to give you have made consulting superstars who they are. Your three most critical marketing principles are as follows:

I. Analyze, discover and continually rediscover the best combination of marketing methods that will generate a critical mass — a significant number of potential client leads.
II. Convert those generated leads into business in the form of contracts, hireable and billable tasks, etc.
III. Create a system for fulfilling consulting services in the highest way possible by subcontracting or delegating your lowest priority tasks to others and executing your highest priority tasks yourself.

Let's look more closely at these areas.

I. FIND THE BEST COMBINATION OF MARKETING METHODS

Your first aim is to discover a handful of media—three to five—which give you the best lead-generating leverage possible. Take time to really study your potential and present clients. The goal is find out how target clients find and hire accountants. You will discover that 70% to 80% of your clients tend to find accountants through special referrals that highlight their expertise. Devoting your resources toward investing in the right media combinations for your specific consulting business means constantly seeking new knowledge about new combinations of marketing methods for use in generating leads for new client projects. Most accountants follow the pack. To market your consulting business on the cutting-edge with tremendous success, it is necessary for you to become an innovative and creative marketer. So then, what marketing methods should you actively pursue to consistently generate a full supply of business leads?

By studying the success factors of the nation's top-earning independent accountants, a tangible success pattern emerges for the selection of marketing methods. It is clear that accountants who achieve higher levels of income use significantly different media combinations than their less successful counterparts. Remember: If you actively study the most successful accountants in the field, their successes leave clues and patterns. The clues discovered significantly eliminate years of trial and error testing for the remaining accounting businesses.

Based on the best marketing methods of the nation's top-performing independent accountants, I have crafted a marketing method selection plan for accountants that can be used to set your course:

A. Create a system of communications that continually asks your present clients for referral business, such as letters, e-mail and other highly personalized methods. The best time to set a foundation for referrals is at the beginning of your relationship with new clients — those who have communicated they are pleased with your service. Mentioning that they could possibly refer 3 or 4 of their friends to you actually predisposes them to doing it when you later ask for specific referrals.

Remember: In larger companies referrals can be internal or external. Internal referrals occur when one department recommends you to another department laterally within the corporation. External referrals are referrals to secondary businesses outside of the primary business relationship. Always look for opportunities to acquire both kinds during all service encounters.

B. Follow up immediately on all potentially new opportunities presented by past clients. Send them a Credibility Boosting Kit that includes:
- Past articles you have published in your field
- Your story in the form of a biographical feature story
- A statement of your philosophy that tells what you do that's different
- A brochure that sells your services
- Testimonials from past clients
- Endorsements from national associations in your specialized field
- A business card with your picture on it

C. Put together a network consisting of other service professionals who are noncompetitive to you. If your specialty is in marketing, unite forces with a Financial Management Consultant and an Operations Management Consultant, thereby forming a team able to share referrals, etc. Be sure to see "chapter on Accounting Cross-Promotion Teams for more information.

D. Giving dynamic presentations to local and national associations, not in your field, but in the field of the market of your clients, provides the highest outcome presentation and the most results-driven information you are capable of developing. Speaking topics that closely relate to the unique benefits your give through the services you offer should also be presented, basing them on your one primary point of difference—that what you offer, no one in your field offers. Refer to Session on Seminars and Presentations.

E. Actively write articles for at least 12 publications in your field per year, including local organizations. Ask your local reference librarian at a good business library to direct you to one of several periodical directories. The periodical directories list a large number of the periodicals germane to your field. I usually adapt material from my published books into articles and automatically submit them to magazine editors on the 12th day of the month. Once you build a relationship with magazine editors they will call or e-mail you ahead of time with ideas regarding the kind of articles they would like you to write for them.

F. Use direct mail to support the above efforts (stated in A–E). Send your published articles to your house list of current clients and past seminar attendees. Test purchased mailing lists of magazine subscribers obtained from niche trade journals, other publications, and association directories. Send your house newsletter or your past published articles to the high-probability subscribers in your local area. Your house list is your best mailing list.

G. As a last priority effort, consider advertising in national and local niche newsletters, magazines, and other publications. Test using smaller ads first. If they pull leads you can move up to test slightly larger ads. The key is to move slowly and advertise in the publications that have the highest probability of being noticed by your target market first. Ask a sample of your potential clients what magazines they read, as well as which ads for service professionals they have responded to in the past. Ascertain the colors and shapes your potential clients like best, and what offers they would respond to most quickly. The use of the right shapes, colors, and offers in your ads is critical. These factors all contribute to the pulling power of the printed advertisement in your niche market. The only way to know the best combinations of ad elements is to do your homework and then test your ads.

If you are a fledgling accountant and new to your field, then you will have to strive even harder to obtain higher levels of visibility. The higher your visibility the more effective your marketing strategies will become for you. If you join an association, you will receive more business referrals by becoming president of that association as opposed to being a back-row participant. The more visibility you receive in your local, regional and national niche area of expertise, the more the above media combinations will produce a catalyzing result for you in generating a flow of leads.

II. EFFICIENTLY CONVERT LEADS INTO BILLABLE JOBS

Your second aim is to efficiently convert your leads into business — in the form of contracts and billable jobs. If you obtain 15 leads for your services per month and you only convert three of these leads into billable business then your conversion ratio is 3 clients out of 15 prospects, or 1 out of 5, this is 20%. In other words, you are spending as much time and effort on the four clients out of five that you are not capturing, as you are to obtain the one that becomes your client.

By creating a new pattern of thinking and changing your approach you can easily convert more prospects into clients, and then more clients into billable jobs. Here are some more ideas for converting more of your leads into actual business:

- Tape record your best interactions with clients. Be aware of what words you use that really hit the hot buttons of the client, and that work a high percentage of the time. As you tape record your client, imagine that your client has a green button and a red button on his or her shirt. Every time you say something that pleases the client you are hitting the green "pleasure button." After taping your most successful attempts to convert clients, transcribe them. Look for the success patterns. The words you used should be boiled down to just the right words — these are the green buttons. The green buttons are the words consistently yielding the highest probability that your prospect will become your client. Create a hot list of "green-button" phrases. For your next 10 prospective interactions, try using the right green-button words that you have discovered. For the next consecutive 10 lead follow-ups, don't use them. Compare the results to see how many more leads you actually convert into clients. Play with this exercise and have fun.
- Make certain that your proposal is created in the most professional way possible. This will help you make a tangible presentation by communicating to the prospect what he or she will be receiving from you.
- Increase your people skills and selling skills. There are many courses you can take to enhance your ability to close sales. Learning International conducts one of the best courses on professional selling that is offered on the market. After you have shared a proposal with the client, try asking for the business. It is often as simple and straightforward as saying, "Ms. Green, we have given you our best-reasoned advice on how to proceed. We are excited about working with you. Would you like to hire us?" The next most obvious question, assuming she says, "yes" is, "How soon?" If she says no, you have to ask, "Why?" That is, if you are as curious as I am about how

and why people respond the way they do. You will be surprised how often people will respond by saying, "yes!"

III. CREATE A SYSTEM FOR PROVIDING SERVICE EXCELLENCE

Your third aim is to create a system for providing your consulting services with progressive excellence, with professional ease, and as efficiently as possible. I suggest that you create a system for each component of professional consulting service that you provide. If you have not yet developed a master plan for delivering your service, you will gain instant delegating leverage. With a written master service plan in place, you can hire an employee or a subcontractor to work the system for that new client scenario. So you must analyze every one of the unique services you provide and create a mini-system for completing each service, without having to provide it yourself.

The best way to start to plan your master consulting system is by taking a careful inventory of your daily tasks. Here is how to create an unbeatable system for providing your services more efficiently:

STEP ONE

Start by listing the tasks you perform each day. Determine the duration of time you invest in completing each task on your list. Then at the end of each day assign each task a "Replacement Cost" (RC) (how much it would cost you to hire someone else to do the work). Total your RC for each day. Let's say your total RC for today is $95. You could hire someone else to do these tasks for about $95 for the day.

STEP TWO

Determine the value of your time per hour. This is called your "Consulting Lifetime Value" (CLV). Now figure out how much your CLV is worth per day. Let's say your billable time is $75 per hour and you worked 8 hours today. Your CLV is $600 ($75 x 8 hours). You could perform your tasks at a cost of $600, if you do them yourself. You should be paying yourself this amount if you choose to do these tasks.

STEP THREE

Compare your Replacement Cost to your Consulting Lifetime Value. What is the difference? Here it is: $600 minus $95, which is $505. This is the price you are paying per day for working the way you are today. By creating a system for these tasks and by delegating or farming them out to someone else you are saving $505 worth of your time.

The question I will now ask you is this: which tasks on your daily lists can be shifted to assistants, farmed out to service firms (i.e. mailing houses, etc.), or given to additional part-time workers? — Which tasks are your highest priority tasks? —and— Do you pay yourself well enough for performing your highest priority tasks?

- Mundane tasks should be shifted to workers whose time is less costly than your own.
- High-priority tasks can be converted into work-producing systems that are to be turned over to capable workers, such as, college interns, junior consultants, etc.
- Highest priority tasks can be done by you, or shifted to exceptionally qualified staff members.

The better you become at executing your Chief Marketing Aim, the better your business becomes for you. Do it effortlessly, efficiently, and with greater speed as you put your Chief Marketing Aim into practice. As your ability to create efficient new systems grows and as you attract new talent to help you run your systems, your business or practice will flourish.

–55–

INCREASE YOUR CLIENT RETENTION RATES

Most businesses I look at have growth opportunities that the owners have overlooked because they haven't taken time to focus on them. One of the most significant is client retention. Every business loses some of its clients throughout the year. This is called "attrition" or "client-loss." One of the first questions I ask my clients during consultations with them is: "How many clients do you tend to lose per year?" Ninety-five percent of the time, they look at me with a blank stare and say, "We're not sure." I inform them that they must know how many clients they are losing on average, because for every 5% to 7% of the regular clients you retain by reversing client-loss, you add 15% to 30% more profit to your bottom line.

The purpose of this session is to help you slowdown the number of clients you lose, and, in effect, to convert them into long-term clients. Your long-term clients are more profitable for the following reasons:

- Regular clients usually cost less to service
- Satisfied clients are more likely to pay premium prices for your services
- Satisfied clients often refer new clients to you at no additional cost
- Retaining more clients means that fewer new clients are needed, and can be acquired less expensively
- The cost of acquiring a new client can be substantial

Everything you do—every service you perform, every client-marketing strategy that you implement, the way you handle phone calls—is a part of your business system. Even if you think you do not have a system for client loyalty, you actually do! Remember: Having "no system" is a system, especially if you regularly rely on "management by the seat of your pants."

Think about how you handle customer loss. Have you worked hard to make as many of your present clients as loyal as possible? I am sure you have. At seminars I usually say, semi-jokingly, that the least loyal kind of client is a lost client. Well, most accountants do not think about their client-loss rates until it is too late to recover lost clients at all.

If you have 500 clients in your practice and you lose 20 percent of them annually, that is a loss of 100 clients per year. Just by taking an action to reduce that loss by half you would, in effect, gain 50 clients that would otherwise have left you during the year. In 10 years' time, just by slowing your client losses by half, you would have, in effect, doubled your practice without any additional marketing efforts.

Understanding the value of reducing the number of clients you normally tend to lose will motivate you to take a series of powerful relationship-building steps that will help you. You need a simple system in place for checking your client loss, so consistent action can be taken to influence them into becoming more loyal. Here are some valuable suggestions:

- Hire a staff member to look through your client database and give you a list of all the clients from whom you have not interacted for three months or more. Set a plan to personally call your clients to ask if anything went wrong and just check on them in the event corrections may be needed for any past consulting performances. This action will usually work well to reduce client loss by between 30 percent and 50 percent all by itself.
- Create a system of continual communication that your staff can implement monthly. Use mailings to send clients articles and books in their areas of interest and to remind them that you are there. I like to send special alert reports that tell clients about significant changes to their industry and give them instant solutions and suggested actions.
- Remember important dates in the history of your relationship with that client. Sometimes showing that you remember special personal things about your client can create connection. Birthdays and anniversaries are always wonderful to remember. One accountant sends his clients a special present on the one-year anniversary of their involvement.

To successfully reverse the effects of client loss you must understand the primary reasons why your clients leave you. Often it is because people have had an unsatisfactory experience with your business. They may have come in for tax preparation and didn't receive the desired outcome. Perhaps they dealt with someone on your staff who was mildly offensive in some way. Maybe the service you sold them was performed a day later than your staff member promised and the client felt upset. Whatever the reason, your client has become unhappy. They no longer associate visiting your business with pleasant feelings because of the problem they experienced. But it can be resolved.

Also, the possibility that a significant change occurred in a client's life may have caused them to interrupt their dealings with you. Perhaps they became ill or went on vacation and, as a result, never returned to you. People sometimes become diverted, overwhelmed, oversaturated with a particular type of service and temporarily stop using it. They may have had the intention of coming back to use your services, but never get around to it.

If you notice that your business has a large percentage of clients who just go away because of attrition, you have a responsibility and an obligation to nurture them to rebuild a relationship with you.

If you can cut your rate of client-loss in half, it is like adding that number of new clients back into your business. If you have 500 regular clients and have been losing an average of 20% of your client base each year, that is 100 clients. If you cut that loss by 50%, it would be as if you added 50 extra clients to your business per year. This means that in ten years, if you used no other strategy except my retention marketing-strategy, then you would double your number of clients. This would occur every 5 years in business because you would add 50% more loyal clients to your business just by using this one idea.

HERE ARE THREE WAYS TO SLOW YOUR CLIENT LOSS BY 30% TO 65% OR MORE

- Contact your inactive clients and ask them, "Is anything wrong?" I suggest that you call them to communicate your concern about why they are no longer doing business with you. Ask them if something happened, or ask, politely, if they have a problem you can address. Determine whether they had an unsatisfactory experience with your people or your business. Tell them that whatever is wrong, you want to know, so that you can support them and resolve any problems. This will free them to visit you again.

- Make certain that you are delivering consistently higher-than-expected levels of service to every client you deal with. You have to ask this question: "What does my client ordinarily expect to receive when they visit me or my competitors?" The important word is, "ordinary." Now move beyond the ordinary into the realm of the extraordinary by systematically exceeding your client's expectation of what ordinary service is.

- The third way to decrease client loss is to communicate frequently and meaningfully with your clients. Many accounting professionals do not understand this valuable step. The phrase "out of sight, out of mind" has never been truer than at this moment in time for many of your clients. Today, people are bombarded with more information than ever before. So you have quite a marketing challenge ahead of you. Your challenge and your biggest opportunity is to keep clients constantly connected to you and your business. You can do this in a number of ways — by calling each client after your service to see if they were happy with the results they. Call your client a week after their visit to see if they have any questions about the service they have received.

MORE WAYS TO SLOW CLIENT LOSS

The critical measurement behind the durability of your accounting practice is your level of client loss. How many clients are lost each year? Most accounting practices tend to lose between 15% to 65% or more of their clients per year.

Your primary point of action is to establish the rate of client loss for your accounting firm. Are you certain how many of last year's clients have failed to call you for service this year? Is your rate of client loss discussed at staff meetings? Tracking client attrition is not always easy because clients usually don't announce the fact that they are leaving you. They slip away quietly. Lost business is usually discovered after a client has fallen through the cracks. Here are some more key points to look at to reduce client loss:

- Put a client tracking system in place. You might want to classify clients based on their tendency to hire you. For example, you can categorize clients by their hiring cycle: "A" through "D." "A" clients may hire you once every month or two. "B" clients may average once every three months. "C" clients may hire once ever six to nine months. "D" clients may be once per year. If your staff has not contacted or been contacted by your "A" clients within six weeks, then you or staff should call the client immediately to bring in the expected business gracefully and with ease. It is easier to correct a missed expectation when it first occurs rather than three months after you have lost the client.

- Call clients you have not heard from in at least three months to inquire how they are and to make a subtle effort to determine if they found your service satisfactory. If you have never attempted this simple but powerful approach you will be amazed at the results that you will receive by taking a special interest in the well-being of your client. If you discover that the reason you have not heard from the client is because something went terribly wrong during your last consulting session, you must do everything in your power to correct it.

If you don't have a system to prevent client loss, then you will never attempt to connect with those clients to nurture that relationship.

–56–

DEVELOP A REFERRAL SYSTEM
THAT ATTRACTS MORE CLIENTS

You must develop a referral strategy that encourages your clients to recommend you to their friends, family, and business associates. Once your clients understand and appreciate clearly what makes your business different and find low-risk, easy and fun ways to ask your present clients to recommend your services to others they know and trust, then the foundation for your referral system will be securely in place.

Do you remember a time when you went to a particular restaurant, and you experienced great value or terrific service? Who did you tell? Did you tell someone special, a friend, colleague, a neighbor, a relative, an employer, and a fellow worker? Do you remember how wonderful you felt when your friend called you and told you how happy they were that you had told them about that restaurant? You owe it to your present clients to give them the same opportunity. You must realize that referrals will climb in significant numbers, but only if you take the initiative to stimulate them. Referrals do several very powerful things for your business:

- Referrals help the referrer and referree appreciate value, results, and benefits that they receive from your business at a much higher level.
- Referrals help your present clients return to you the appreciation they feel for the advantage you give them.
- Referrals give your present clients a way to improve and enrich the lives of others through their experiences with your business.

INCREASE YOUR SERVICE LEVELS—GIVE MORE VALUE TO CLIENTS THAN EVER BEFORE

The key to making your referral system work is to understand the benefits, and advantages that your clients value most.

Before implementing your referral system, you must ask yourself some important questions, such as: Am I giving the best possible value (or benefit or advantage) to my clients? Do I genuinely care about my clients' best interests and needs at the level I should or could? Is my staff extending every ounce of effort to service our clients? Are we always genuinely thinking about clients' interests above our own? You must focus all of your thoughts and all of your actions on the best interest of your clients in an all-encompassing way. When you make the shift to focus your attention on the needs of your clients, your referral system then has a credible base on which to function. Then your business will have the foundation you need to take the next step in generating referrals because your clients will be very proud and happy to tell others about you. Otherwise they just won't make that effort to tell others. Or worse, they will tell others the things about your business that make them unhappy. Make certain that your team is performing with excellence at all times because this also sets an important foundation upon which client referrals are based. It is so easy to miss the mark in one or two key areas of your service and not realize how much clients notice what they are missing.

MAKE REFERRALS A MUST FOR YOUR CLIENTS

There are many ways to almost automate your referral system so that your clients will follow through by talking to others about your services.

When new clients come in for a consultation, explain to them what they can expect to receive from their experience with you. If they are very happy with their service, perhaps you might ask if they would refer you to at least three other people. Persuading clients to take action is the key. Try saying this to your clients, "Our policy is to continue to give you superior service, because we anticipate that you'd be happy to tell at least three good friends about how much we've helped you when you leave. Would you be willing to do that, Sandra?"

Give your new clients incentives to refer others to your business. One smart marketer I know gives each new client three business cards and tells clients that if they will write their name on the cards and give them to five good friends who come in for service that they will receive a free tax preparation service. This accountant keeps careful records of all the referrals each client makes.

DEVELOP AN EXCEPTIONAL REFERRAL BUSINESS

Paying for referrals is unethical in the professions; the alternative is to give value for consideration. In other words, make yourself available to provide valuable services to groups or individuals with the understanding that you're extending yourself, and anticipating they would be willing to reciprocate.

You could go to businesses and offer to be the resident accountant for the employees, giving lectures on a scheduled frequency, such as monthly or quarterly, and perhaps holding special programs for whole weekends.

At these times you knowingly and willingly give at no cost, what a client would normally pay $100 or $200 to receive, with the knowledge that you are accessing to a great many people, some of whom could ultimately become your loyal clients.

This same pattern can be followed with fraternal groups. Being very up-front, you might say, "I'd like to build my practice. The way I do this by getting endorsement of organizations that have members who can truly benefit fro the tax-saving information I share. If you will allow me to access your members by sending them information, holding a lecture, or speaking at one of your gatherings, I'll provide information that would normally be worth $50 or $100 if they bought general books on the topic of tax-planning—actually most of the inside information about significant savings that I share simply isn't available in any books." The key is to be forthright when you approach the organization with your proposal to reach their members. This is the ultimate referral.

There are also other ways to gain referrals. Although you cannot pay percentages, you could pay for leads. You can contact various people, such as a list of your fellow business members of a local professional organization, and say very simply, "You know me by my reputation. You know that I'm a talented accountant. I know that a lot of your clients (customers, employees, members, etc.) could benefit from improved accounting services. I have a service to offer: a free consultation (or a free report or a free copy of my tape) to anyone who would send for it. I will pay for the leads that come from it at a rate of $X per lead."

I used to have a standing offer. I was interested in obtaining a certain kind of clientele. In an effort to do this, I offered one hundred qualified people 15 minutes of my time for free with the knowledge that I was looking for a single client out of those hundred. I always tell my contacts that they can give my time to their customers as a gift. I give them a vehicle from which they benefit because they will all receive a 15-minute consultation, and I in exchange for the exposure.

Go to your contacts and say, "I'll give my time and my expertise freely to as many of your customers, prospects or friends as you want, provided they meet my specified qualifications. They receive something, win, lose or draw, whether any business comes to me or not. They receive a tutorial on accounting that would cost them $50 if they came into my office. It's my way of showing that I want their business and can provide effective service." Tell them your motives up front.

ADVANCED REFERRAL STRATEGIES

A REFERRAL SYSTEM THAT WORKS BY MAILING LETTERS

This is another powerful strategy for capturing additional prospects. Write your customers and offer them a special gift — perhaps a silver dollar or a commemorative coin — if they will give you the name of a prospective client. Ask them to refer a friend or relative to whom you could send your literature, and in turn offer to mail them a gift.

Although you won't pull great numbers, because these referred prospects will not be highly qualified, the ones you obtain will become choice clients because of their connection to the referrer.

You should also personalize the outside of the envelope with a teaser that names the person who referred you to them. For example, if Bob Jones referred you to Jana Ruffi, the teaser could read:

"Hi Jana, Here's something that I wanted to share with you.
— Your friend, Bob Jones."

USE AN ASSUMPTIVE LETTER SYSTEM AFTER REFERRALS HAVE BEEN OBTAINED

Once you have referrals or other hot leads, you can use the assumptive letter approach.

The essence of this technique is to aim your letter solely at those people who are seriously thinking about using your services. This is unlike most direct-mail sales letters or lead- generating devices, which ask a question such as: "Are you thinking about hiring a new accountant?"

The assumptive approach actually assumes that prospects are inexorably desirous of acquiring your services. For example, in an assumptive letter you might write:

"The other day your friend, Bob Jones, was in my office and mentioned your name. The thought was that you might be within weeks of having your federal income tax return prepared; however, I don't know whether you have taken the appropriate steps to avoid over-paying your taxes. Bob and I just created a special strategy to reduce his tax burden by 25%. I just want to let you know that before you contact an accountant this year, I'd like you to consider trying my free 20-minute tax-reduction consultation. Here's how it worked successfully for your friend, Bob..."

The main factors that differentiate an assumptive letter from a typical general sales letter are that it assumes every recipient is firmly in the market for your accounting services. To be most effective, the assumptive letter should be personalized with the person's name and address and laser printed. Furthermore, the assumptive letter should offer some enormously informative and educational benefits—for example, a seminar, a consultation, free advice, a free audit, or even a book or report. These things must genuinely provide valuable techniques that will help the recipients become more knowledgeable, better informed, and better prepared to buy—even if they don't seek to do business with your firm.

It is critically important that you make a noble informational offer in the assumptive letter. Also, clearly inform the recipient that your offer of free information education is being rendered on a no-obligation, totally risk-free basis.

Finally, you must clearly and openly reveal the methods to your seeming madness of offering information that the recipients can benefit from even if they don't buy from you. Simply state the fact that, all things being equal, you've found that once you honestly and conscientiously inform and educate someone, they become a far more discerning buyer — and more often than not they turn to your firm once they are educated to what you're all about.

Conclude an assumptive letter with a clear, concerned request for action. For example:

"Whether you're ready to re-evaluate if you are over-paying your federal income tax today or in two weeks, you'll make a better buying decision once you learn these facts. To get this information, or to set up the free consultation call me or my assistant, Kim, at 323-555-1234 or send me the enclosed card in the postage-paid envelope I've enclosed."

The idea here is to personalize your letter to leverage the connection that the letter recipient has with the person who referred you to them. Your can use your laser printer and the mail merge feature in Microsoft Word to personalize all your letters in a very compelling way. Personalized assumptive letters make "cold" marketing "hot" — and that improves your results dramatically.

–57–

DEVELOP ACCOUNTING CROSS-PROMOTION TEAMS

Oftentimes during consultations, accountants and bookkeeping business owners ask me how to get better results with rented mailing lists of potential clients. I will share with you the same thing I share with them. Sometimes the smartest thing to do is not to direct mail to cold mailing lists at all. A cold mailing list is a list of random names and addresses that have not requested information from you, and may or may not need or be interested in your services.

One of the best strategies accountants can use to obtain better qualified clients is to develop Accounting Cross-Promotion Teams. This involves finding a group of other business owners and professionals who are seeking to target a similar market to yours. Once the team is formed you can share advertising space/time, referrals, do direct mailings to endorse each other's business, etc.

Quite literary the list of potential business building team tactics is only limited by your imagination. Employing Cross-Promotion Teams can easily triple the marketing power of your business in a short time without employing any other efforts. But you have got to select the right team members. Then you have to influence them to cooperate selflessly, but strategically, to faithfully promote the business of the other teams members.

HOW TO DEVELOP CONSULTING CROSS-PROMOTION TEAMS

- Search for at least four to six other professionals who have consulting practices or businesses in areas that are a complement to your field of expertise, but who do not directly compete with you. Make certain that the other professionals you have selected to team up with have extensive practices with a plethora of clients. Make certain that the clients they have attracted are the same kind of clients that you draw to your practice. These consultants will become your potential Cross-Promotion Team Partners. As an accounting professional may decide to start by approaching a non-CPA tax attorney, a marketing consultant, the controller of a management consulting firm, a small business development director from a local SBA office, and/or a successful insurance professional. You can set the rules of your team member selection in any direction you feel you should go. Make a large list of potential team members.

- Don't hesitate to approach these professionals to discuss the possibility of setting up a customer-referral system. Many of your own clients may have requested referrals and have been seeking professionals in other fields. You are also in a position to work together with these other professionals in other areas to offer them the benefit joint print ads, cooperative mailings, plus share other benefits. Perhaps you know that a attorney has been running small, unnoticed print ads in the back of a local upscale magazine. Consider selling them on the idea of taking out a full-page ad and splitting the cost among five other noncompeting professionals. This is justifiable because you can run the larger ad in the front of the publication. The ad will be likely to receive more attention with a higher potential of pulling more business for the attorney. In addition, all of the Cross-Promotion Team members who agree to run the ad together may also decide to share the new leads with all of the team members. This suggests that the team might want to consider performing a cooperative mailing with the pooled leads that each member receives from the full-page print ad. Having each team member simply hire a mailing service to stuff their brochure into the same envelope together considerably reduces the mailing cost for everyone. For one-fifth of the marketing cost you and your team members receive more than one-hundred percent of the effect.

Here is another way to apply this idea to your business :

As a marketing consultant I have successfully influenced accounting firms to fund special events for their business clients during which I have been highlighted as a keynote speaker. The accounting firms' intention was to reward their clients by giving them better ideas and methods to grow their businesses. The accounting firms usually rent a country club, cater a meal, and invite me to speak. It is not unusual for me to pick-up three or four high-paying business consulting clients per event. The accounting firms enjoy doing these events during the slow seasons of the year because it adds so much extra-value for their present clients. You could do something similar for business consulting firms, or any other business or professional sharing your target clients.

Here's another success story using the Cross-Promotion Teams idea from my files:

> I know an accountant who selected the director of a local chapter of an association of American business women to be on his Cross-Promotion Partner. He did this because he wanted to target and attract more business women to his accounting practice. He simply referred all of his present female business clients to the association and handed them information on the chapter suggesting that they go to a free meeting to network. Reciprocating kindly, the association director referred all their members to the accountant to and asked him to speak at their largest attended chapter meeting.

Think about who the best and most compatible potential Accounting Cross-Promotion Teams partners might be for your business. Consider other types of noncompeting consultants and business partners who already have the kind of clients you would like to attract. If the basis of your marketing programs involved approaching those businesses to share client lists and/or referrals by simply writing letters of referral to each other's clients, that alone would be powerful. Once you have your Accounting Cross-Promotion Team partners in place you may not need any of the other marketing ideas in this book. This idea alone is worth the price of this book, hundreds of times over.

You could also develop Cross-Promotion Teams engaging members who are lawyers, bankers, and any other business professionals that your clients tend to visit before and after they are with you.

Make you own exhaustive list of potential Cross-Promotion Team partners, and then approach each of them boldly with the resource-saving and promotion-enhancing tactics that you have come up with.

-58-

GENERATE MORE BUSINESS BY WRITING TO YOUR CLIENTS

You can send direct mail or e-mail to your clients—and to people you know who are interested in your services—rather than wasting money running expensive ads that may only reach those who may not be interested in what you have to offer.

Instead of wasting time and money mailing to a general resident list, personalized, direct mail, e-mail messages, and promotional letters may be sent out. E-zines—newsletters sent by e-mail containing valuable articles—can also be distributed to your client "e-list" for free. A cold rented mailing list or unsolicited e-mail list is an ineffective, untargeted, shot-in-the-dark waste—yet that is the main promotional thrust most naive business people opt for. By sending out a special, "preferred-client" mailing to people who are familiar with your business, you can be sure that you are reaching people who are interested in what you have to offer.

In your promotional letters to your customers, you can offer services that are not yet offered, "preselling" all kinds of merchandise and services before you invest a single dollar. You can take deposits from customers, or they can prepay the full price. All of these ideas won't work for you, but some will, and when they do you will understand that they are pure genius.

And, if you know a lot about each client, send specific letters to specific segments of your customer base, offering them the precise type, kind, or subject matter of products or services you know the customer is most interested in. Let's say, for example that 200 of your 1,000 customers are small businesses who hire you to perform two services when they visit you. You could write a simple letter exclusively to these 200 small businesses, offering them either the newest updated service that are most like the ones they usually hire you to perform. Chances are, if your letter is crafted correctly (and I'm providing proven sample letters in the next session) as many as 50 or 100 of these 200 clients could be enticed to use these additional services. And if the average client purchases $50 worth of services or products every time you mail to them, you would add $2,500 to $5,000 in additional sales to your business—and conceivably a lot more if 150 people purchased instead of 100.

But let's say a mere 50 clients hire you or buy from you because of a simple letter you send out. The $2,500 in added sales only cost you $90 to produce (that's what it cost to mail print and mail the letter), yet it yields over $2,000 in pure profit. And if you, like many business people, triple your markup, it may even yield as much as $3,500 in profit.

Just for risking a "whopping" $90 on a letter, you could make $2,500 to $3,500-plus—extra profit—from mailing one letter to one segment of your customer list. And most customer lists can be segmented (or broken down) into at least four or five different categories—each of which can receive a single type of mailing at least once every month or two.

I won't take up important space in this section by listing all of the direct mail math of a typical accounting business. But it is not at all uncommon for a business to have 1,000 to 10,000 customers they've never mailed to before, have mailed to very infrequently, or mailed a boring approach that did not work.

By the way, you don't have to be a huge firm for my concepts to work. The previous example is for a small to medium-size local accountants—not only large firms. Now it is time to delve a little deeper.

I have provided you with special sample letters in the next session that reflect even more of the success principles that will help you improve your efforts to sell more services to more clients.

–59–

SUCCESSFUL MARKETERS SEND FOLLOW-UP MAILINGS TO THEIR CLIENTS REGULARLY

Once you have developed a customer list, you have the most cost-effective, direct access to the single best source of future business there is. All you have to do is intelligently work that list, and rework it over and over again. By intelligently, I mean logically.

First, contact the customer by letter acknowledging his or her importance, and make a powerful and compelling case giving the "reason why" (this is critically important) the customer should be interested in taking advantage of the service you are now offering. Make certain you can actually offer a reason why (or multiple reasons why) they should accept your offer. Then lead the customer to action, by explaining why to buy, how to buy, what to do, and why it should be done now.

These points must be stated compellingly and simply—until you can smoothly, confidently, powerfully, and intimately express them in a manner people will respect, believe and, most importantly, respond to!

Leverage off of the reasons that your customers previously purchased from you, and repeat the essence of those reasons once more.

Most business people cease all communication with past customers, and those who attempt to communicate, do so using only a fraction of their potential in renewing interest.

Satisfied customers like to be, want to be and are already favorably predisposed toward working with you or doing business with you. They are simply silently begging to be led. By that, I mean they want to repurchase—ironically, they really do. But it is up to you to expend the effort, the energy and the necessary overture to lead the customer back. There is an infinite number of ways this can be accomplished. For example: Offer your customers preferential pricing to induce them to do business with you again.

The following sample letters will guide you in creating successful follow-up mailings to your clients. Frankly, now may not be the best time to carefully read these letters. You may want to skip them for now and read them the day you sit down to write your next marketing letter to your clients. You can tailor these letters for your own use. They are guides to what you will want to mail out in your business.

LETTER ONE: CREATIVE ACCOUNTING SERVICES LETTER

CREATIVE ACCOUNTING SERVICES
800-555-4081

Mr. Bill H. Customer
1209 Arlington Avenue
Milton, Iowa 00000

Dear Mr. Customer,

I've been thinking about you a great deal, and I've decided to do something a little bold but perhaps very much appreciated by you, once you understand the method behind it.

Simply put, I've just started an automatic, ongoing, subscription-based service that I'm inviting my most valued customers to take advantage of. We are now able to offer the convenience of an automatic rendering of our accounting service for a pre-established time and at the appropriate intervals designated by you.

Our staff will come to you, determine through a brief consultation the exact level of continuing service you require, and at the same time every month (or every week or every three months) and then automatically perform that service for you.

We'll keep your business operating at the level of perfection you want and expect, automatically, without your having to worry about contacting us.

(OVER)

In addition to scheduling our consultations to perform your monthly payroll (or personal bill paying service, or state tax filing) and financial check-ups at the appropriate intervals, when you sign up for this service, you'll also receive, free-of-charge, our interim catastrophe insurance. In other words, if something happens in your business, we will work with you overtime on your challenge at no charge. If you need extra help or advice at any time, one of our staff members will be there for you.

What's all this cost? A lot less than you might imagine, and certainly a lot less per visit than it would if you engaged our services one-time only.

Why is it such a savings? The answer is very logical, actually. I have employees on my payroll whom I have to pay whether they work or not, and for some inexplicable reason, most clients want to avail themselves of my services on Mondays and Wednesdays Not everyone avails themselves of our services on Tuesday, Thursdays, and Fridays so there are occasional time slots available. My employees are still kept on the payroll, so from a utilization standpoint, it's to my advantage to have them bringing in revenue during those times—even if it's not maximum revenue—on the off-days.

If you will allow me to schedule these services at times that are more convenient to us but fairly appropriate for you, we would be delighted to pass on a savings to you. By the way, when you agree to allow me to set you up on this ongoing service, you're never obligated to continue.

At any time, if the service is no longer appropriate, or our performance is no longer satisfactory, or you have any problem of dissatisfaction, you can cancel on the spot. Moreover, if ever our service doesn't measure up to the discriminating standards you expect, all you have to do is call me personally, and I'll either re-perform the service or refund your money, whichever you prefer.

Knowing how important a smooth-running business (or having bills paid automatically) is to you, this service will be particularly appreciated. I think you'll also love the annual savings—both in time and money.

Unless I hear otherwise from you, I'll be contacting you in the next two or three days just to set up the schedule and work out your requirements. Or, if you would rather not have me phone you, simply send back the enclosed reply card with your specifications.

Sincerely,

John Overhill
Overhill Accounting

LETTER TWO: NOTIFY YOUR CUSTOMERS OF SALES OR SPECIALS AHEAD OF THE GENERAL PUBLIC.

Your offer must be so compelling that they prioritize your product or service. You have to convince them that your product or service can help them. And your offer must support this by making it unusually easy or affordable for them to conduct business with you.

Offer better customers a limited number of appointments or exclusive availability first.

Here is an example of how to alert customers to a limited-availability item.

CREATIVE ACCOUNTING SERVICES
800-555-4081

I've Got to Get This Off My Chest Before I Explode!

Mr. Bill H. Customer
1209 Arlington Avenue
Milton, Iowa 00000

Dear Mr. Customer,

I'm writing to alert you to an opportunity that I think is very appealing (or very significant or applies to you, etc.) This year, Overhill Accounting got in a jam because we overproduce certain hi-performance tax and personal finance organizers. Now we've got to figure out what to do with the extra organizers.

Our firm is the only accounting firm in the area that provides clients, not only with service, but the tools they need to become organized and stay that way. Last year we had 35 extra performance organizers. We contacted our preferred customers to alert them about this. We sold every one of them within 48 hours. In fact, we actually oversold by 25, which we could have fulfilled if we had the product. This year we have 64 extra "fire-resistant molded document safes" that the manufacturer has discontinued. They asked if I wanted them. Of course I said, "yes."

I have 500 clients. I'm sending this letter only to my preferred clients — those 121 clients I think would most appreciate them and to whom I would like to pass on the most value.

These are the very same organizers you'd pay $450 for. They carry the same lifetime 'no questions-asked' guarantee and are insured for up to one-million dollars if they fail to protect your documents in the event of a fire. They are the same, except for the fact that the manufacturer has decided to discontinue manufacturing this model, so they're no longer on the market, although the guarantee on them is for life. If you'd bought them from any dealer (including us) last year, you would have paid $450 to $850.

Because we pay cash and because the manufacturer knows we won't indiscriminately promote them in the marketplace, we were able to buy their last remaining inventory of safe organizers at such an advantageous price, we can pass the savings on to you. We can sell the same $350 to $850 safe organizers for $176, and if you have any reticence about it being appropriate for you, you can use it for 30 days at our risk. If it's not an absolutely wonderfully-performing document safe, you can send it back to me because I'm certain to have 25 or 30 other clients waiting on a stand-by list for it.

> Nevertheless, we have these 64 safe organizers available—
> they'll be in our warehouse in seven days. I'm sending this
> letter out to only a handful of preferred customers whom I
> really want to do a service for. You're one of them. If you're
> interested, please call me personally — or call my assistant,
> Gina Montana, within the next two days, because frankly,
> there aren't going to be that many left. I hope you're able
> to take advantage of it.
>
> John Overhill
> Overhill Accounting

I could go on and on about working your current and past customers. But remember this:

It may have cost you $100 or $1,000 initially to buy or acquire a new customer, considering the cost of running ads, commercials, including your sales efforts and dividing it into the number of resulting sales. However, the cost of reselling an existing customer once you have acquired them is negligible.

It costs $100 or $1,000 to generate a customer, but only 34- to 70-cents to mail them a powerful and personal letter once you have captured their business.

Also, it only costs a few dollars to call that customer on the phone and, perhaps, $15 or $20 to visit them in person. All this is far less than you'd have to spend on the outside market to bring in a new customer.

So first, and foremost, work your existing and inactive customers hard and often. It is easy, inexpensive and immediate. The return will out-produce any other option you have available.

Before you begin marketing these new programs to your customers you may want to briefly take another look at your customers and their needs.

Ninety percent of the businesses I look at never precisely determine the needs, desires, or requirements of the people to whom they are trying to sell.

How can you expect to adequately fill someone's needs if you never take the time to understand them? Yet few companies seek to meet their customers' needs. Those who do seem to end up with all the business. You can end up with all the business, too, if you'll take the time to learn what your customers need and want.

To induce someone to favor you with their business, you normally have to offer them some need-filling advantage. Let's review just a few of the possible needs people want filled:

They want services that offer to save them money. They desire services that save time, give them greater control of their money, and perform more functions with state-of-the-art technology. They are attracted to ideas that generate more money, or make them more effective.

What do your customers want or need most in the services that you offer? Do they want the convenience of knowing they can go down the block and get it from you, or the knowledge that your firm offers more services, (or products) than any other company? Do they want the top-of-the-line service options? Do they want highly personalized service, attention, advice, and instruction?

Perhaps they merely want to acquire the kind of services you sell at the lowest possible price. Or maybe price alone isn't what they're after—maybe they want the best guarantee or the best ongoing service to support the their initial service experience.

I do not know which need, or which combination of needs, your potential client seeks but that client does seek fulfillment of some singular need or combination of needs, and sometimes he or she doesn't even fully realize it. But once you find and fill that need, you will have your business niche.

If you do not know what needs your customer most wants you to fill, start by recognizing that no one can be all things to all people. You will dilute your image as a need-filler if you try to do that. So, first determine which needs you can fill, consistent with who you are, what your business is, and how you operate.

Then talk to clients, prospects, and customers, and have your salespeople do the same. Experiment with the image you convey in your advertising and promotion. Monitor the consensus and gauge the feedback. Let your customers tell you which specific needs they most want filled, then determine which of those needs you can actually fill.

Then, do not merely fill those needs silently. Make sure your customers, prospects, salespeople, and your entire marketplace learn that your business listened and that you finally did something to satisfy your customer's needs. Continuously (tactfully) inform, educate, and forthrightly point out that your company is filling those needs for your customers. Change your ads to feature these specific need-filling advantages. Have your field or in-office staff point out what you are doing. Send out letters that do the same. Phone your customers and inform them that you're prepared to fulfill their needs.

Once you determine precisely what their needs are, and you commit to fulfilling, then do it.

If you decide that service is the critical element, offer the best service, the fastest service, the most skilled service people, and the most knowledgeable staff. If top quality is the need you decide to fill, don't offer mediocre goods. If you claim to be the best-quality accounting service in your market, make certain you are a regular "fuss-budget" about your approach to provide service. If you provide the lowest price, keep that promise. Integrity requires it. If you don't genuinely fill the needs you purport to fill, your customers will soon abandon you.

-60-

COMMUNITY INVOLVEMENT:
THE WAY GAIN MORE EXPOSURE

You and your business should be actively involved in the community, because giving something back to society is the right thing to do. Community involvement can also provide you with more exposure, which will increase client loyalty, sales, and profits. Local folks want to give business to accounting and bookkeeping firms that care about them. Although it is not possible to directly contact everyone in the community to show them how much you care, you can clearly and powerfully demonstrate your concern for specific community causes and issues in other highly visible ways.

You must always have a goal for your community-involvement activities. Choosing community events randomly is senseless because you want to gain exposure in areas that will put you directly into the hearts and minds of your target market. You want your target market to notice you in a very special way.

I know an accountant who volunteered her entire staff to perform services for a local theater-project charity. They consulted and gave away services to help the theater. It was a very time-consuming task, and it was a little discouraging for the accountant when she realized how long it would take to finish the project. The accountant finally finished as promised, and the theater was very happy with the end result. Because the staff donated all of their time and materials, the theater manager gave them special recognition in the form of free advertising in the theater's printed programs for all future plays. As a result, the accountant's name was viewed by thousands of influential community members, many of whom hired the accountant in the months that followed. Their work had clearly paid off.

WAYS TO USE COMMUNITY INVOLVEMENT TO GET NOTICED
- Contact your local Chamber of Commerce and ask them

to mail you information about local charities, their contact names and telephone numbers. Many organizations, such as the American Lung Association, have multiple events and they need volunteer committee members to help with their programs. Volunteer to become chair of a committee.

- Sponsor an event for people who need the most help in your community. Consider developing a golf tournament or other event for a local charity, such as the Make-A-Wish foundation.

- Send press releases about the community events and activities that you are working on to all local media contacts. Take media professionals out to lunch to build strong relationships with them so that you will be top on their mind for covering your charitable event(s) for certain stories they are writing.

- Consider creating publicity stunts for charity. You could rent a crane and hold $10 bungee jumps from a platform. Have local radio station personalities bungee jump live "on the air" during drive times. You could have $10 hot-air balloon rides in your parking lot. Advertise that all of the proceeds go to a favorite charity.

TIME DONATIONS CAN BRING MAXIMUM MARKETING DIVIDENDS

Most professionals have a desire to give of themselves for noble causes. If you structure your giving to showcase your expertise, it will be more beneficial. There are many noble causes you could dedicate your time and services to. If you embrace the philosophy of leveraging your opportunities, choose the ones that have the highest probability of generating future clients.

Give your services in a way that showcases your ability. As long as your schedule will permit, offer those in attendance at your events or seminars the opportunity to meet with you later for free advice. People are silently begging to be led. If you dedicate yourself to working with a charitable organization, offer to speak to the group free of charge during an evening- or lunch-meeting, as a service to the organization. In the course of your speaking engagement, subtly suggest that if anyone has a problem, needs advice or has questions that need clarification, you would be happy, as a service to the organization, to talk on the phone with them or even to meet with them in your office. Start planting the seeds. Lead them. Encourage them.

You can also dedicate your time or services as a fundraiser. You can present a clinic or a seminar and donate the money that would have come to you. Structure it in such a way that you perform a noble service for the organization and then the organization will unknowingly perform a wonderful service for you through your association with members and associates.

-61-

USING SEMINARS AND CLINICS
TO DRAW NEW CLIENTS

Free lectures and seminars attract potential clients. The cost lies in some preliminary advertising or mailing and the cost of a hall. Your audience may already be concerned about the topic you choose and are looking for solutions.

By making the seminar or lecture free, you engender goodwill from your audience. By addressing issues of concern to them, you are validating their perceptions that the topic is an important one. By offering good, sound, and thorough advice, you establish yourself as an expert.

Give complete information in conjunction with your self-promotion. Do not hold back, do not offer just enough to titillate their interest. Elaborate on each topic you choose, supplementing theoretical information with case studies or anecdotes. Establish depth of knowledge along with experience.

You won't gain 100% of the attendees as clients. Some people attend such events out of general interest rather than particular need. But If you dedicate two or three hours of your time one or two evenings a month to addressing subjects with which you are already very familiar, you will see an increase in your client base and that will repay your minimal expense and effort.

How do you design the campaign to promote your seminar? It's very simple.

Create an ad or mailing piece announcing a free 90- or 120-minute lecture on a topic of wide general interest. Relate the presentation to your specialty. As a tax accountant you could present a seminar on sheltering income.

After a headline announcing the topic, the copy chronicles your credentials, your accomplishments, achievements, professional memberships, and articles about your practice and specialty:

"Accountant John Bournes is a specialist in this subject. He's conducted research and he's perfected financial and tax burden-reduction techniques. He will present a lecture for people interested in the topic but who do not know the facts. This lecture will be held from 6:30 p.m. to 8:00 p.m. on Tuesday, January 7th."

One successful accountant has created a seminar on estate taxes. He invites guests from all over the community to attend at a local upscale steakhouse. He sends out invitations as free-standing inserts in a local business journal. He offers to buy each attendee a free steak dinner for attending. His marketing highly targets retirees who are working through estate-related issues. He has been highly successful in mining new clients.

If you are doing something simliar, admission should be free but instruct interested people to reserve tickets and give them a number to call, thereby capturing their names and addresses for future mailings. Or you could collect names at the door, which is simpler. Be sure to require advance reservations, because restaurants need to know how many people to expect.

Another way to create an audience for a seminar is to go to affinity groups, social groups, fraternal groups, business groups and so on. Offer to speak on subjects of importance to that group. For example, a CPA might offer to speak on loopholes still available to corporations after recent tax changes. It should be something provocative so that when the group invites its members, they will all be inclined to come.

Your lecture should be split into two parts. In the first half, titillate them with anecdotal information. Then break for coffee. Mingle with the audience, distributing your business card and an information package you have put together, which could include the reports that we've talked about and a statement on your practice.

In the second half, offer some service that's free but designed to capture valuable information. For example, conduct a quick tax knowledge survey on your audience. Have them respond to 25 basic questions, providing their name, address and telephone number on the questionnaire. Your office will tabulate the results and send a brief summary back to them. Offer to perform a quick business accounting survey to see whether they're using all the accounting opportunities available to them. Ask twenty or thirty primary questions and obtain their names and addresses.

At the end of the seminar, you will have established initial contact for an ongoing dialogue. Do not let the lecture be a one-shot deal. You should have solicited names and addresses to add to your mailing list of high-probability potential clients. You could have the attendees register at the door — this is a better time to get names than at the end when they may be thinking of their next appointment, their errands, or simply going home to bed. It makes attendance at the lecture hinge on providing some easy information.

Another approach is to require pre-registration. Stipulate in your advertising that admission is free but that tickets are required. The interested reader then calls your office and your staff can obtain those vital names and addresses. This method is also good because it gives you an advance idea of audience size. Also, because the attendees then have something physical (the ticket) to remind them of the place and time of your presentation, it will ensure the attendance of a larger percentage of respondents.

Once you have names and addresses, do not file them away. Use them! Maintain the dialogue that you have begun. Send the attendees follow-up packages. A simple questionnaire two weeks later on the quality of the seminar will continue to strengthen your tenuous relationship, as well as possibly eliciting some testimonials you can use in the future. An announcement of future free seminars will reinforce your image as a concerned professional. A newsletter can allow you to elaborate on some areas you touched on in the presentation.

Whatever method you choose, do not let go of these highly-motivated individuals once you establish a dialogue. The more often they see your name, the more likely they are to think of you when they need your professional services.

TAPES AND TRANSCRIPTS OF SEMINARS AS POWERFUL TOOLS

Whether a seminar is successful or unsuccessful, it has residual value if you record or transcribe the text. You can make transcripts or recordings available to both current and potential clients.

Send the tape of the transcript to prospective clients, along with a cover letter telling them that a great many people tell you that they learned a lot from the presentation, that it changed their attitudes on accounting or on how to use an accountant to legally pay much less tax. Indicate that you've taken the liberty of sending them a transcript or a recording of your speech or lecture in its entirety, including questions and answers, in hopes that they will benefit as well. Encourage them to read it or listen to it and stress that you hope that they will find it useful and informative. If they find that they have questions, assure them that you are available to respond.

If they are interested in your services, offer to talk to them in person or by phone to explain your philosophy and how you operate. Provide some case studies. Tell them that you think the best way for people to learn about how a professional operates is to listen to what he says and to meet him or her. Since they were unable to attend your seminar, this tape or transcript is second best. And always encourage them to feel free to call with questions.

You can use the transcript or tape in several ways. You can offer it through your Yellow Pages ad, through your display ad, to the groups to whom you give presentations on other topics, or to the referrals you have obtained. You can mail it to residents of entire neighborhoods. If portions of it are of current interest or time-sensitive, you can eliminate or occasionally update those parts. If you make a tape or transcript once, you have a valuable product that you can use for a long time.

You do not even need to hold an actual seminar. You can simply record a session as though people had attended. You can then offer the tape or transcripts in promotion, advertising or mailing so then you can say:

> This private seminar is worth $400 (or whatever you perceive its value to be) and it is worth every cent. But to me it is worth giving you $400 of my expertise to provide you with a chance to familiarize yourself with how I think and how I work.

SEMINARS FOR PROFIT

Valuable information sells. That's clear! And what better way is there to sell your ideas than to the largest groups of people in a single place? You can sell the information focusing on your sub-specialty to large groups as easily as to single clients.

Of course, specific application to individual problems requires a one-on-one approach, but there is nothing wrong with dispensing general information of widespread appeal to people for their personal use. And, if you structure the seminar properly, you can respond to questions asked in public or afterwards in private.

The information you provide will be the bedrock of your profession and will not require extensive research and hours to prepare. It is more a question of organizing the style of presentation, the flow of information, and the organization and assembly of any materials for distribution. But do not skimp on the information — be sure to over-deliver — and present lots of practical hard facts. Just remember that to make a significant impression on the non-professional attendees will require the repetition of what you consider to be the extremely obvious or well-known facts. The point is to make a few really important points stick, not to make your listeners instant experts on a particular corner of your profession.

Organize a two- or three-hour information-packed seminar, adding bonus packages, such as personalized counsel, financial savings plans, tax reduction ideas, etc.

Advertise your seminar in a newspaper or issue direct mailings to your clients or your prospects. Hire a man or woman on a percentage basis to promote it over the telephone to groups, organizations or companies. Experiment with different promotional media and organizations available to you until you find the right market, promotional device or company.

Hold the programs at the frequency you desire, allowing others to do the work for you. You can come up with ads and run them as often as you like. Each time you present a seminar, you bring in 50 or 150 people and charge each of them $50. After promotional expenses, your only expense is for the facility you use.

Again the ad should start with a provocative headline such as:

> **HOW TO SAVE AN ADDITIONAL 15% TO 25% PER YEAR ON YOUR TAXES**

Then introduce the content of the seminar by listing about twenty bulleted topics to be covered. End with a succinct but provocative biography of yourself or the speakers that you will be presenting.

You can simply sponsor the seminar, bringing in other speakers with the ad detailing their expertise:

> Dr. Jordan Russel is the most knowledgeable specialist in tax strategies in Essex County, having concentrated on his topic for the last thirty years. He has personally counseled 3,000 people with an 89% success rate. He has developed tax strategies, which, in most cases, reduce taxes paid by 15% to 25% beginning the first year. In this session he will present his philosophies, his techniques and a tax reduction plan that could be used by anyone to radically reduce their present tax burden.

Specify the seminar location and time. Explain how to register and what steps to take to attend your seminar. Identify attendees' payment options—prepayment, telephone payment, and pay at the door, etc. Direct people by explaining what actions they should take. Offer tapes or transcripts if they cannot attend at the designated time.

POWER IDEA:

You can also develop seminars in cooperation with corporations as sponsors for their clients. As an accountant, if you know that XYZ Corporation is introducing new products and services that help businesses save money on taxes, go to XYZ and say, "I would like you to sponsor a seminar that I will hold on corporate tax savings. I would like you to furnish me with your mailing list, pay the postage and prepare a letter of invitation from you to your clients. Explain in the letter that this program would normally cost them $1000 but that XYZ have engaged you, a highly knowledgeable accountant, to give this seminar as a service to XYZ clients." The point of leverage that you have with XYZ is that you will weave into your presentation the benefits of using their newly introduced tax-saving products and services. Thus, you will be assisting XYZ greatly in providing their clients objective knowledge and advice that leads to the purchase of their offerings.

Negotiate with XYZ. Tell them that you can conduct a three-hour presentation; break for lunch; and then do three more hours of the seminar, after which you will provide counseling. Tell them you want $1,500 (or some other reasonable fee), plus the list of attendees (you may want to solicit them later yourself).

Show the company that they are giving every one of their customers a free $1000 gift. This will predispose these customers toward the sponsoring company and will encourage them to reciprocate with future business. You will be paid for the privilege of soliciting people.

After the seminar, write a letter to each participant saying:

*Thank you. I am pleased tha t you had an inter est in the subject.
I hope I helped y ou, I enjoyed talking with y ou.*

Encourage them to contact you if they have questions or need the service you offer on a permanent basis. Offer a no-cost initial consultation prior to any long-term arrangement. If offering evening or weekend office hours would gain you clients, make sure they are aware of this.

You should also offer special seminars to current clients. First, review your client base and identify subjects appealing to most of them. If you offered an intensive three-hour seminar every Saturday on a topic or cluster of topics and had 100 people each week, you would turn a nice profit. You could send a letter monthly including a list of the next twelve weeks conferences. Charge $50 or $100 per person to attend the seminar. You would probably have thirty or forty people attend each seminar.

CLINICS TO INCREASE PROFITS

Conducting clinics is similar to the seminar approach. It can be presented in either of two ways: 1) by accessing existing clients, or 2) through promotion and advertising.

List the most provocative, significant subjects in your profession: tax shelters, tax savings audits and penalties.

Then create clinics that you promote, either internally or externally through endorsements from organizations. These will be weekend or evening clinics. You invite a lot of people to attend and they receive lectures and special treatment. As an accountant you might provide prepared forms or one-on-one counseling to review tax returns. Distribute forms to compute savings, printed plans of action, reports on topics of current interest.

You might offer a weekly or monthly small business clinic. Hold the clinic in a room in your office or rent space in a community center, church or hotel.

Then send out a mailer or solicit your clients by phone, saying, "This Saturday, Accountant Jim Russell will hold a clinic costing $50. You are invited to attend his lecture on "100 ways you can save 15% to 25% more on taxes". During the second part of lecture, you will be shown easy and effective exercises. Third, you will receive a cursory financial check-up, including financial analysis. Fourth, you will receive action assignments for improved financial planning. Fifth, you will be provided with a supply of easy-to-use monthly organizing forms to take home."

You can do this in an infinite number of ways, limited only by your imagination. You can also go the other way, taking a topic with limited appeal and charging a premium for highly specialized information.

CREATE SPECIAL EVENTS FOR YOUR CLIENTS

One of the organizing principles of accounting marketing involves creating extraordinary ways to communicate the value-rich benefits you give to your clients. One of the most enriching experiences you will ever create for your clients involves hosting a special event. It could be an educational evening conducted in a seminar format hosted for clients and nonclients. It could be as simple as a special dinner party hosted to thank your clients for their patronage. When you host a special event you demonstrate the distinctiveness of your clients by acknowledging them in a special way. Large or small, special events give something wonderful back to your clients and hosting them can be fun.

TYING A SPECIAL EVENT TO A HOLIDAY

I know an accountant who runs a special event four times a year. He has one large annual Christmas holiday dinner party and three smaller seminar group events. He's a real motivated person, and sends out several waves of invitations and announcements to his best clients well in advance of the event. At the special holiday event, his most exclusive clients experience something extraordinary. His event is fully catered, includes a classical chamber music quartet and usually one very dynamic speaker. One year he hired David Brenner to entertain. Another year he hired Zig Ziglar to speak. Every year his holiday event becomes bigger and better. He always invites the local press to cover the event and the caliber of speakers that he hires warrants a full compliment of local news reporters, which gives him a lot of publicity.

USING A SPECIAL-EVENT SEMINAR FORMAT TO SELL

A tax attorney, who is a CPA, does something even more profitable using special events. He has licensed the "source code" of a popular accounting software company. He hired a computer programmer to give the accounting software a facelift—meaning that he repackaged it with his own brand name. He changed the way the windows looked on the computer, added his logo to it, changed the brand name of the software and created new packaging. The new software performs all of the same functions as the original software from the accounting Software Company. All that's different about the software is the way it looks. Over the course of only a few weeks he had a special new accounting software product to market. The only way he markets his product is through special events. He started marketing the software by inviting his biggest clients to a fully catered dinner at his country club. He hired a juggler, magician and flutist to perform during dinner. After dinner he gave a full-color computer demonstration of his new software package on a huge projection screen. He then closed the evening by making an offer to his guests to install the new package on their client server, to train the client's staff on how to use it, and to process the client's taxes free for the year all for one flat fee. Because he bundled his services into the price of the software, the clients instantly understood that they were receiving a tremendous value. He promises his clients that if they are unhappy with the new software, he will not only remove it, but also put their old software back in place and still do their taxes for free. This is what I call a better-than-risk-free guarantee because it not only lowers the risk that clients perceive about trying the product, but it also gives them an additional incentive. The offer was irresistible to his clients. That evening and over the course of first nine months he sold 85 software packages that netted him just under a quarter of a million extra dollars in additional revenue using special events as his sole form of marketing.

FOCUS ON WHICH OPPORTUNITIES ARE MOST COMPATIBLE WITH YOUR BUSINESS

In order to stimulate your thinking about selecting a possible special event ask yourself two key questions:

- What kinds of different promotional or event-oriented opportunities could you create for your clients to make them feel special?
- How can you create a bundle of highly profitable, unique accounting services and/or products at an irresistible price that could be sold at a special event?

Your event doesn't have to be expensive or fancy. You should start on a small scale. You can sponsor an inexpensive-to-run free seminar that gives people valuable information. You can build your event as your success in conducting the seminar grows.

Special events create such excitement that it is often a great idea to make highly-irresistible special offers to participants during the event. You can use special events to bring together combinations of powerful motivating elements—entertainment, great food and drink, social interaction—in an atmosphere that increases "wow-factor" for your clients. This combination of elements tends to increase social proof that your offer is right in the collective minds of your attendees. Because you are giving something back to your client that is truly valuable, in the form of this special event experience, you will be very well received by them.

If you cannot think of a type of special event that you feel comfortable developing, you can use holiday celebrations or your business anniversary as opportunities to thank your clients by having an open house. I have another client who holds a "special invitation-only" annual Christmas party for all of her best clients. She gives the event as a special holiday gift to clients, and as a return holiday present, she asks each invited guest to bring at least one friend who might be interested in her services. Her last party had 250 people in attendance. She attracts a lot of customers from these events.

Another way to create a special event is to hold a class, workshop, or seminar for your clients with the purpose of educating them in a way so unique they receive an incredible value. The possibilities for event themes are endless. One client has succeeded by doing seminars on the topic of "sources of small business start-up funding." I know another accountant who simply offers to conduct a free seminar for church groups, business clubs and any group who will listen on the topic "How to Keep More of What You earn." He obtains at least 12 new clients per one-hour event. The seminars were so successful that he began to charge for them and has created several more spin-off themes.

Have fun with these ideas and create events that add value and excitement for your clients.

−62−

USE WORD-OF-MOUTH MARKETING STIMULATORS

Your most successful marketing methods will tend to combine to create a word-of-mouth stir that will be noticeably profound at certain times. This will become apparent at certain moments when you will discover that you have obtained increased business without any extra effort or investment. I call this phenomenon the "envelope of client uptake." Word-of-mouth marketing tactics have become points-of-key marketing discussions over the past couple of decades in certain industries. Do you realize that some businesses successfully and solely rely on word-of-mouth as their primary form of marketing?

While most business owners realize that word-of-mouth is a valuable tool, most do not understand that it often comes synergistically from combined media efforts in surprising ways.

You must identify the primary advantage clients receive from you. To generate word-of-mouth, you must set the stage for your business by carefully crafting your unique selling proposition— the statement of why your business is unique. Once you do that, a large key to successful word-of-mouth marketing occurs; because when you are able to communicate what makes your business unique to your clients, you are teaching your clients "how to tell others about your uniqueness." That is the fundamental element of successful word-of-mouth marketing that many business owners never understand.

WORD-OF-MOUTH STIMULATORS

- Use synergistic combinations of media to saturate your specific market. Develop a profile of your high-probability client. This is a detailed description of the kind of client likely to do business with you. Armed with this profile, attempt to locate all of the media, mailing lists, and marketing opportunities that help you send messages to this unique group of clients. The people in this group are frankly the best marketing investment you can make because your messages will be directed to them in a very pointed and targeted way. Next, select a mixture of the best media for sending messages to this tightly targeted niche market. You might decide to rent a mailing list of addresses of people from this niche from certain neighborhoods and send them newsletters and postcards, alternating the kind of mailing that you send to them every other month. You might elect to distribute doorhangers in these neighborhoods. You might buy 15-minutes of radio time of this niche market's favorite talk-radio station talking about topics they love during drive times. You might mail them invitations to listen to your radio show. If you are smart you will choose as many marketing methods as possible, as many as you can afford, in order to buy a significant piece of your target market. You will lace together as many media messages as possible, using only the media that target your specific high-probability target. If you have a doubt that you have selected an ad medium that may not contain a large enough number of people in the audience who are in your specific target, then "drop it fast" before your lose money on a wasted ad. Only use media that have a proven track record of successfully reaching your specific high-probability clients. In a short time you will have saturated your customized market. You can layer media together in a big way, or on a small scale depending on the size of your firm.

- Use your business cards to power your word-of-mouth strategies. One bookkeeping business owner I know puts three business cards into every direct mail piece she sends, and asks clients if they are happy with her service to do her a favor by giving the extra cards to close friends. This works well for her. Turn your business card into a mini-billboard.
- Ask for referrals. Mention to your clients: "If you are satisfied with the service you receive, I'd appreciate it if you would tell a friend about our business being the fastest bookkeeping service in town." Do this consistently with all your clients. They will help you generate word-of-mouth.

- Always do an incredible job. The best way to stimulate word-of-mouth is to regularly astound, wow and amaze your clients. Go beyond their expectations. Give 100 times more than your clients expect on even the smallest request, and you will create such a positive impression that your clients won't be able to stop themselves from sharing you with their friends.

EXCEED YOUR CLIENTS' EXPECTATIONS:

- Include extra service or financial check-ups to ensure the well-being of clients as a bonus.
- Load your clients up with lots and lots of samples of new products that you sell
- Give your clients gourmet coffee, wine, hors d'ourves and other delicacies upon entering your doors
- Have a magazine a rack with exclusive magazines
- Use ergonomic office chairs for clients

On subsequent client visits, remember the extra services that they liked and have them waiting for them. This will powerfully move your clients.

–63–

MORE ON DEVELOPING AN INCREDIBLE CLIENT EDUCATION SYSTEM

You must increase your level of marketing sophistication far beyond the normal advertising methods used by most accounting firms. Too many accountants use conventional ads on a hit or miss basis that draws poorly. Bad results discourage them from continuing to market and promote themselves. This can kill any hope of success.

You must market more wisely and astutely than your competitors. You must make every dollar you spend as effective and as prolific as you can. The success of your business depends on how well you seek out new marketing approaches and sales avenues.

The foundation of your marketing plan should be to educate your clients. You first educate them about your products and services. Let's say you market a payroll service for small businesses. All the interesting details regarding the way your program has been developed should be included in your advertising and promotional material. Next, you should have a booklet, report or video on how to save time and money on payroll, and this can be used in a variety of promotions. Finally, you could create a report on how to buy or what to look for in an existing payroll service, or a book on payroll basics, or payroll savings that explains ways to expedite the payroll process for greater results. In other words, you educate them on your product and your firm; you educate them on the field in a way that's useful to them and you broadly educate them on tangentially-related subjects which have the effect of endearing you to them.

One of the saddest marketing mistakes I see is the failure of accountants to educate their customers about the unique advantages offered to them. If you've reviewed and critiqued the services of 100 other different accounting businesses, let your customers know that. The fact that you've screened out services that haven't the quality, endurance, warranty, support, service guarantees, or dependability they desire will impress them. Perhaps your guarantee is three times longer, or covers five times more of the problems. Your customer will never know that unless you tactfully point this out by educating them.

When you educate your customers, you will see your profits accelerate. Think about when you buy or consider buying any item or service—for yourself, your home, your family, as a gift, or for your business—you often don't know as much as you would like about the item. If you have unanswered questions about a product, you are less likely to buy it.

When a company or professional takes the time and initiative to objectively educate you on all the products in the field that you are considering purchasing, they gain your trust and favor.

Education is a powerful marketing technique. Educate your prospective buyer about everything (including a few of the less positive aspects of your products and services) and you will sell to almost twice as many people as you do now.

This concept of educating your customers will give you an inordinate advantage over your competitors.

TAKE YOUR CLIENT BY THE HAND

Few businesses realize that they must lead the customer to take a very specific action. In addition, few businesses develop a compelling marketing plan.

People need to be explicitly told how to obtain your product or service. Therefore—and this is incredibly important—every marketing approach, letter, commercial, or personal contact should make the case for your services. Give prospects a brief education, then take them by the hand, figuratively speaking, and tell them what specific action to take next.

If your offer is for a limited time, tell your prospect to get in touch with you immediately. And do not be abstract about it. If you deal by phone, tell them to pick up the phone and call a specific number.

TELL THEM WHY

Whenever you make an offer, ask for a sale, run an ad, have a salesperson make a proposition to a customer or prospect, or offer a product or service for sale at a specific price, always tell the reason why you are offering the value that you provide at an advantageous price.

Why can you sell your services at a lower price than your competitors? Does your business have lower overhead? Do you buy odd-lot inventories of the software that you provide to clients? Do you not give all the services, rather only the important ones? Why is your price so good?

If your price is high, tell the customer or prospect why. Do you offer a service that is far superior to the norm? Is your service provided with demonstrably better expertise? Is your product designed to last or perform 2 1/2 times longer than your competitors?

Why is your price high? Is your service performed with exceptional painstaking accuracy? Does your staff perform your service with three times more care than similar accounting firms?

If your price or the package of services is an especially appealing value, tell the client why you are making this offer. Is it because the client is going to order from you for the first time, and it's an exclusive offer to first-time customers? Or, is it because you have new equipment that makes your work five times more efficient and you want to pass the savings on to the client? Is it because you're overstocked or overstaffed, so you're willing to initially sell at a loss to capture more excellent clients?

Please, tell your clients the reasons why! Why should they patronize you instead of your competitors? Tell them what you are doing that makes favoring your accounting firm better for them. Why can your staff handle the work better than someone else can?

Tell me more reasons why I, as your potential client should use your services. The more factual, believable, credible, and plausible reasons you give me for dealing with you, the more compelled I am to favor you with my business.

When I write a mailing piece, I do something most other people do not do consider—I let my readers in on a special secret. I tell them why I am making the offer to them and what it is all about. Then I admit that I do not know for sure if it is good for them. So after they order, they have a choice. If it works, they can accept the results we have obtained for them. If they are unsure, then they can receive reasonable compensation.

Most people just say, "buy from me," in their ads. If their offering is expensive, they do not say why it is expensive. For example, a product may be constructed with 12 times more material, triple-reinforced and made with the best material available. Educate your public and they will become as moldable as putty in your hands.

An accountant once came to me because he was stuck with a large inventory of business productivity enhancement software he had purchased. His original goal was to sell it through magazine ads. He had sold very few of the pieces of software. It seemed as though nobody wanted the product. He had paid over $250,000 for the inventory of software that he had been storing in his small warehouse. They cut the price and still no one bought them.

In a final effort they hired me to help them liquidate their software on this failing business venture. I turned around and began talking directly to the reader. I said, "Here are the facts. We paid over $250,000 to develop this very unique software product. Our manufacturer over-produced the number of software packages. If you bought them through your favorite computer mail-order catalog, you would have paid $750,000 for all of them. Right now we are selling them for $450,000. If you took them to your local office product dealer, he would buy them for $600,000. Here was the "why" proposition offer that was used:

"If you have ever wanted a business-productivity tool that saves you time and money by tracking your schedule and helping you make better decisions, this is the steal of a lifetime."

"If you want to add 15 extra hours to your week by using this new computer tool to increase productivity, pick up the phone and call 800-555-1234. Select the version that is best for you. If you do not feel that the software gives you at least two or thee times worth of greater productivity, send it back."

Attempting to build the case one step at a time, I concluded with an offer that if the software works for them, they would keep it, if it doesn't work for them, they would not.

Educate people to appreciate the value of your products and services. It worked for this company. The software sold out in five business days.

Your clients cannot appreciate value in a vacuum. You cannot appreciate anything until you're educated about it. Most people forget this when it comes to marketing, and they lose millions of dollars.

I am frequently asked to help a company out of a problem. Often, I help businesses out of inventory overstocks or I stimulate patronage for some service or product that has not been selling.

How do I do it? What's my secret? The answer is basic, simple and obvious. I tell my clients to tell their customers and prospects the truth.

For example, if you've had 10,000 widgets gathering dust in your warehouse for six months, and you have $90,000 tied up in them, but no one's asking for widgets, write a letter, or display ad, television or radio commercial that tells potential clients that:

1) You have a huge inventory of widgets
2) The widgets are good for such-and-such
3) You are interested in selling them retail
4) Their quality composition/construction and service functions and performance criteria are such-and-such.

Then inform them as to what other retailers or wholesalers would normally offer these or comparable widgets for, the price you're willing to sell a widget or a specific quantity of widgets for, and why you're selling the widgets to them so cheaply — the real reason — but with a delightful embellishment.

For example, tell the prospect the truth — that you have 10,000 widgets in your warehouse and the real rush for them is over until next fall, so you'll sell them for your actual cost or even for cost-less-20%. But add to that explanation a parenthetical exclusive qualifier such as...

- But we are only offering this value to our best customers as a reward for patronage.
- Or... But we're only making this offer to new, first-time customers who buy an equal amount of other products or services.
- Or... We are only making this offer available to people who buy (some other specific product).

An important point—in fact, it is vitally essential—that your clients and prospects will not understand or appreciate a value, or a bargain, or a service, or a benefit, unless, and until, you first educate them to appreciate it. Merely offering a product or service at a specific price (even the best price) does not generate excitement or a response until you tell people what they are receiving, what a value it is compared to other products and services, and why you can offer such value.

This applies to any marketing problem.

When your business has a problem (say you've taken money or advances for a product or service) and something goes wrong, precluding you from fully rendering that service, never fail to acknowledge your mistake. Otherwise that is a sure way to commit integrity suicide. Be up-front and honest. Call, write, or individually approach your customers and inform them of the situation.

Let them know precisely what you were supposed to do, and why you are unable to fulfill your obligations. Tell them with certainty when you will be able to perform.

Real consideration should be given to compensate them for their inconvenience. Perhaps a small gift that costs a lot less than the profit you will lose if you are forced to return their money. Send a discount coupon, or rebate a portion of their original purchase price. Whatever consideration you offer, explain why you are doing it. Apologize for what went wrong, thank them for their business, and assure them honestly that you can and will rectify the problem—that everything will be put right by a specific and certain time or method.

-64-

USING YELLOW PAGES ADS
TO MARKET YOUR BUSINESS

Did you know that most people in the United States refer to their yellow page directories close to 20 billion times per year? In fact, professional services are one of the top categories that people use their yellow pages for. In addition, yellow pages are everywhere—in phone booths, in homes, in offices, at local businesses. Therefore potential clients have many opportunities to access your yellow pages ad. Your local yellow pages can be a powerful way to reach your clients.

There are five kinds of directories that you can advertise in, depending upon what is available in your local market. If you have researched your yellow pages options well you will discover many more directories than you thought existed. Don't be coaxed into paying for ads in directories that don't have pulling power. For reference here is a list of the different kinds of directories that you will find in your area, however, there will usually be one directory that out pulls all others. It is usually the one in which most of your competitors appear and it can vary by local area. The directories include:

- Utility Directories - provided by telephone companies in your local area.
- Area Wide Directories - combining areas covered by smaller local directories
- Suburban Or Neighborhood Directories - covers smaller segments of communities and can assist you in targeting special segments of your area
- Special Interest Directories - target specific markets of consumers, such as foreign language directories, woman's directories, African-American directories, university directories.

- Business-to-Business Directories - targeting the needs of business people in specific areas.

When selecting a yellow pages directory, use one rule: Look for your competitors and advertise where most of them are advertising. Their ads are there for a reason. Many accountants and bookkeepers have attributed their entire success to yellow pages ads. I have also met many small business owners who under-use them as advertising vehicles. When you consider yellow pages ads you must be very careful because the ads are difficult to test. Publishers of yellow page directories will often restrict your ad with a lot of rules about how the ad must be run. Yellow pages sales reps can be very helpful, but they often have a strong motivation to sell you the largest possible ad, whether you need it or not. So be careful when shopping for yellow pages ads. I recommend asking for the directory publisher to mail or fax information to you about the rules, rates and most popular accounting-bookkeeping category listings for your area.

PUMP-UP THE PERFORMANCE OF YOUR YELLOW PAGES AD

AD SIZE

I suggest that you look at all of the yellow pages ads your business competes against within the yellow pages directory. Your best bet is to have one of the largest ads presented in your category. Use your budget to guide you through the decision process. Larger ads give you room to convey more of the advantages and benefits of your business and persuade clients to contact you. In several general business studies conducted on yellow pages advertising, a large percentage of yellow page users claimed to have call businesses that display the largest ads first. If there are a lot of competitors competing for the attention of yellow pages readers then larger and more benefit-rich ads may be necessary to persuade readers to select your ad.

AD PLACEMENT

Your yellow pages ad performance will vary according to "heading" development. If your business is a bookkeeping firm and there are few competitive listings under "bookkeepers" in your area, then you may be in a good competitive position. But you should make certain that this isn't a sign that the directory is not good. The bulk of your competitors might be advertising in a better directory. You can list the benefits of each service that you offer as a first step in teaching your market to make your business different from your direct competitors. If your business name does not begin with the letter "A," which would put your company at the top of the category listing, consider a small display ad near the top of the category heading. You want to position your ad where reader's eyes will be. One of the rules of advertising is that dollars tend to follow eyeballs. Yellow pages space ads that are placed near the category heading, will achieve more selections than ads placed further back in the heading. This implies that proximity to the category heading is important.

AD FLOW/DESIGN

Usually the design of your yellow pages ad flows well if you can place your finger where your attention is drawn first, and then move through all of the information in the ad without lifting your finger. Your goal is to keep your readers eyes moving toward the phone number. Vary the size of your type from bold to medium, and from large to small to keep your readers interest. Never use reversed type, i.e. yellow letters on a black box, because the mind tends to not notice them. Avoid type styles that are hard to read quickly or that might distract your reader, such as Old English. Try highlighting your phone number with bold type to draw more attention to it. Use enough white space to keep the ad clean.

AD HEADLINE

Make sure that your headline captures your readers' attention and draws them into the ad. Make a bold statement or ask a question to fully grab reader interest. You may decide to use your Unique Selling Proposition by stating the primary advantage that you offer in your headline or under your logo.

AD COPY

The content of your yellow page ad will influence the number of selections that you receive. Remember, ad content is determined in part by the ad size. Larger ads allow you more space for copy graphics, business location information, and the features, advantages and benefits of your accounting services. Don't hesitate to use long copy. Research demonstrates that long copy tends to make the reader of yellow page ads feel more comfortable about calling your business. This of course implies that you may be taking out larger ads to accommodate for longer copy, which may not be appropriate for the size and budget of your business. But the point is that even if you use a small or medium-sized ad, don't be afraid to expound a bit in the ad on what makes your business different. People love to hear the compelling story about what you do for them through your business that is completely unique.

AD GRAPHICS AND PHOTOS

Ad graphics are one of the most effective ways to attract your customers' attention. Use large black & white line art. Photographs tend to look bad when reproduced in phone books because the printing resolution is usually moderate to poor. Line art illustrations (solid black) tend to reproduce better in yellow page ads because the photographic resolution tends to be low. Make sure illustrations point into your ad not towards the ad of a competing business. Use distinctive borders to create a positive mood. Thick black bold borders work well for accounting businesses. If all of the other ads on the page use bold borders, then hairline borders in another color, such as red, may set off your ad more effectively. Avoid really silly cartoons, puns or clever slogans, or your children's or grandchildren's pictures.

INCLUDE THE UNIQUE BENEFITS AND ADVANTAGES THAT YOUR BUSINESS OFFERS

Here are the kinds of features, advantages, and benefits that you can include in your yellow pages ad about your accounting business:

RELIABILITY OF YOUR BUSINESS
- Years in Business in Your Market - demonstrates longevity, gives clients a sense of security
- Association Memberships - demonstrates your expertise
- Size and Scope of Your Business - if large, you can emphasize a variety of talent and services. If small, you can emphasize intimacy and personalized attention

AUTHORIZED SERVICES
- Accreditation Services - associate the benefits of the special services that you are qualified to provide

SPECIAL ASPECTS OF YOUR SERVICE
- Open Sundays or During Special Times - use it to give clients a sense of reliability

COMPLETENESS OF SERVICE
- Hours, Delivery, Parking, Satisfaction Guarantees, etc. - use this information to give clients a sense of receiving a complete experience

ILLUSTRATION AND COPY
- Use Artwork with Image Appeal - give clients proof source of service excellence
- Prove You Are Different -give clients independent proof of the unique advantage you give
- Your Unique Selling Proposition – make a slogan telling the primary advantage you offer that no other competitor offers

LOCATION AND AREA SERVED
- Mention Prominent Landmarks - use outstanding visual cues that people will recognize while driving
- Accessibility - how to access difficult locations
- Include a Map and Street Address - give people resources to find your office

Smaller ads, which are crammed with too much information, can result in few readers selecting your yellow pages ad. If you have complex messages or several office locations, you may need a larger ad to capture all of that information.

TEST YOUR YELLOW PAGES ADS
You can run a metered yellow pages ad, which is like an a/b split ad. When you run a metered ad, your phone service provider will assign an extra telephone number to your business that is printed in every other your yellow page ad. The extra number rings over your present telephone number so that you receive calls to both numbers. Each month, your telephone service provider will send you a printout of the number of calls made to the extra phone number, as well as to your main phone number. This is a great service because this enables you to test two different headlines in the same yellow pages distribution area. I suggest that you use the metered ad in your yellow pages ads continually, each time testing one new element. The metered ad method is most often used to test different size ads. You could make your "A" ad a smaller ad with headline "A". Your "B" ad would contain headline "B" keeping all other information in the ad the same. By metering phone calls to each ad using a different

phone number, you will usually discover that one ad pulls better than the other does. And it may surprise you to discover which elements yield higher responses for your specific business given your unique competitive factors.

INSIDER SECRETS FOR MAXIMIZING YOUR YELLOW PAGES AD SUCCESS

The critical concept in Yellow Pages advertising is to set your name apart from the crowd. Do not consider a simple listing. That's fine if the potential client knows your name but then they could look you up in the White Pages. You do not want people to call you at random. If you are an accountant specializing in small business clients, you may not want phone calls from people in need of estate planning advice.

There is no question that display yellow pages ads draw more business than simple directory entries. Maximize the full potential your ad to for greatest effectiveness. Yellow page ads should be value-oriented and offer risk transference—so that you are lowering the risk for clients to try your services.

I have crafted a kind of Yellow pages ad for accountants that have only been used a few times during my consultations with a large level of success. I have designed the ad to instantly lower the risk for the reader. I also use a process throughout the ad to give the client a preview of what they should expect from the accountant. You'll notice that I say words such as "I'll give you…" or "I'll ask you…" to help the potential gauge their expectations. This kind of approach warms up a normally cold yellow pages ad approach. You can use a similar process for any other ad that you create as well.

A HIGHLY UNUSUAL YELLOW PAGES AD SPECIALIZING IN PROMOTING A FINANCIAL PLANNING PROFESSIONAL

The ad that appears on the next page is one that was used successfully by a financial specialist. It was done as a full-page ad, but the concept could just as easily be adapted as a half- or quarter-page ad. Although it appears to break every rule of traditional yellow pages advertising, it pulled 1,500% better than most ads in the same category. I feel that the reason it was so successful is that it stands out from all other ads, almost appearing as a highly informative article with in the yellow pages directory. It presents the specialist in such a balanced and personal way, which gives him a favorably superior competitive position.

As you can observe, the aim of this yellow pages ad is to create a point of difference by using a large noticeable ad that communicates directly and intimately to the reader by helping to shape their expectations. Use the ideas from the above yellow pages ad to create your own unique ad.

−65−

TIPS, TRICKS, AND TECHNIQUES FOR SUCCESSFUL PRINT ADS IN MAGAZINES AND NEWSPAPERS

Unfortunately, the marketing of many accounting and bookkeeping professionals sometimes doesn't work as well as it could. Sometimes the marketer's efforts aren't uniquely connecting him or her to the market, yet a "connection" is necessary for before someone will consider using your firm. Many times business professionals choose to advertise in publications that simply do not provide enough exposure to the right potential clients. My rule for using print ads is this: Simply do not choose to advertise in any newspaper, magazine or local niche publication if you aren't 99.99% certain that your well-paid-for ad will be seen by a high enough percent of the specific niche customers you are seeking to attract. If you have a doubt don't buy the print ad, unless the cost of it is so marginal that you are willing to gamble in the face of your doubt. In the latter case, you will test your ad fearlessly.

You must always determine whether the publication will reach your target market by testing your ad(s) on a small scale to first measure your response rates. Your test will confirm which publications tend to work best for you and which ones are worth avoiding. Your test results will lead you to find successful publications, which will become the basis for running further successful ads. Your test results will sometimes lead you to learn the "hard knocks" lessons of failed ads. Have no fear you will learn a lot more from failure than you first expect.

Testing different publications is important because if your print ad doesn't connect with your target market—they don't tend to notice it—then the ad is not a wise income-producing asset. The ad merely becomes an expense. When that happens you are throwing your money away painfully. The sooner that you realize that different publications attract different readers and therefore, different potential clients. It behooves you to study the readers of different publications that you have thought about running ads in to make certain they are people you ultimately want to attract as clients.

Printed publications give you considerable flexibility because you can change your ad up to two or three days before it goes to press. And there are more specialized newspapers and local magazines in one's market than most accountants realize. Obtain a list of local publications from your local chamber of commerce, choosing the best local publications—that help you reach your niche market—perhaps testing small print ads in as many of them as possible.

HOW TO AVOID AD-KILLING BLUNDERS THAT REDUCE YOUR SUCCESS

NOT TARGETING YOUR AD

You must know your customers, and know how to target them within the publications. Learn which publications are read, which specific words in your headlines are most appealing, and which offers induce readers to take the greatest action. If, for example, your target market includes affluent females, ages 26 to 48, test your ads in the more upscale magazines in your community. If you are targeting small business professionals, consider testing your ads in local business publications, Small Business Development Council newsletters, and other local small business association newsletters. Ask your present clients which publications they read to determine the best publications to select. Then run test ads with highly irresistible offers in those publications.

TIMING YOUR ADS

Make sure that your services are in sync with the season in which your ad will appear. Look over your business records to determine your "hot ad months" which include the time just prior to, as well as, during tax season. Depending upon the other services you offer, if you check your business records carefully while looking for seasonal patterns, you will find other hot months that will pull better ad responses than others You can use this information to better target your print advertising. In general, it is wise to increase the intensity and frequency of your advertisements before and during your seasonal hot months.

CREATE IRRESISTIBLE OFFERS

One way to pull more clients through your ads is to make irresistible offers. The best way to do this is to look at the offers of your competitors. What are your competitors offering? Add three times more value to the offer. Are they offering the first month of bookkeeping service free if a client signs up this month? If so, your can offer three months free, plus 30% off of all tax-preparation services during the client's first year. Perhaps you can make your offer irresistible by keeping your prices the same as your competitors, but make your point of difference giving them season tickets to a local symphony. You must add more value to your existing offers to induce clients to try more of your services. You should create irresistible offers for your existing clients to induce them to try extra services they have never tried. Instead of offering a cheap price for your services through your ads, try adding extra value-rich benefits to persuade others to give your firm a try.

USE REPETITION

The primary law you must become familiar with in marketing your business is called the "Rule of Seven." Running a single print ad will probably not benefit your business greatly. Your prospective clients need time to learn to trust you. Your clients are usually not ready to buy when you are ready to sell. If you present your message to your target audience in as many different ways as possible, then you will increase the chances of making a strong connection with your clients. The idea here is to layer as many media as possible together. You can put your web site address into your ads. You can mail out inexpensive postcards to those people who respond to your ads every few months to remind them that you are there. By layering marketing methods in this fashion and using the more of ideas that you derive from this book to remind your mailing list of potential clients about the reason why you are different, people will learn to trust you more over time. Develop a well-rounded strategy of layered marketing methods that continue to tell clients who have responded to you at least once what makes you different from other accounting and bookkeeping firms.

MAKE SURE THAT EVERYTHING IN THE AD EMPHASIZES BENEFITS

The two most important aspects of your ad are: (1) The advantage or benefit that your accounting firm offers and that no other competitors offer, which is usually put into the headline, and (2) The call to action that explains what your reader has to do to obtain the irresistible advantage or benefit that you are offering, usually in the form of a special inducement offer that is highly compelling.

Make sure that your ad designer creates your ad so that the readers' eyes are drawn to key points by making mini-headlines throughout the ad. If your key advantage is to free clients from the pain of performing their own payroll, then consider using dramatic photographs of a long row of business people being released from prison, while still holding payroll books. Use pictures of people who look relieved to have been set free by your services. Increase the power of your ad by infusing a compelling headline into the ad, such as:

FREE YOURSELF FROM THE SELF-IMPOSED PRISON OF PAYROLL

Can you sense the "pulling" power of this ad?

Once you have created the primary headline then get ready to deliver more advantages to the reader in your sub-headlines. Make the benefits palatable; don't just balk the benefits at the reader. Involve as many of the five senses in the sub-headlines of the ad as possible. You should include at least three sub-headings throughout your ad. Here are some unique ideas for sub-headlines continuing with the theme of selling payroll services:

SMELL THE FRESH AIR THAT SIGNALS YOUR FREEDOM.
FEEL THE RAYS OF THE SUN WARMING YOU AGAIN.
LET US DO YOUR PAYROLL AND GET YOUR LIFE BACK.

Then create the body-copy for your ad. Use "action" words in the copy of the ad. Tell your story. If your ad is about freeing clients from the self-imposed prison of doing their own payroll, then explain how you will free them. Explain the steps clients must take to unlock themselves from the prison of their own making by using your accounting services. Tell them what they will experience when they take the one action that makes the most sense for them, which is to call you or visit you to receive the one key service that will release them from the prison-like time trap they feel fettered by. When you are create your body-copy, you are in essence taking the premise that has been created by your main headline and sub-headlines, and then using the body-copy to tell a complete story.

And of course the happy ending of the story that your ad tells through the powerful offer that motivates the potential client is to take action to get the results you have promised. In the above "self-imposed prison example" you could offer to give your readers a special key that is attached to a valuable key chain as an incentive for calling for an introductory appointment. You could offer to give free tickets to a local IMAX theater showing a great tie-in movie theme entitled "The Freedom of Flight." You could create an incentive that is in keeping with your theme of freedom. The incentive must offer enough value to induce clients to try your services.

Your ad is competing for your reader's attention against banks, airlines, car dealers, beverage companies, and many other advertisers within the publication. You must give your ads a distinctive style. Hire an experienced graphic designer to create just the right look for your ad. Your graphic artist must create an advertising presence that uses pictures, headlines and body copy to extend and expand your unique selling proposition—which is your point of difference, your slogan, your statement of primary benefit that you give to your specific clients.

WHAT SIZE AD SHOULD YOU BUY?

If you have the marketing budget, test a full-page ad because it attracts the most attention. This is rarely a practical option for accountants to do. Consistency in running ads within the right publication is usually much more valuable than ad size but you must consider both factors. Readers will most often notice your ad when they perceive a need for your services. By consistently running smaller ads that get a lot of attention you may find that you have greater consistency and better overall market saturation because you will be able you afford more ads in more publications. If you choose to run a half-page ad, realize that it can often have more impact for you over time than a full-page ad because you can run more of them for the same cost. When you decide to run any size print ad, find information on the advertising cost of running smaller ads. Calculate the cost of running a smaller ad more frequently and compare it to the larger ad alternative. Some advertisers test the cost and effectiveness of running several smaller ads in one publication in comparison to one larger ad. Until you test both alternatives you will never know which is most effective for you. I have one client who decided to stop running a one half-page ad and ran three strategically placed one-third page ads instead. The result was that readers noticed the ads 15% more often for approximately the same ad cost as one large ad. So test and play with different combinations of ad sizes. Some advertisers have had success by beginning with small classified ads and making them profitable and then moving up to small display ads after they have had some success with the classified ads. If classified ads work well for you then consider using them as reminder ads—ads that suggest clients look on a certain page for a coupon or gift certificate, or use them to pull readers to your Internet web site, if you have one.

Before you plan a complete print ad campaign, call the appropriate publication advertising offices and request a media kit. Look at the rates for display ads. Publications charge for ads by the column inch. There are 14-lines per inch. If a newspaper charges 50¢ per line, you will pay $7 per inch. If you want your ad to be 3-inches high and 2-columns wide, you multiply $7 by 3-inches, giving you $21. Now multiply the $21 by two columns, giving you an ad cost of $42. Run some calculations before calling the publication to place your ad. Have a rock solid idea of how often and when you want to advertise before you call.

PICK THE BEST DAYS FOR YOUR ADVERTISEMENT

Make your ads first appear on days when your business is open. People will see your ad, determine whether they have a need or not, and respond immediately. Target your advertising in conjunction with the editorial. Monday's sports pages attract male readers. The food section runs on Wednesdays. People tend to read newspapers for the entertainment section on Fridays. Test your ad in appropriate sections of the magazines and newspapers.

Newspapers charge more for Sunday ads because they attract the highest readership on that day. If you place a Sunday ad, test it to make sure it is worth the cost. To do this, run one ad on a weekday and one on a Sunday. Then ask clients which publication or day they saw your ad and keep a tally of the results.

Some of your best print advertising opportunities will be to place ads in small tightly targeted newsletters and small local publications. Most communities have Small Business Development Council offices. Consider advertising in their newsletter. Church bulletins can be very effective for generating additional business. Private businesses in your community have newsletters. Submit articles to them. Request to place an ad in their newsletter. For example, your local utilities company most likely publishes a newsletter that goes out quarterly to everyone in your community. By submitting a special article to the newsletter editor showing people how to budget and pay their utility bills more efficiently, you will probably receive mention of your practice at minimum, if your ideas are published. The cost of your publicity is the time you invest to write the article. Your "payment" for writing the article comes in the form of a bio box at the end of the article providing contact information about you and your firm.

TIPS FOR INCREDIBLE PRINT ADS

- Use the word FREE and repeat it where possible. Yes, it still works well for many advertisers.
- Show a graph or picture of the results that your business delivers.
- Try using testimonials of satisfied clients. Show the superior results they have received from your business. Try using a "before-and-after" approach.
- Make limited-time offers to persuade readers to visit now.
- Use a border around a small ad to make it look larger.
- Add color to your ads. The color red tends to receive more attention than blue or brown, which are also recommended.
- Run your ad until it no longer pulls. Even if you are sick and tired of looking at your ad, do not change it if it brings in clients. You, your staff, your friends and family will get tired of a good ad long before your audience stops responding to it.
- Obtain prime page space. Put your ad in the front section of the newspaper or as close to the front of the publication on the right-hand side of the page, above the fold or halfway point. This position tends to receive more reader attention.
- Use more copy than less. Ads with more copy tend to pull better then those with less. Tell the story of the advantages you give and give readers the "reasons why" you are in business. They will tend to be more drawn to you.
- Say something newsworthy in your ad. Format your ad to make it look like a news story. This technique is called an advertorial ad and can work well for you. Say something that is timely.
- Always include your business address and phone number so your client knows how to contact you.

HEAT UP YOUR PRINT ADS WITH HOT HEADLINE TIPS:

- Convey your business' primary benefit in the headline to intrigue your reader to read further.
- Speak directly to one reader at a time. Write one-on-one. Use the word "you" as often as possible. Create a sense of personal intimacy and immediacy in the headline.
- Write your headline as a news headline. Study daily headlines to learn power words — words such as "announcing" or "new" and put appropriate action words into your headline.
- Announce your free offer. Create an offer of the month. Readers will come to rely on looking for your ad to see what new offers you make.
- Create a sense of urgency. Try: "Act Now for Free Tax Credits" — "Limited Appointments Available."

Remember your headline is the most important element in your print ad. Often improving the headline will usually result in between 40% to over a 2,000% improvement in the pulling-power of the ad. Try to find one or two words that sum-up the one distinct advantage that your accounting firm gives that is different from competitors. If you can mentally boil down your advantage to just these two words then your marketing communication has obtained the clarity you need to develop the right headline. Your headline should never be more than 6 words long, in general. The second most important element of your print ad is the sub-headlines. Theses are also like mini-advertisements within the print ad. They act to get attention and communicate your advantages instantly.

Many accounting professionals who are able to run print ads have had good success especially during tax season. One very good way to learn a lot about running print ads is by clipping ads that have consistently appeared in each issue of the publications you have an interest in. Advertisers who consistently run their ads time after time are probably pulling profitably. Study these ads. Look at the headlines. Determine precisely what is making them work so well. Call the advertising sales offices of the publications and ask the sales manager why these client's ads are doing so well. Listen to what the manager says to see if you can ferret out a few grains of truth amidst his or her sales rhetoric. Then, form your own conclusions about why the ads work well. Make this process of ad analysis a continual study to determine the optimal way that you can successfully adapt print ads into your marketing program.

TARGETED TECHNIQUES FOR LOCAL MAGAZINE PRINT ADS

Local magazines provide an excellent way for you to promote your business. I want to present a few key distinctions that are essential for you to know when running magazine ads. Start by using small ads, until you have tested the magazine extensively. A well-produced magazine ad will give your business a high level of credibility because magazines are more upscale than newspapers. Remember, for your magazine ad to work well, you must run your ad over and over. Readers are leery of one-time magazine ads and often will respond after four to seven exposures to your ad.

Magazines will often create split-run ads for you so that you can test one element, such as the offer or headline. If local magazines in your area provide split-run ads then take advantage of this feature of the publication. Consider running two different but powerful compelling headlines. You must "key" your ad perhaps with a different suite address or code number at the bottom of the ad. When clients call you, ask them for the code number to track which ad headline attracted more readers. This will give you a tremendous opportunity to compare results. The two best ad elements to test separately are your offer and your headline. Use your creativity and test a variety of offers and headlines over time.

HOW TO DESIGN SIZZLING ADS

- Avoid using ALL CAPS in your ad body copy because they are hard to read.
- Use Sans Serif fonts in headlines and subheadings. San Serif fonts include Helvetica, Futuri, Impact, or any "block" font.
- Use one typeface for body copy and one for headlines to reduce visual clutter.
- Check to determine if the typeface is large enough to be read easily.
- If you use a coupon or gift certificate, use dashed lines around it instead of dots. Dashed lines or a box tends to make people desire to clip it out of the publication with scissors.
- Use photos that tangibilize the benefit that your business offers.
- A two-page magazine ad attracts 25% more attention than a one-page ad. Therefore, after testing, if you build up to a one-page ad and it pulls well, consider testing a two-page ad.

- A half-page magazine ad is usually about two-thirds more effective than a one-page ad.
- A full-page color magazine ad tends to attract 40% more readers than a full-page black-and-white ad, on average.
- The best magazine ad positions for accounting business print ads (from best to worst):
  1. First right-hand page or on back cover
  2. Second right-hand page
  3. Third right-hand page or inside of back cover
  4. Fourth right-hand page or page facing inside of back cover
- Position your ad as close to the front or back of magazine if no other choices are available.
- Photographs are more effective than drawings. Photos that show clients gaining benefits from you are better than a picture of your building from the outside or of empty office chairs. And ads with photos of people in them have higher response rates than ads without people.

CHECKLIST TO IMPROVE YOUR PRINT AD

- Does your headline clearly communicate your unique selling proposition (USP), the primary advantage your accounting firm gives that no other firm gives. Have you communicated the core benefit that your business is known for?
- Do your sub-headlines expand on your USP, or extend the benefit or advantage that you give?
- Does your the first paragraph of your ad expand on your primary business advantage (USP) even further?
- Do your have subheadings that break up your copy and make it easy to read. Is your ad stimulating, visually appealing and interesting?
- Are the paragraphs of your ad short? Is your copy to the point?
- Have you made an irresistible offer to your reader?
- Have you spoken the language of your target market?
- Use testimonials from satisfied clients to add credibility to the ad.
- Is the overall language of the ad fun? Does overall tone of the ad feel alive to the reader?
- Can you cut any trite phrases from the ad?
- Does the ad, as a whole, tell the reader what your accounting business can give them that no other

accounting firm in your market provides? If not, you must rethink whether you want to have a mundane business that is not very well differentiated. If you decide that you would rather develop a unique business, then recreate your business approaches. Offer distinctive kinds of services that give tremendous levels of extra value to your clients.

TRICKS OF THE TRADE FOR BUYING PRINT AD SPACE

Here are some questions to ponder to help you save resources on print ads:

- Does the magazine have "remnant ad" space available? Remnant space is space that is left over near the end of the magazine or newspaper's print deadline. You can often negotiate 50% to 60% off of the regular ad rate this way.
- Is there a frequency discount or a dollar volume discount for running ads? Many publications will give you a volume credit discount for running two ads in one issue.
- Do they have seasonal discounts during low advertising months? You usually have to ask.
- Do they have spread discounts when running two or more pages in one issue? Often you can obtain up to a 60% discount on the second page. If they have never offered this, persuade them to test the idea with you. If they need advertisers, they will probably be agreeable.

−66−

USING INSERTS AND PIGGYBACKS TO PROMOTE YOUR BUSINESS

Piggybacks and inserts can be an inexpensive and very effective way to promote your accounting business to your target market. All you have to do is find a marketing partner in your area who is already reaching your target market using a specific medium, such as direct mail, and pay them for the privilege of enclosing your message to their clients along with theirs. Then you'll be piggybacking your message to your target market at a reduced cost to you. Your partner should be a non-competitive business that reaches local people in your target market with marketing materials or products regularly. Your marketing partner could be a local magazine or an attorney. Your program could involve piggybacking with a retail-marketing partner who stuffs flyers for your services into their shopping bags at their cash register. It could consist of an oversized postcard stuffed into a local magazine. There are all kinds of clever ways that you can piggyback your materials into the hands of your market at a reduced cost to you.

One of the keys is to make sure that potential customers who have a strong need for the benefits you offer receive your inserted materials. Inserts can lower your marketing costs dramatically, but you must select opportunities carefully. Your objective is to obtain clients who are of high quality. High quality potential clients are those who will be the most satisfied by your services and who have the highest probability of becoming loyal clients. Obtaining high-quality clients, by choosing the most compatible insert and piggyback partners, is more important than the number of recipients your piggyback effort goes to. You must conduct a lot of research and do a lot of planning and testing before you will be able to properly choose a long-term piggyback opportunity.

Your insert must have powerful visual impact, and must be saturated with benefit-driven messages about the primary services that your business offers. And your offer must drive home the benefit in such an irresistible way that your reader is driven to respond to the offer that you are making.

CREATIVE WAYS TO USE DIFFERENT KINDS OF INSERTS AND PIGGYBACKS

RIDE-ALONGS

Ride-Alongs are direct mail piggyback pieces that are already being mailed to your potential market by other companies that you can cooperate with. I know an upscale accountant who has a relationship with an upscale culinary and gourmet shop. The accountant piggybacks a special full-color flyer inside the regular mail-outs of the shops and pays the shop owners a small portion of the direct-mailing costs for the privilege of using the ride-along. The association of her business with the shop adds immeasurable marketing credibility and value for her because it positions her business with their special interests. The flyer is directed toward 2,000 of the shop's clients, and makes an exclusive offer only to them. Include gourmet hors d'ouvres and wines that delight the senses during every consultation. The accountant has an arrangement with the most expensive caterer in her area. The caterer flies in fresh Maine lobster and crab daily. Because the gourmet shop's clients are interested in creating gourmet food experiences, they love the combination of food and self-improvement. It is a powerful upscale program that works very well for this select group of potential clients. The trick to a successful ride-along program is to identify other businesses that regularly approach the same target market as your accounting firm, but from a totally different angle. Some accountants offer to pay the partner's total mailing cost for the privilege of having access to their client base. Others split the costs evenly or are given some other fair cost-sharing compromise, allowing the partner to have access to their client base by reciprocating the ride-along arrangement.

FREE-STANDING INSERTS

Free-Standing Inserts (FSI), are promotional pieces—like flyers—giving information about your business that are put into specific publications reaching people in your market. Test using FSIs with large local newspapers, small specialty newspapers, corporate newsletters, and special interest magazines. FSI programs are—often conducted by large publishers—to cover significant geographic markets with coupons or flyers announcing special sales. You can use this idea in multiple ways to test narrower aspects of your local market. To use FSIs in a more targeted fashion, you need to obtain a list of every local newspaper, newsletter, magazine, and specialized targeted publication. Your local library's research librarian can provide you with this information. In order to develop your own personalized FSI program, simply approach the circulation manager or editor-in-chief of a publication(s) whose readership description accurately matches your target market. Ask the manager if she would be interested in a way to reduce their distribution costs. Tell them you will pay them to stuff your preprinted brochures into a specific section of their publication. You can sharpen your targeting ability by requesting that inserts go only to certain geographic areas. This is important because you might only want to attract potential clients who live only within a certain radius of your office instead of people living in every area of your city. You could also select your insert targets by zip code. If you can find smaller niche publications and newsletters in your area that cater to potential clients, it may work well for you. You can insert flyers, postcards, gift certificates, scratch-off discount cards and anything else you can think of.

You can promote your business by creating your own customized insert-program by approaching a business who is already successful at reaching your market. Just remember to test your efforts on a small scale first, and then broaden your efforts only after you obtain proven results. Don't waste your resources. Have fun playing with this wonderful idea and use it wisely.

−67−

USING DOORHANGERS
TO ATTRACT MORE BUSINESS

Because a large percentage of your business is driven by your geographic proximity to your clients, one of the most unique and effective promotion tools that you can test is a doorhanger. Doorhangers are like mini-billboards, which can be hung on the front doorknobs of people's homes in high-value market areas. They are inexpensive to print and distribute, and they help you connect with your potential clients at home on a one-to-one basis. Doorhangers remind existing clients of your presence in their lives in a tangible way. The doorhanger says, "I was here personally, and I have a special message to share with you, for you are important enough to my business that we took the time to come to you in a special way." Creating a doorhanger program for your business can be fun because it is such a different way to market your business.

I know of one accounting and bookkeeping firm that used a creative marketing campaign involving a "bounce-back door hanger." The doorhanger contained a tear-off postage paid mailer that encouraged the recipient to fill out their name and place it into their mail box. The doorhanger promised reliable, quick and easy in-home tax preparation at a special advantageous and irresistible price. The firm hired high school students to distribute the doorhangers. The marketing piece pulled a response of 2 out of 14 for the bounce back mailing and then 25% of those who mailed back accepted the offer. Considering the lifetime value of the clients obtained the promotion had tremendous long-term success as a market saturation technique that covered only the geographic areas that the firm wanted to target.

I know of another businessperson who distributed doorhanger video boxes that contained a 20 minute well-produced video on the topic of "keeping more of the money you earn." This businessperson targeted hardworking people in a few upscale neighborhoods. Well-done video tends to have high appeal and excellent "pass-along" value. On the video, the accountant showed viewers a simple plan for reducing the likelihood of overpaying taxes. The message was simple, touched a strong need amidst his market and people responded in droves.

Your first step in creating a successful doorhanger program is to select a few geographic areas with a very high concentration of target prospects. Starting at the neighborhood level is your best bet because people with similar social and economic status tend to cluster in the same areas. By looking at and modeling the neighborhoods and street profiles of your best clients, you will see that a pattern emerges. This pattern will lead you to the best places for distributing doorhangers with your compelling messages on them. Refer to our session on geographic analysis to fully examine your existing client base to find the best local neighborhoods that are "hot spots" for your business.

The key to a successful doorhanger program involves thinking about the lifestyles of your market before you create your doorhanger. Imagine the person receiving your doorhanger coming home from a long hard day at the office. Or perhaps they are returning home from a tiring workout — maybe a weight training workout, a long jog, or a step aerobics class. They have sore muscles and they feel tired. Maybe it is a hot day and your recipient has been grocery shopping and is feeling fatigued from making four trips to their car to put groceries away. The question that you must ask yourself is, "What can I communicate to my target market on a doorhanger to fully appeal to them in the highest and most favorable way." Again, as in all of your marketing efforts, you must rely on your Unique Selling Proposition (USP) to guide you to describe your prime benefit. All of the words and pictures on your doorhanger should aim to extend the one specific advantage that is represented in your USP. Do you recall the primary advantage/benefit your business gives to your clients? It is not just accounting or bookkeeping services. Your primary advantage will consist of the benefit of freedom, stress-release, saving time, and/or keeping more of what you earn, and the like. Drive home your one primary benefit throughout your doorhanger copy. Use pictures to entice your recipient to act on your offer.

The most powerful doorhangers are oversized. They resemble extra large "Do Not Disturb" signs. The most important part of your doorhanger is your headline, which is the first thing your recipient sees. "Firsts" are usually the most important part of any advertising campaign. The trick is to have a positive and immediate impact on the person who pulls the doorhanger off the doorknob. If you design your doorhanger well, your recipient will most likely read it in full. The instant the person picks it up, your message is communicated. That's powerful advertising. Your headline could also be your primary call to action: "Call Us Now To Start Saving Payroll and Tax Dollars Today."

You should hire high-school students to hang the door hangers in select areas. Make sure you give them a stack of enough doorhangers and explicit instructions on how to find the neighborhoods that you are targeting. Include a map of how to get there and highlight the streets each student worker must cover.

TIPS ON DOORHANGER DESIGN

- Use a short punchy headline to communicate your unique selling proposition (USP) quickly.
- Do not cut corners on printing. Print the doorhanger on heavy card stock and add one or two colors, full-color is preferable. Use powerful black and white or full-color photographs that exude the ultimate benefit of your business.
- Print testimonials (on the door hanger) from satisfied clients and the results that they received
- Discuss your staff's qualifications for providing excellent service so that people will know your business is professional and not a fly-by-night operation.
- Make a strong offer — a discount, a free 20-minute tax-savings consultation, or a gift certificate (coupon). Entice your prospect to call you. Add an expiration date to your offer for faster redemption response.

−68−

RUNNING CONTESTS AND SWEEPSTAKES

People love to play games and have fun. For a small amount of money you can create a sweepstakes or a contest that will cause people to focus their attention on your accounting business in a unique and different way. Contests will build traffic, encourage people to try your services, and generate word-of-mouth advertising.

One smart accounting firm manager developed a cross-promotion with a travel agency. Together the accounting firm and the agency gave away a cruise for two as a ax-season incentive to visit both businesses. The travel agency owner wanted to encourage potential clients of the accounting to use their tax refund to buy a vacation. The accounting firm wanted the exposure to the clients of the upscale travel agency. All anyone had to do to register was to come into either office and register for the event. The primary benefit the accounting firm owner wanted to emphasize was that it was fun to do business with the accounting firm. The promotion worked very well for both businesses. Foot traffic and sales increased by about 25% for several months.

SOME IMPORTANT FACTS AND GUIDELINES

There are many US laws prohibiting private lotteries, which are different from contests and sweepstakes. If you remember never to require participants to "pay to play" or to "purchase to play," you will be safe. Some states consider mail-in contests illegal because it requires a "paid postage stamp to play." The main thrust of controversy is that there is a prize, which is given away. In general, the larger the prize the more scrutiny you could potentially face.

Contests: *Games of skill* that involve a
                       registration fee. They are legal but
                       often tough to execute.

Sweepstakes:	*Games of chance* that require *no purchase for registration.* This is the most common form of game promotion. Very legal.
Lotteries:	*Games of chance* that require a *registration fee.* Lotteries are very illegal.

SIZZLING CONTEST AND SWEEPSTAKES TIPS

- Require registration to enter. Create registration cards requiring people to give you their names, addresses and phone numbers to enter. People who are very reluctant to give their names, addresses and telephone numbers will often do so to make a sweepstakes entry.
- Publicize the winner on radio, television, or newspaper, and tell entrants that they will appear in local ads and press releases if they win.
- Use incredible prizes to entice entrants. Cash usually is not motivational unless you give a lot away. Consider developing cross-promotions with other businesses. This might enable you to put a package together consisting of a mix of your accounting services and your partners' products and services. Offer a wonderful array of your own services as a prize.
- Run large and small sweepstakes throughout the year. Use smaller sweepstakes such as survey mechanisms that ask clients 3 to 5 questions about issues that will give you a greater understanding of their needs. Give away smaller combinations of services more frequently. Develop large sweepstakes that give away more significantly higher-value packages at key times throughout the year.
- Make sure that everyone thinks they have a good chance of winning something. Try adding a skill component to the contest to encourage people to register.

FUN SWEEPSTAKES THAT YOU CAN USE TO BUILD YOUR MAILING LIST

1. Endorsements/testimonials

    Ask your clients to submit a "30-word-or-less" suggestion for improving your service or giving you a compliment about why they enjoy visiting your business. Use your favorite compliment(s) in your advertising as client testimonials, by asking the client's permission.

Conduct a random drawing for gift certificates towards free services.

2. Cross-promotion Contests

   Find three other businesses whose client base compliments yours. Find businesses that attract the same kind of clients that you attract and which are noncompetitive to you. Each business will throw in a product or service to the contest prize winnings. The contest will be run at all partnering business locations. A separate drawing can be held at each of the locations, and three separate prize packages awarded. Each business will share contest names, client lists, and media coverage. This kind of sweepstakes creates a tremendous synergy, which gives each participating business much more than it invests.

3. Instant Win Entries

   There are many variations on this sweepstakes idea. This idea has been used even by fast-food restaurants, such as McDonald's pull and peel contests. One way to create "instant win" contests is by putting an extra-large fish bowl on your front counter filled will numbered chips. Each client is asked to select a chip after his or her visit. If the number on the chip matches the day of the month (or a pre-selected number posted on the wall), the client wins something, a fruit basket, a dinner for two, etc.

MORE SWEEPSTAKES AND CONTEST GUIDELINES

The Direct Marketing Association suggests guidelines for contests. The following is a partial list of their guidelines. Always double check with a lawyer or law service to ensure that you are not breaking any laws through improper contest procedures. Your state attorney general can refer you to appropriate information on state regulations. You should formalize the following rules and communicate them to your sweepstakes or contest participants:

- State that no purchase is necessary to register or win a prize.
- Clearly state the procedure for registering in the sweepstakes.
- State the termination date for eligibility in the sweepstakes, and whether it is the actual date of mailing or the receipt of entry deadline.

- Disclose the number, retail value, and detailed description of prizes offered, and whether cash may be awarded instead of merchandise. If a cash prize is to be awarded in installments, that fact should be clearly disclosed, along with the nature and timing of the payments.
- State the approximate odds of winning a prize, or statement that such odds depend on the number of entrants.
- Mention the method by which winners will be selected.
- Disclose the geographic area covered by the sweepstakes and any areas where the offer is void.
- Spell out all eligibility requirements, if there are any.
- Approximate dates when winners will be selected and procedures by which they will be chosen.
- Disclose publicity rights regarding the winner's name.
- State that taxes are the responsibility of the winner.
- State the provision of the mailing address to allow consumers to receive a list of winners of prizes over $25.00 value.
- No promotion, or contest, or sweepstakes should ever specifically state or imply that a recipient has won a prize when it is not the case. Winner selection should be conducted in accordance with the laws of chance.

–69–

USE POINT-OF-PURCHASE IDEAS
TO INCREASE SALES

Point-of-purchase (POP) displays include signs and countertop displays. POP signs can be used to carry a message to your clients at the point of sale in a unique way—often to create an impulse buy or reminder purchase. These displays can have a profound effect on your bottom-line sales.

You may have never thought of it before but the little corner of your receptionist's desk and the corner of your desk is valuable space. It can be used to pique the interest of your clients to actually try one or two of your services they normally wouldn't try because it may never have occurred to them.

I know an accountant who began selling a new kind of software that helped his clients manage their small businesses better. This astute accountant put little signs on the desks of his employees, who were regularly consulting with clients. The signs read: "Small business decision-making software trial —Only $29.99— Saves you at least $350 per month or it's FREE." The signs made clients curious enough to ask what kinds of decisions the software helped with. This, of course, opened the door for the consultants to make a special desktop presentation of the software, offering the trial version with the condition of buying the software if they were satisfied. The accountant's sales of the software increased from $400 per month to just under $3,700 per month over the course of the first month. This result occurred because the signs created a non-threatening opportunity to sell the software.

TRY FUN SIGNS TO SUGGEST THAT YOUR CLIENTS TRY SPECIAL SERVICES

A very clever accountant bought a fluorescent backlit wipe-off sign that is used at restaurants to communicate lunch specials. The top of the sign said "Today's Special" and the he wrote a different service on the sign each day. One day the special might be a consultation for a great price. Another time it might announce a new seminar they were sponsoring. Clients always read the sign before sitting down in the waiting area, because they know, as with their favorite restaurants, greater value is always received when paying attention to "specials".

I have a client who tried a subtle approach to POP signs. She put a classy, but simple, marble sign at the front counter where clients would check in. The sign made an offer for giving free financial check-ups to any client who wanted to improve their financial well-being. Her office saw at least 300 people per month in estimated foot-traffic. The signs created 300 new opportunities per month to offer clients new services after the initial visit.

USE DISPLAYS TO BRING CLIENTS TO YOUR DOOR FASTER

Nothing is more frustrating for a new client than trying to find the office of a well-hidden accounting firm. If you are in a shopping mall, a strip mall, or another such location that is exposed to a lot of drive-by or walk-in traffic, yet despite all your efforts, no one knows you are there, try a VisionQuest Display frame stand in front of your door. VisionQuest Displays makes various sizes of banner stands that can be positioned from every angle to inform walk-bys or drive-bys of your business name, a special offering, your USP, or anything else that attracts people's attention. Contact VisionQuest Displays for free information on their attention-getting frame banner products:

VisionQuest Displays
7591 Atherton Way
Eden Prairie, MN 55346
612-906-9121 phone
612-906-9122 fax

Here are resources for small desktop displays, call or write for a catalog:

Beemak Plastics, Inc.
16639 South Gramercy Plaza
800-421-4393 toll-free
310-768-0750 phone
310-538-4393 fax

–70–

MARKETING WITH NEWSLETTERS

N ewsletters are a very efficient way to remind your clients about your business. Newsletters are a low- cost way to gain an inroad into the lives of people in your market, because newsletters both educate your clients and remind them about your services. When you position your business as a source of information, as well as an excellent service, your clients will become more loyal and respect you so much more. Newsletters can be a lot of fun to create; and creating them in a layout program such as Pagemaker®, InDesign®, or QuarkXpress® can be very simple. Have a graphic artist create a newsletter template that includes your masthead/business nameplate at the top. This way, all you need to do is write the short articles for each issue, take your computer disk to your local printer, and you are done.

Newsletters are a great way to stay in touch with clients and sell more to existing clients. They add more value to your services, reinforce your specialty (see USP), increase word-of-mouth referrals, inform and educate at higher levels. You can even use them to publicize your business to your local media contacts.

TIPS FOR LOW-COST NEWSLETTER DISTRIBUTION

Consider creating and sending recipients an electronic, paperless version of your newsletter either by posting the file on your web site to be downloaded by visitors or by e-mailing it directly to them. To do this you will need to purchase a program called Adobe Acrobat®. Acrobat enables you to create electronic brochures and newsletter, etc. from your favorite programs (i.e. MS Word®) into readable PDF-files (portable document format) that can be downloaded and read by any computer platform. Your clients can read your e-newsletter by obtaining a free-version of Acrobat Reader® at the www.adobe.com web site. This greatly reduces your cost of distributing your newsletter. When a new issue of your newsletter is finished, you can send an e-mail reminder to your clients to visit your web site to download it.

NEWSLETTERS HELP YOU TARGET YOUR MARKET IN EXCITING NEW WAYS

If your accounting business caters to local business people, you can target local business professionals directly. Go to your local Chamber of Commerce; obtain a list of presidents, vice-presidents, association leaders, business-club officers, and other key influential people in your market. Send them a newsletter full of anecdotal stories from professionals who use your services to improve their bottom line and give tips on how to free up their time so that they can do other things. You should cite benefits and use testimonials about your services throughout the newsletter. Make it easy for readers to contact you for more information. Include a gift certificate or a special offer.

Use your newsletter as a powerful vehicle for testimonials of satisfied clients. To do this, highlight certain clients with photos, and include their comments about how you have changed their lives. If you have clients who are highly visible and influential role models in your community, be certain to highlight them because your association with them will influence the opinions of others to try your services.

Remember to use the concept of cross-promotion (see cross-promotion chapter) in your newsletter effort. Find several other businesses that complement yours, because you share the same kinds of clients and combine all efforts by creating one newsletter that will benefit all of the businesses. You can even sell advertising to other noncompeting businesses. By combining mailing lists, you will have substantial exposure to each other's clients overnight. And you can reduce printing and mailing expenses considerably by sharing them.

Your newsletter articles will consist of valuable tips that significantly enhance the lives of your clients. Throughout your newsletter give examples of successful consultations that you have performed.

If your newsletter appeals to your market you can begin to sell products by developing a catalog section of clever and unique products. You can sell your clients all kinds of fun products.

TIPS FOR CREATING HOT NEWSLETTERS

- People like newsletters with interesting subjects, short articles, excellent visuals, easy-to-skim design, bulleted lists, organized calendars, and special offers.
- People tend to dislike newsletters with intimidating pages (technical articles with small type and no graphics), disorganized information, long articles, overly frequent mailings, irrelevant content, impersonal tone, chaotic page design, or too many pages.
- Once your client receives your newsletter, you have 15 seconds to grab their attention through use of intriguing or emotional photographs, illustrations, charts or graphs which condense your message, Use captions that pull the reader into the article. Consider using fun cartoons that illustrate your promotional message, concise calendars, headlines that suggest the benefits of reading an article, subheadings that list your mail ideas at a glance, "pull quotes" that interest the reader, and the "emotional" elements of paper, color, and design.
- Create a nameplate. Put your business name in the name

of your newsletter, if your business name is "Progressive Bookkeeping," you could call your newsletter "Progressive Ideas." Add a tagline to your nameplate. A tagline is a phrase that describes the benefit your business provides. Your tagline should flow from your Unique Selling Proposition. Also, add a dateline to your newsletter month — June 1999; Season-Spring, Summer, Fall, Winter 1999; Quarter One, Two Three or Four 1999, etc.

- Use kickers, a two- to three-word phrase that gives the subject of the information that follows, above different sections of the newsletter to entice readers. Use large bold headlines that jump right out at the reader. Use a deck, which is the subtitle of the article, under each headline to give the reader more information about the article at a glance. Drop caps - an enlarged letter from the first letter of the first word of an opening paragraph - add a little style and bring the eye to the beginning of the paragraph. Use the highest quality photos and illustrations possible. Always use captions with your photographs. Bulleted lists also provide readers with more easily digestible information and tips. Use a pull quote, a direct quotation from an authority that is pulled away from a paragraph and usually enlarged to add visual appeal, to add an extra personal touch.

- Use interesting content to stimulate your readers' desire to read more. Introduce new products and services, tell your success stories in case histories, recognize top clients and employees, report on your involvement as a business owner in lively editorial, give lots of how-to information, provide technical advice in "question and answer" columns, and share lots of "insider's secrets" and pertinent information.

- Use inserts to add impact. Provide a pull-out calendar about fun activities offered through your business. Include a survey, insert an article reprint from local or regional publicity you received, insert an ad reprint, include a subscription form, insert a sales letter or a thank you letter, give how-to inserts in the form of free guides or special reports, or insert a special edition.

- Offer clients a free newsletter subscription in exchange for their business card or name and address.

- Use the newsletter to announce on upcoming postcard campaign offering discounts, or to announce mini-seminars that you can conduct at your business on how to look your best. Discuss contests and sweepstakes that your business will be having.

- Start small. Begin with a one page, two sided newsletter printed in black & white. It should only cost you about $38 per 100 newsletters, and you can start immediately.
- Save on postage. Add a zip-plus-four to your list — a zip code with four extra digits added for accurate post office delivery — and convert them to postal bar codes. Clean your mailing list by checking for duplicates and incomplete addresses. Use metered postage. Use an automated lettershop to print, collate, address, and mail your newsletter. Use your lettershop's bulk-mail permit to save money, and rent lists on disk instead of labels.
- To find content for your business newsletter, you should contact trade associations, trade journals, and specific books written about current trends, and conduct interviews with local experts.
- Use fact boxes throughout your newsletter to capsulize vital details of a story in a few lines or paragraphs.
- Use mailing panel. When you fold your newsletter for mailing, you will affix your client's address to the mailing panel. Add other graphic tools to the mailing panel that will make reading easier for the recipient. You can add a map that leads clients to your doorstep, which also includes your business name and address, your logo, your business phone number, an "inside-this-issue box" with bullet points that tease the recipient to read the newsletter. If you have space, include a short news brief, the hours of business operation, and your Unique Selling Proposition.
- Use your newsletter as a sales and educational tool. Include a phone number and information about how to find your business on every page. Fill the newsletter with information-rich copy that gives real value, and lots of it.
- Generate editorial content that considers every aspect of your readers' lifestyles, interests, opinions, and attitudes. If you know that your readers love a certain hobby, add information about how to enjoy that hobby more. Your readers will respond very favorably to your insights about their interest. Connect with your readers by encouraging them to suggest articles and even write them for you. Even if you can't use them, they will give you tremendous insight about your readers.

- Have your newsletter proofread by a professional editor before going to press. The smallest spelling or punctuation error can reduce your credibility instantly and turn the reader off fast. Take this advice seriously. Pay an experienced editor well if you have to. You can often hire a local newspaper editor to free-lance for you.

HOW TO PRODUCE A HIGH-CLASS NEWSLETTER

- Select High Quality Paper. Your printer can show you various paper swatches that you can choose from. Avoid glossy stock because it is too shiny for newsletters that use heavy text. For paper, choose a #1 or #2 matte finish, or a dull-coat white sheet, or a premium grade uncoated paper stock.
- Add An Extra Ink Color. Unusual colors such as black plum, dark coffee, eggplant, or forest green for headlines, body type or photos can look wonderful in place of traditional black ink. Contrast this with aqua, peach, or celery for screens, artwork, clip-art, page numbers, and initial caps. Make sure body type is close to black for legibility.
- Use Full-Color Reproduction. If your business caters to a very rich local market, or has services that require vivid photos, using full-color will better reflect the quality of your business service. You can reduce your printing costs by having color photos only on the front cover.
- Use High-Resolution Output. If you layout your own newsletter on a computer, make certain that you have prepared files for your printer that will output on their imagesetter at a high resolution. Your desktop laser printer will output at 300 to 600 dots per inch. However, your computer files must be able to handle the 2400+ dots per inch of your printer's image setter. This is especially important for graduated tints and photos.
- Use Professional Photographs. For the best photographs of your facilities and your staff, hire a news photographer to shoot your staff using black & white format (2 and a 1/4) sized negatives.
- Use Quality Page Design. For initial design concepts, hire a professional graphic artist skilled in the subtleties of publication design. Your readers will probably be very turned off by amateur design. Make sure that your nameplate (header) is of the highest quality possible. Also make sure that your mailing panel is as small as possible to allow for maximum content in the rest of your brochure.

USING NEWSLETTERS AS AN EFFECTIVE MARKETING TOOL

The best way to market is to educate, inform and give a foretaste of your service to prospects. Newsletters are a productive marketing tool for accomplishing this. And as you will see in the "Internet Marketing for Accountants" chapters of this book, you can create electronic newsletters that are highly productive and inexpensive to publish. Marketing with newsletters is effective because it gives you a large amount of space in which to present vignettes of non-proprietary, non-confidential case studies or to issue short courses or primers. In the course of writing that newsletter, give the recipient the value that you would render if someone paid you $1,000 privately for a short consultation.

The newsletter should be, ideally, approximately four to eight single-spaced typewritten pages, photo offset. The inclination of shortsighted people is to titillate, hold back and provide full information only when paid. I adhere to the opposite school of thought. Give so much valuable information freely that it becomes apparent that you are the person to turn to when more extensive information is needed. This strategy has two advantages:

1. It establishes credibility and expertise.
2. Human nature draws us naturally to reciprocate. If you give something of value, the recipient has a tendency to want to reciprocate. The best way they can do that is to patronize you.

In your newsletter, write in a one-on-one style. Avoid formality and technical terminology. Write as if your reader were sitting across the sofa from you in your living room. Tell them what's going on in your practice, about innovations and problems in your field. You might say, "I'd like to share an interesting or a curious story about a particular situation," and then tell stories that make you human; perhaps that tell specifically how you helped someone, how you solved a unique problem, or resolved a personal financial crisis for someone. Choose a common dilemma that could apply to many of your readers.

Give examples and techniques that could help them in their business, their life or their profession. Then present a specific offer. For example: a great many people are concerned about a certain aspect of their financial future. As a response, you can use the newsletter as a vehicle for your clients. Perhaps you will offer a prepared booklet, a report, a tape or a session on the subject at your office every Saturday, to which they are invited to attend.

Make it clear that if they are already a client, you are always available to consult with them. If they have never used you, you are always available for an initial consultation to see if you can be of use to them. Encourage them to call, write or visit. Always enclose a response card inside the newsletter that they can send in for something that will maintain their interest and keep this dialogue part of an ongoing process.

You should send a cover letter with all of your unsolicited newsletters:

John O'Toole CPA
125 East Mountain Lane
Naples, FL 32799
(555)555-4563

Dear Mr. George Iorio:

My name is John O'Toole. I am an accountant in your community. I have developed a substantial practice. My clients enjoy receiving the monthly newsletter that we publish because, as they tell us, it is informative, interesting and gives ideas that help them save a lot of money. We've enhanced people's financial situations, and they tell us that they have stopped over-paying taxes.

I don't know if we can help you, too, but I thought you might enjoy reviewing a few copies. I have arranged to send you a copy with my compliments for the next three months. I am hoping that it enlightens you and that it is a valuable resource for you. I know it will warrant your spending five, ten or fifteen minutes a month reading it because of the ways to will help make you more financially literate. Most of all, I hope it allows you to reflect on and achieve your overall financial goal.

After reading it, if you feel that I could be of service to you, I would be delighted to discuss your particular situation. I would be happy to arrange an appointment. As always I would be glad to confer with you for half an hour, at no cost to you, to determine whether I can be of service. At that time I will share some of the things I have done for others, and perhaps discuss some ways you can keep more of the money you earn.

In the meantime, I publish several reports, booklets and tapes on subjects of interest to people like you. I have listed them on the enclosed card. If you send it back, I will send you any of them with my compliments. I hope I can be of service to you; moreover, I hope that what I have already included can benefit you. The next two newsletters will arrive with my compliments, so enjoy!

With my Compliments,
John O'Toole CPA

SPECIAL NOTE:

You can send your newsletters to present clients to stay in touch. Perhaps you will send them to a list of VIPs in your community that you derive from your Chamber of Commerce, or other local associations you might be involved with. This will usually do a lot to get the word out about your expertise in your locale. You should also send newsletters to the list of referrals that you actively obtain from all of your present clients.

−71−

USE "TAKE-ONE" TECHNOLOGIES
TO PROMOTE YOUR BUSINESS

Take-one technologies will influence more clients to visit you more often, buy more of your services and pass along information to friends. Take-one technologies can be as simple as putting a rack of one-page information sheets you publish on a special display in your waiting area to educate clients about your services. You can create, in essence, mini-billboards with "take-one" information sheets you put inside of office supply stores and other businesses in your area to promote your services while providing valuable information to potential clients. Do you realize the power you have to reach your clients by using multiple "Take-one" technology applications?

You can use special take-one racks and displays in your office to provide clients with information-filled fact sheets or booklets about your special accounting and consulting services. You can also use take-one racks filled with information-rich fact-sheets and booklets inside other businesses. The more information you give to people in your target market, the more they will think of you as an expert. Sooner or later they will seek you out to help with specific questions and concerns.

BEGIN BY DEVELOPING A "TAKE-ONE" PROGRAM INSIDE YOUR BUSINESS

Create 25 to 50 different one page, front and back, information sheets for specific problem areas, such as, audit survival, money saving ideas, budgeting tricks, tax-burden reduction tips, etc. Create the information sheets with a header that is similar to your newsletter and one that provides free, up-to-the-minute information that people can use instantly to obtain results.

The process of generating information can be as simple as subscribing to trade journals in your field, to find tips and problem-solving information that your local market delights to discover.

As long as you cite your sources, you can include the information from these magazines, as direct quotes or as bullet points. I know many accounting professionals who compile tips from back issues of trade journals. Subscribe to as many trade journals as possible that cater to your target market—not only to capture material that you will share with your clients in the form of a "take-one" program—but also to obtain as much knowledge as possible about your market.

Generate a list of the most commonly asked questions or problem areas that your clients experience. Divide the list into 10 to 50 of the most common topics. Some accountants will poll clients to ask them what information they value the most. Then you have a better idea about which specific information is most valuable to potential clients. Give lists of remedies that readers can use to solve their most pressing problems. Be certain to include information about how readers can contact you an expert who will provide them with your best-reasoned advice.

Once you have written your factsheets, you are ready to purchase a literature display for your information. You can use a magazine rack or buy an in-store display. Make sure you keep your take-one information center stocked full and accessible to all clients. Encourage people to use your factsheets by leading them to your display and recommending that they take anything that will help them.

Topics that may work well for you may include:

- How To Avoid Paying More In Federal Taxes Than You Need To—An Insider's Report
- How To Budget Your Way To Your Dream Home
- How To Retire A Millionaire
- How Take A Tax-Free Vacation Each Year And Write It Off

TAKING MESSAGES ABOUT YOUR BUSINESS INTO OTHER BUSINESSES

Now here is the most fun and creative part of your program. I want you to identify as many potential partners outside of your business as possible to participate in your take-one program.

Here are some valuable special applications for your take-one program that can be adapted inside of other businesses:

- Offer to put a rack with free fact-sheets and other information inside local bookstores. Each factsheet will recommend different books that reflect the best books the store carries to help clients achieve a certain purpose. You may decide to create factsheets on small business problems, some on avoiding audits, some on personal finance issues. All of the factsheets will read: "Sponsored by Your Firm," with complete contact information. You will buy the rack, stock it and reload the factsheets when it becomes empty. Extra-value idea: Create fast information cards in the form of bookmarks that lead clients to best books in local bookstores on certain financial-related sub-topics.

- Put your racks in public libraries, local small business development centers, special libraries in local association chapter offices, and other places that people go to obtain information. Write your factsheet on hot topics that aim to protect and inform the specific people who visit each of these places. Each factsheet must always have a way to contact your offices for more information.

- Put your racks in the business establishments of other key non-competing businesses. You may choose to cooperate with a lawyer whose clients are also in your target market. If you have to pay that particular professional a flat fee for the privilege of placing your factsheet display inside his or her waiting area, it may well be worth it.

USING FACTSHEETS TO PROMOTE YOUR BUSINESS IN UNIQUE WAYS

Once you have generated a sizable amount of problem-solving information, you can begin to reform it and distribute it in creative new ways. Consider putting the factsheet information onto videocassette, or audiocassette giving it to clients who would benefit the most from it. One accountant that I know gives clients audiocassettes on "small business start-up finance resources and procedures" that are available in his local community free of charge. You could also use all of this information as the basis of material for two- to five-minute radio spots. And, you can use it on your web site to publish information about your expertise there.

For information about purchasing displays for your information sheets contact:

Art-Phyl Creations
P.O. Box 5457
Hialeah, FL 33014-1457
800-327-8318 Toll-free Phone
305-624-2333 Phone
305-621-4093 Fax
web: www.art-phyl.com

POP Plastics
2225 Faraday Avenue, Suite C
Carlsbad, CA 92008
800-767-7220 Toll-free Phone
888-767-1444 Toll-free Fax

web: www.popplastics.com

-72-

USE PREMIUMS, INCENTIVES, AND GIVEAWAYS AS MINI-BILLBOARDS

If used appropriately, give-a-ways can generate daily reminders of the advantages and high-quality service your accounting and bookkeeping business delivers. If you keep your benefit-rich, emotionally- appealing message in front of your prospects long enough, your business will become part of your prospects' and clients' lifestyle.

There are two basic categories of give-a-ways: Premiums and Advertising Specialties. Premiums are offered to increase the perceived value of your service because they tend to be higher quality give-a-ways. Advertising Specialties are very inexpensive and are designed to display your logo and business name and perhaps some contact information.

Many businesses use premiums to increase traffic at their place of business by offering a low-cost gift to everyone who visits. Sometimes gifts are given at special events, such as open houses or trade shows, because the business name is imprinted on the gift. Premiums serve as a reminder to patronize your business after the prospect has gone home. Premiums can sometimes be certificates for free services that are given in exchange for frequent visits. They can be high-quality gifts, such as, clocks or calendars displaying your business name.

For our purposes here, we will refer to all of them as premiums and incentives. When you buy from suppliers, you will want to remember the difference between the two.

As your business becomes more competitive, you may decide to add an extra touch to the service you give by using premiums and incentives. Remember that your potential clients are subconsciously asking themselves one primary question when they are presented with information about which bookkeeper or accountant to patronize, the question is: "What benefit will I receive by going there?" They are driven by this question whenever they spend money on any service. Incentives give your clients good reasons to visit you. They are opportunities to get something extra that makes using your services special. Incentives provide extra motivation that answers the "What will I get?" question every client silently asks themselves once they perceive a need for the kind of services you offer.

You can use incentives as an "added ingredient" creating a tangible benefit that encourages your client to:

- Buy more services in greater quantity.
- Try a new service for the first time.
- Make regular purchases over a period of time.
- Decide for a more expensive service or special combination of services.

Regardless of the give-a-way or incentive you choose to test in your business, be certain to remember that your clients must perceive the item as something very "special." Perhaps you will decide to use an incentive that people are not able to buy or obtain anywhere else.

SET SPECIAL GOALS FOR USING INCENTIVES

Before you spend any amount of hard earned cash on incentives and give-a-ways, clearly identify what you want them to do for you. You might want them to:

- Bring people to your doorstep. Attracting a crowd is a surefire way to increase your business fast. Be sure that you have adequate supplies of incentives for your promotion.
- Try to spark the attention of special groups who congregate in special places. At public events, people take special notice of what others are wearing. If everyone on the beach has your business logo on their hat, you make a strong impression. But, will this translate into business for you? It may or it may not. Be sure to test your incentives on a small scale to see if they will work for you. If you display at local events, and trade shows, use appropriate incentives, such as thick colorful note pads with your business name, to appeal to this captive audience.
- Create a special position for your business in the minds of your clients. Establishing your business image by tangiblizing the primary advantage your business gives

in the minds of clients can take a long time, and it can be costly for you. The right premium incentive can do this for you very quickly. Make sure that the incentive you select matches your Unique Selling Proposition (USP). *See USP.* If you are trying to establish your business as "the premier business," you could give out special high-end calculators that display your business name, logo and phone number when you turn them on. A video on how to systematically organize one's personal finances and their estate or portfolio may have the same effect on your market. These incentives will establish you as someone who cares about helping your clients lower their stress level and better their lives.

- Offer a premium incentive with each service to help focus client attention on your products and services. Cosmetic companies do this all the time: They offer a make-up case or a free bottle of perfume with a significant purchase. You can bundle your services together in the same way to create an incentive for clients to try more services.

Incentives will help you place your name and phone number in front of potential clients when they need you. One creative marketer had $2.00 phone cards made up and gave them to her best clients. She made an arrangement with a local telephone company to buy 500 of them. They put her business name, phone, logo, telephone number, and card amount on them. She gave them to her clients and told them that it was for their protection in case they were ever in an emergency situation. Those who received them kept them handy, because they were perceived as informative as well as monetarily valuable.

I know a mortgage broker who sent thousands of her home-buying clients a 9-volt battery as a premium. She sent a letter asking homeowners to take a moment to change the battery in their smoke detectors to ensure their safety. This was a powerful way for her to keep in touch with clients and communicate how much she cared for them. This created immeasurable value and also gave her a reason for enclosing several business cards with a request to share them with friends for referrals. She received hundreds of referrals.

Another idea for a premium is to have wall clocks made with your business name and location on them. Few people would ever throw this premium away—and of course people will look at them thousands of times per year. You can use refrigerator magnets, hats or baseball caps, tee-shirts, scratch pads, pens, and other items. See some helpful resource companies below.

HOW TO USE PREMIUM INCENTIVES IN A SUCCESSFUL PROMOTION

- Select a premium give-a-way that your recipients need, want, and desire. You must select items that cause people in your target market to respond very favorably. Items that can cause people to become emotionally excited will usually create the strongest word-of-mouth response. If your recipients do not consider the item useful, they will probably trash it soon after the novelty wears off.
- Plan how you will distribute the premium. You can distribute the premium before or during a client visit depending upon your purpose for using the premium.
- Choose a product that complements the primary benefit your business offers.
- Put your phone number on the premium so that people can readily access your phone number and call for an appointment. Remember that your aim is to turn your goodwill gesture of offering the premium to clients into actual increases in sales.
- Make certain that the quality of the premium you choose is at least as good as the quality of your service—from your clients' point of view. Contact the companies listed below to request a copy of their catalog. Clip pictures that are compatible with your business, and ask a few clients which gifts they feel best match and communicate the quality of your service. As you know, a broken clock with your name on it makes you look bad.

Resources For Premiums and Incentives Providers

American Premium Corp.
125 Walnut Street
Watertown, MA 02172
(617) 923-1111phone
(617) 923-9939
Premium Provider

Gift Creations
10310 Norris Ave.
Arleta, CA 91331
800-468-0713
(818) 993-0001 phone
(818) 993-0020 fax
Gift/ Specialty Provider

-73-

USE TESTIMONIALS AND ENDORSEMENTS

When your customers say good things about your business it is so much more powerful and convincing to potential clients than the good things you say about your business. Trust and credibility are slowly being lost by skepticism and a lack of faith in marketing claims in the United States. Some marketers say that it takes longer than it once did to persuade potential clients they should give you their business. That is why smart marketers use testimonials in every appropriate communication with potential clients.

Marketing must be founded upon credibility in order to be believable. People are afraid to switch from the accountant or bookkeeper they currently patronize—even if they are not completely satisfied. They do this because they fear they might have a worse experience with someone else. People are afraid of feeling silly by making bad choices, and will avoid spending money, continue to receive poor service, or eliminate taking new risks. Trust becomes the critical factor when potential clients choose to do business with you. Your aim is to reduce the barrier of risk between you and your client. You do this by creating a tangible representation of the benefits, advantages, and enrichment that your current clients receive from you.

The best way to generate trust is clear, but often it intimidates business owners and they often hesitate to follow through on the method I am about to reveal to you. Please don't fall into the category of nonresponsive accountants and bookkeepers who throw away this precious golden nugget idea by not taking action to test this concept.

Consider assembling a notebook of letters from existing clients who have recommended your services to new clients. Create an outstanding presentation by putting the letters in the most expensive binder you can find. Use plastic protector pages or have the pages laminated. Perhaps you will want to reproduce your best letters and hang them on the wall in your waiting area. Your goal is to show prospects that these testimonials are from real people on actual letterhead. These are powerful proof sources of the unique advantages that your business gives clients that others do not.

The hardest part of this for most people is asking clients to write letters that describe some of the best service encounters with your firm. Asking your clients for feedback about your service may reveal more complaints. This is often a marketer's biggest fear, but complaints can quickly become like true friends, if you use them to improve your service. The few complaints you're likely to receive will give you the opportunity to elevate your service to the highest level possible. Ask clients directly for testimonials. You will be very pleasantly surprised at the results.

DEVELOPING A POWERFUL TESTIMONIAL AND ENDORSEMENT PROGRAM

- If you are hesitant to ask clients to write a testimonial letter, send a survey to your clients or hand one to them on their next visit instead. Ask them a few multiple-choice questions about the quality of your service. Then end the survey with this:

  "If you feel that our service has been exceptional, we would love to know about it. We would consider it a tremendous favor if you would let us know by enclosing a statement that we could share with prospective clients. Try to write one that will give others an idea of the benefits, advantages, and enriching experiences you have discovered by doing business with us."

- Show prospective clients the statements and letters that you gather. It is important for them to know that this is how your current clients feel about your service and that you will work just as hard to provide them with a similar experience.

- Use this three-step plan:
  1. Write down the names of people who command the highest respect among those in your core market. They can be local celebrities, or immediately recognizable local personalities.

2. Approach the people on your list and ask for their endorsement of your service. Some local celebrities request fees for endorsements used in ads. You may be able to trade-out or barter your services for their endorsement.
3. Obtain the most powerful and specific claim they can make about your business. Use it in all of your advertising and promotion.

HOW TO USE TESTIMONIALS AND ENDORSEMENTS

- Print up booklets or factsheets that include a few of your best testimonials and send them to your mailing list of prospects, loyal clients and local media.
- Use testimonials in all of your print advertising.
- Dedicate one full section in your brochures to testimonials from clients.
- Use voice-overs from actual clients giving testimonials in your radio commercials.
- Put audio testimonials into "on-hold" marketing efforts so that people can hear them when they call into your office.
- Consider headlining an ad with nothing but powerful testimonials about your business.
- If a particular client has had an incredible experience or result with you, don't hesitate to rewrite their experience for them into a powerful testimonial that they may be willing to endorse.

SEVEN TIPS FOR DEVELOPING CREDIBLE TESTIMONIALS

1. Tell the truth. It is illegal and immoral to fabricate a testimonial.
2. Reveal the source — give the entire name, not just initials. Using only initials lessens your credibility.
3. Show endorser's status. If the endorsement or testimonial is from a city councilperson mention it with their permission.
4. Get specific testimonials that talk about the real value that clients have received from you. Saying, "The service was terrific" is too vague and therefore is a weak testimonial. "The service saved me hundreds of hours worth of time and effort and helped me avoid losing time and money on a devastating audit." is powerful because it tells why your service gives clients an advantage.

5. Use natural sounding testimonials. Testimonials don't have to be "grammar perfect." If they sound like everyday conversation, they will tend to be more effective and believable.

6. Demonstrate clear specific advantages and results. "Perfect Bookkeeping saved me a lot of money" explains an advantage in a mediocre manner. Look at what occurs when you combine this advantage with a very specific description of results. "Perfect Bookkeeping saved me $7,000 this year in payroll costs, and my first consultation was at no risk... it was free." The latter example makes people want to reach for the phone because the advantage is spelled out for them and appeals to their self-interest.

7. Put testimonials and endorsements in quotes. This signals to readers that someone actually said the words within quotation marks. Also, the quotation marks tend to look visually appealing in the graphic element.

–74–

BUILDING YOUR MAILING LIST

Developing a client mailing list in a usable form provides the means to connect with your clients. Most accounting and bookkeeping firms do not adequately and properly optimize the marketing value of their mailing lists. Your client list is the gold mine of your business. Using your client list to maintain and build consistent relationships with your existing clients is easier than constantly trying to bring in new clients who are less familiar, or may not value you as much as your most loyal clients. Few accounting businesses invest the time to utilize every client's name, address, and phone number to the best marketing advantage. The ideal marketing situation is to begin collecting names from the day you start your business, continually building your mailing list, and then using your precious mailing list to connect with your clients in more meaningful ways.

BUILDING AND USING YOUR MAILING LIST

- Whenever you receive a phone call from a client who wants to make an appointment, or who walks in for service, make it your formal procedure to take their name, address, and phone number.
- If someone calls to ask a question abut your services, ask them if they would like to be placed on your mailing list to receive a free report on how to guarantee they won't overpay on their taxes. Give potential clients an incentive to share their contact information with you. Send everyone who inquires about your business a special free-gift certificate for full service or partial service and tell them about it.
- Ask any callers inquiring about your services if they would like to receive a brochure to learn more about your business.

- Run contests for free services and products that require customers to fill out response cards. Another great way to build a mailing list of new clients quickly is to cross-promote. Find a cross-promotion partner who targets the same clients that you do, but is not an accountant or bookkeeper. You could match up with an attorney or insurance agent. Ask them to run a contest giving away a combination of services. You could offer free monthly service to three winners or a complete tax preparation for one lucky winner. You could easily obtain 150 to 400 names through your collective contest. Share all names and addresses gathered through the promotion with your partners. Send a special offer to participants on your list after the contest is over. You could realistically convert 50 to 100 of them into loyal clients using the right offer in a month.
- Install a "suggestions box" at your office. Capture the contact information of your clients. Always follow-up suggestions that clients submit to you with acknowledgment of your clients' ideas and a thank you note. This shows your desire to be responsive to the suggestion. And send a sincere thank you to your client for doing their part in making your service excellent. Hand-written notes work well.
- Offer to send free newsletters to your clients in exchange for their names, addresses, and phone numbers.
- Whenever clients hand you checks to pay for services, capture their contact information and put them on your mailing list. If they pay by credit card, make it your formal policy to ask them to write their name and address on the merchant slip they sign. Put this contact information in your database.
- Contact your local chamber of commerce to determine if your city has a mini-trade show for small businesses. Consider displaying it. If you participate in a trade show put a fishbowl at your display booth to capture the business cards of booth visitors. Remember you will have mostly business men and women in attendance. Ask your local Visitors & Convention Bureau for a listing of local trade shows. Consider displaying at trade shows to attract your target market. While displaying at a show, run a contest or give away free merchandise in exchange for throwing their business card in your fishbowl.

- Put a small sign on your front counter next to a business card fishbowl for clients to drop in their card to win free lunches at local restaurants.
- Swap lists with other cooperating businesses that target the same market as yours, yet who do not compete with you.

MORE CREATIVE USES FOR YOUR MAILING LIST

- Mail a gift certificate good for 10% to 25% off any of your services to prospects who have inquired of your services but have never purchased with you. Emphasize different aspects of your services and be sure to attach an expiration date for the certificate to persuade people to visit your business now.
- Clip articles from trade journals in your industry related to different services that you offer for clients who have purchased a similar service from you to confirm that they have made a good decision. Try to select articles that discuss the benefits of the services they like or other services they have taken an interest in. This requires you to remember and capture information about client interests in addition to contact information.
- Send a greeting card to every client on special days. Remember holidays, birthdays (usually can be captured with check ID), weddings, anniversaries, etc.
- Send a thank-you note after your staff performs services.
- Create a newsletter. Feature topics related to the hot interests of your clients. Don't be afraid to include lifestyle tips related to your primary market. Certain times of the year will suggest particular editorial. Your Winter/Spring issues can contain tax preparation ideas. Use your newsletter to position yourself as an expert in your local market.
- Send premium incentives to your best clients: clocks with your business name on them, tax planning kits, organization kits and systems, computer programs that make daily tasks easier, gift certificates for Daytimer products, etc. You can also send free article clippings that relate to the interests of your clients. I know an accountant who sends books in specific areas of interest to a hand-picked list of clients. He uses this to stay relevant to his clients. Make sure that the items you select match the image of your business and do not cheapen it.

- Consider sending 10% to 20% of your best clients a magazine subscription. You can contact appropriate magazines to obtain a group subscription rate. This may mean that you send 25 to 50 subscriptions as gifts. If you use this promotional idea, make sure you send a special letter and personalized gift certificate to them. Explain to each client that you are gifting him or her with a subscription because you value their business and you want to show how grateful you are for it. Tell them that you actually want to show your gratitude in a tangible way. Ask them to contact you when they receive their first issue to make sure the magazine was sent to them.

−75−

USING RADIO TO TARGET YOUR CLIENTS

Radio can be an excellent way to reach potential clients in your market. If you have not yet strategically determined the kind and caliber of clients you want to attract to your business, review our discussions in the first few chapters of this book dealing with the topic of strategy, positioning and client focus.

By clearly identifying your target market, you give yourself a tremendous advantage. You must figure out which radio shows your target market listens to and when they tune in. You must learn what kinds of radio programming your clients tend to be attracted to during drive times and in their spare time. Radio connects you to your target market using another one of their senses—hearing. Radio commercials enable you to use music, audio effects, testimonials and other unique devices to heighten listeners' emotional response to your message.

I like radio advertising for accountants and bookkeepers for another reason, a personal one. I know many accounting business owners who successfully barter with radio stations exchanging family and employee bookkeeping and tax services for radio ads. Radio stations also like to give friends special deals on remnant air time, air time that is reduced 40% to 60%, playing your commercials "run of the station," during unpurchased air time. This can give you up to 200% to 300% more coverage over normal advertising for the same cost. This may work well for your business. A little luck and moderate testing will confirm this for you.

Your radio commercials have the following marketing purposes: To bring new people from your target audience into your office or to influence them to call you for an appointment or remind past clients to revisit your business.

HOW TO CREATE AN EXCELLENT RADIO AD

Remember that your radio commercial has a beginning, middle, and an end. At the beginning of the commercial, use an opening that appeals to your target market. Use your USP (unique selling proposition) to guide you by centering the ad around your primary point of difference—the advantage that you give that no other competitor gives. The middle of your commercial can expand on the unique benefits and advantages your business offers that no other accounting service offers using benefit-rich, enticing detail with a special offer to take action. The middle portion of the ad could be used to give your best-reasoned advice in the form of an "Expertorial" ad giving tips on how to reduce the chances of an IRS audit. The ending of the commercial must contain a call to action — mention an extra bonus, give your location, give your phone number, and recommend a specific service the listener should hire you to obtain. Always mention your phone number at least 3 to 5 times throughout the commercial.

TWO KINDS OF BASIC, BUT POWERFUL, RADIO COMMERCIALS

1. New Client Commercials - These are designed to bring new clients into your business. The opening statement of this kind of radio commercial might be: "Paychecks Bookkeeping Service offers one free month of service to all new clients PLUS three free car washes at the "Car Detailer." We'll do your mundane tasks so you can concentrate in the important stuff in life."

2. Reminder Commercials - These commercials are designed to remind past clients to revisit your business. You could use this kind of an opening statement: (in an echoed male voice) "Dear Mom, I just returned from Paychecks Bookkeeping Service, I was so impressed with how well they took care of me that I just had to write. They helped me get my bills paid on time, gave me money-saving tax tips, and helped in so many ways... it kinda reminded me of being home again. Any way I just wanted to remind you go to the Paychecks Office near your home to get your tax returns done this season. Oh, and the danish and coffee were almost as good as yours." (warm female announcer's voice says:) "Paychecks Bookkeeping Service — you're home when you're with us."

TRY TESTING "EXPERTORIAL ADS" ON RADIO

I know a bookkeeping business owner in Texas who has been very successful in running radio commercials. One of the ways he attracts new clients to his business is by conducting a special kind of radio commercial I call an "Expertorial" commercial. His target market consists of entrepreneurs aged 25 to 45, who are starting up businesses. He runs radio commercials during key drive times—when his market is in their cars listening to their radios on a local business radio station. He spends 2-3 minutes giving his best-reasoned advice and tips entrepreneurs can use to save time and money in significant ways. All of the ideas relate to the services that he offers. The mini-show's format works well because he attracts young to middle-aged businesspeople, whether or not they are self-employed. He is perceived as an articulate expert. The radio station manages the commercial for him by producing all of the music and introductory material. The station-advertising manager calls him and records his radio commercial segments from his office right over the phone so the ad spots are not time-consuming for him to create at all. Best of all, 35% of his new clients come to him because of direct or indirect exposure to this radio commercial.

POWER POINTERS FOR YOUR RADIO COMMERCIALS

- Make sure that you choose the right radio station. Make sure that you have researched and found the stations with listener programming that matches your profile of target clients.
- Radio works better in combination with other media. Use it with other promotions that you are performing, such as direct mail. Or if you are holding a special event, use radio as a support to other media efforts.
- Remember that radio listeners are usually doing something else while listening to your commercials. They may be washing dishes, driving, or washing their cars. They are probably listening to your commercial with only one ear. This means that your sales message must be more simple and clear than through any other form of advertising. Clarity is vital because you have only a short time to catch your listener.
- Radio ads can be a good investment for your business' promotion effort. Short commercials can build name recognition in your community. Longer commercials give you time to tell your story. Fill your radio ad with exciting news and information about the advantages of your

accounting or bookkeeping business. A sixty-second ad is plenty of time to create a strong upscale presence.

- Study radio commercials of advertisers who are promoting products and services similar to yours. If your business targets males and females, aged 24 to 48, married and working, then find another business that also targets this market. Find out what radio stations they use — listen and study their ads. If you decide that their ads are sound, you can ask the radio station to piggyback your radio ads behind theirs. Test doing this against other possible times, and compare your results.
- Repetition is very important to the success of your radio ads. Find the best time slots to use to hit your target audience. Drive times - when a high concentration of people commute to or from work - tend to work well for most businesses. Saturday radio reminders can pull clients in at the last minute during tax season. You must reach potential clients an average of seven times (using different media) before their will respond to your advertising efforts. Once again, they may be busy in traffic, driving under a bridge, or be talking on a cellular phone during your ad.
- Feel free to barter with the radio station. In exchange for airtime offer free services or offer to buy lunch for the deejays in exchange for two mentions of your business per day on the air.
- Radio stations can create the ads for your business; however, if you create your own ads or hire a free-lance copywriter to create them, you will be entitled to a 15% agency discount.
- If you pay a high rate for drive-time commercials, make certain that you negotiate some free time. Insist that the station add-in extra commercial air time during off-hours.
- Sponsor contests, weather updates, news, or other updates on the radio station that reaches the bulk of your target audience. Sponsor a radio program on your local public radio station. You could even create a radio talk show that discusses topics related to bookkeeping, money or finances. Or you could conduct telephone interviews with guests from all over the country who are experts, authors, and consultants.
- Create a "media stir" with the live appeal of radio. Have a local radio station conduct a "live remote broadcast" from your office building offering give-a-ways.

- Once you have advertised with a radio station, and after you have tested your ad and you are confident about its success, offer to pay the station for remnant airtime, which is normally discounted unsold airtime. This way you receive more exposure for your business and the station recoups some money for otherwise unsold airtime.

RADIO COMMERCIAL POWER SUGGESTIONS

- You must obtain the attention of the listener within five to seven seconds or you will lose him or her for the duration of the commercial.
- Mention your business name five to seven times and your phone number at least three times during a 30-second commercial. If you don't, people probably won't connect your accounting or bookkeeping business to the commercial, or may think that you are another competitor.
- Develop a radio presence for your business. You want listeners to identify the ad as yours even if they do not hear the entire ad.
- Boil your radio-station selections down to one or two stations so that you can focus on saturating your market consistently without spreading your marketing budget too thin.
- Use distinctive voices, sounds, a variety of audio and musical textures that appeal to your target market and which capture the flavor of your service experience and your unique selling proposition.
- Do not refer your listeners to your yellow pages ad unless you have the largest ad in the category in which your advertisement appears.
- Ask your radio station to give you technical support to record your commercial for highest- quality results.

TESTING YOUR RADIO COMMERCIAL

Testing radio commercials is easy if you remember that to test anything you must use two versions of the same commercial, changing only one aspect of the ad and holding everything else the same. The most important aspect you should test is the first sentence of your radio commercial because this is the equivalent of the headline of the commercial.

Create two identical versions of your radio ad and change the first sentence to appeal to your target audience in a different way.

You might test statements of pleasure against statements of pain. For example, Radio Ad "A" may start off with: "When you thought about doing your own taxes this morning, did you feel a pang in the pit of your stomach?" Radio Ad "B" could be "Are you ready to feel the freedom of knowing that your taxes are completed and you have one less task to do this month?" Hold everything else in the commercial constant and test each one for a one- or-two week period to see which one receives the better response.

Your commercial must appropriately reach out and grab your target audience and give them a strong advantage or benefit.

QUICK TIPS FOR CREATING YOUR RADIO COMMERCIALS

- Repeat your business name constantly throughout the ad.
- Use simple straightforward sentences. See if an eight-year-old can understand your ad, if so, you're message is getting through clearly.
- If you offer your services at a special price, only mention one specific service item and one price offer.
- If your ad ends with a phone number, mention it at least three times and build up to it by saying something, such as, Get ready to write down this number..."
- Write out numbers so that radio announcers won't stumble when producing your commercial – "202 Happy Street" phonetically becomes "Two-oh-two Happy Street."
- If you are your own announcer or are doing an Expertorial Ad, pronounce "the" as "thee" before words starting with a vowel. Pronounce "the" as "thuh" before a word starting with a consonant.

-76-

BARTERING SERVICES TO LEVERAGE YOUR MARKETING POWER

B artering is a very effective way to leverage your total marketing power. If you think that advertising and other marketing expenses are available only for cash, think again. Your services are valuable enough for people to spend their hard-earned money on. In the same way, if offered in trade, they carry that same value.

And since your services are not something that most people walk out of your office with on a one-shot deal, your "payments" in the form of services through bartering can be automatically financed over a potentially long period of time—interest free. This frees up resources for other areas where cash is required such as your personal salary, administrative costs, and so on.

Another advantage to bartering is that, as a professional, you charge clients primarily for your time, rather than the actual cost of materials, so your "mark-up" is based only on administrative expenses (e.g. office space, staff salaries, and other current expenses). Five hundred dollars of your service may cost you only $150 in actual cash lay out. So in effect you are purchasing $500 dollars in advertising for only $150. Compound this discount with the normal situation where your service is not requested until weeks or months later and you have created a situation of marketing leverage where you gain a tremendous long-term financial advantage while reaping the short-term benefit you need.

Think of barter as a real alternative to cash and credit purchases, not just for marketing efforts, but for other purchases that could pinch your cash flow.

WHAT ARE THE BASICS OF CREATIVE BARTERING?

You can barter to purchase anything you would normally buy for cash. If you present seminars as part of your marketing plan, offer to trade your services for seminar space. If you do not want to personally perform the work with which you have bartered, divert the job to an associate or employee. Let's say you employ an accountant who costs you $20 an hour and your firm's billing rate is $200 an hour. If you trade $20-an-hour accounting services for a $200 ad, you've bought that asset for one-tenth of its market value. Moreover, you finance it interest-free over perhaps a year, while reaping the benefits right away.

You could take it one step further. If the vendor you are seeking to exchange services with does not want your services directly, suggest triangulation. In other words, go to a radio station with the intent of purchasing $5,000 in advertising and offer $5,000 worth of your services. If they do not want the service themselves, suggest that they package it into a promotion to be offered to somebody who buys $5000 worth of advertising. They benefit in that way.

It is unorthodox, but it provides a way for the ultimate user to benefit. If he cannot benefit himself, show him how to sell it, trade it, and package it to a third party. If you can help him find a way to profit from your services, he may be happy to exchange.

You can also barter for other items and services in addition to those related to your marketing plan. Go to a car dealer and offer to trade the car dealer $20,000 worth of prepaid services to his employees for a car. If he had to give employees raises, he'd have to pay for them in cash. You can offer your services at your full rate.

In bartering, it's critically important to recognize somebody's margin. If you went to a car dealer and wanted to trade credits for professional accounting services for a car, it may not be so appealing because they don't work on the margin. A $20,000 car probably costs the dealer $15,000. The way to make it work is to say, "I'll give you one-and-a-half times the value of the car in my credits."

It is very important that you know your real margins, your real cost to render a dollar's worth of service. If rendering a dollar's worth of service costs you twenty-five cents and you trade that for something you'd normally buy for cash, you are still making seventy-five cents on the dollar.

As long as you understand this, you have unlimited potential. Of course, barter agreements assume that your practice is not being used to capacity. If your practice is saturated to capacity, then you would be giving up real money. But up to the point where you would become saturated or where you can take an associate into your practice, whenever you obtain something in trade that costs you less than a dollar, trade it for something else that's worth a dollar.

Go to the printer, to radio stations, to newspapers, to local magazines, to anybody who can provide advertising exposure to reach the desired market, whether it is business people or the masses. Explain to your target that you are willing to exchange your professional services at retail for their product or service at retail.

This is how it works. You want to place an ad in the local newspaper that would cost $2000. You get your ad right away and issue a credit that the newspaper can use forever. The later they use the credit, the less it really costs you to fulfill. The $2000 worth of your time today is worth more than $2000 of your time a year from now after inflation and when your rates have increased.

If the credit as issued specifies a dollar value (as it should) and no time constraints the recipient won't be eager to use it right away. You have made your purchase with soft dollars. What does it cost you as a service provider to render the service to pay for your past purchase? You could answer - nothing. Whatever the cost, you're buying it at a discount over cash, financed interest-free for as long as it takes them to use the credit, while you receive the benefit of the advertisement, the mailing or the radio advertising immediately.

The following is an application of barter: Make an offer to other owners of a big office complex or to a big company that owns perhaps half the building and has employees on site. Offer to trade your services to the employees in exchange for office space.

The company can offer this benefit as a perk or in lieu of raises. If average $100 raises are due next month, that could translate to a $1200 expense per employee over the course of a year. Offer to give each employee a $600 credit with you to provide service. In exchange, you obtain $600 rent credit for every employee.

You may be able to trade service for office space you don't want.

If you trade a $50 visit (that costs you $10) for $50 worth of rent, you can rent to a third party for $40. You're taking something that costs you $10 and making 300% profit, while your renter enjoys a 20% discount. You can trade for all sorts of things whether you want them or not; you can always sell them off to somebody else. You could have a practice built on trade and still make a fortune. You may never see a dime in cash come from clients. All your income could come from the way you dispose of assets you have traded services for. You are only limited by your imagination and ingenuity.

-77-

USING YOUR BUSINESS CARD
AS A PROMOTION TOOL

You should use inexpensive business cards to separate your accounting or bookkeeping business from the rest of your competitors in the market. Your business card can become a powerful tool for promotion if you think about how to use it to attract people's attention and give advantage-rich information about how your service is competitively different.

Your business card should at minimum include your name, the name of your business, your office address, phone number, fax number, and your unique selling proposition (USP). Your business card version of your USP should be an encapsulated statement of the primary advantage you offer that no other competitor offers. If you communicate the advantages and distinctive benefits that you give in a powerful and sharp manner on your business card, this will help your clients understand what makes you stand out. You'll be giving your clients a powerful marketing tool, not only for understanding your point-of-difference, but also for increasing their ability to help you generate referrals.

Consider putting your personal phone number on your business card to establish a personal service touch. This will separate you from everyone else. If you are afraid to try this, you can add an extra personal phone line in your home for this purpose so that you can still maintain some anonymity and security while reaching out in a unique way to your clientele.

Never skimp or cut corners when producing your business card. Use the best paper you can afford, and make sure that the quality of the card is consistent with that of your business. Make sure that colors match your office decor, paper textures are attractive, that the ink color can be read quickly on the card stock you have chosen, etc. You will obtain the most attention with a full-color business card with your photograph and logo on it. Hire the best graphic designer available in your area. If you rely solely on your local printer for design, you may end up with a card design that is less than desirable.

Use your business card as if it is a mini-billboard. You can use the back of the card for a very small extra charge and provide a wealth of information about the benefits, and advantages you provide. You may want to put a reminder checklist of items to bring to your office to facilitate smooth federal-tax filing. Use persuasive copy on your business cards. Think of your business card as a mini advertisement. Your aim is to have the people who read it to call you for an appointment.

INFORMATION THAT YOU CAN INCLUDE ON YOUR BUSINESS CARD

- Your unique selling proposition (USP) - a description of the prime benefit your business gives clients.
- Your list of specialized service benefits and corresponding advantages.
- Details of the unique advantages you give your market over an above those associated with your services (i.e. you give your clients tickets to local sporting events).
- A map to your door - your location and how to get there.
- Provide lists of toll-free numbers for local or national information services your market is interested in (i.e. travel information, weather advisory services, emergency services, etc.).
- Put a one-year calendar on one side to ensure that clients will keep your card throughout the year.
- Profile of key employees and their expertise. Or you could create an Infocard or a multi-panel card for each of your staff members along with their photos, lists of their interests, and fun ideas that appeal to your market.
- Include testimonials of clients who have been successful in some key way because of your efforts. Tell their success stories.
- Tell the story of your business in a few words. If you have a dramatic history or a heartwarming story about why you went into your business, share the story. Explain how your business grew. Share your overall philosophy describing your love for clients and your business.
- Provide a list of titles of the free factsheets available at your office.
- Show a photograph of you and your staff working with clients.

- Put an offer for a free service on the back of the card, and be sure to tell people about it when distributing the cards.

Turn your business card into a frequent-visitor card. You can design it so that there is a place to punch the card. Or you can use your business card to offer other special discounts. A successful accounting firm I know gives a 15% discount to anyone presenting a business card at the front desk. This makes the business card valuable to all clients.

−78−

USE VIDEO BROCHURES TO DRAW ATTENTION TO YOUR BUSINESS

Videocassettes provide a low cost way of communicating with your local market. Video brochures can often be produced for a very low product cost, if using a small, but competent production firm. Creating a video brochure for your business is more fun and often easier than most people realize, as long as you choose a creative local video-production company to help you capture the advantages that your business offers on video.

I suggest that you consider creating one basic promotional video that tells your company story. You may also wish to make a series of 15- to 30-minute videos that give a video-seminar on special topics that are of considerable interest to your market. You could create them on valuable educational topics, such as:

- "How To Survive Or Avoid An Audit: Your Step-By-Step Guide"
- "How To Reduce Your Overhead If You Own A Small Business"
- "How To Retire With A Pension That Is 25% Bigger Than It Otherwise Would Be"
- "How To Organize Your Total Financial Portfolio"

The key is to present yourself and your firm as an authority on the topics that you are covering. If you make the video topic a hot, highly valuable and much sought-after one, then people will associate the expertise that you provide on the video with your business. The educational video approach is self-serving to the client and usually is better than a dull video that showcases desks, computers and an office full of stuffed shirts telling them about a bunch of boring services that are being offered.

Interestingly, you don't even have to create your materials yourself. You can license the ideas and information of local, regional or national speakers. The local chapter of the National Speakers' Association (NSA) will be able to provide you with many people who may be willing to license and present material for you on your videos. You can visit the NSA web site at www.nsa.org.

One of the best advantages of using video is the long shelf life and high pass-a-long value of a well-produced video-seminar. People will refer to the information multiple times if it is valuable enough to them. Many public libraries, college research centers, university libraries and small business associations will keep your information-rich video seminars in their collections for the public to borrow Consider giving your videos to these powerful information dissemination centers to use in their lending libraries. You can offer free videos at your web site to anyone who asks. You can offer them at free community seminars. If you are giving a seminar at your local small business development council center to 30 small businesses, then you are in a prime position to offer your video on start-up financing resources, perhaps entitled, "Getting The Money Your Need To Succeed."

Your video should give a rich amount of valuable information as promised by the title of the video. And you should also spend a small amount of time selling your services. Use the last few minutes of the video to talk about your unique selling proposition (USP). It should reveal the core value that your business offers to your clients. The trick is to create powerful images of the most tangible benefits that your business provides. When people watch your videos, they have to feel it emotionally. The impact of your message has to grab them instantly to the point that they truly desire the value that you give.

The advantage that a video gives your business is that it can position your business as the prime source of information on the topic in your local market. This gives you a distinct advantage over using only a printed brochure. If you have just expanded your service and your facility to offer higher-end services, or plan to, consider using the video brochure to inform a select group of high-end clients about the higher-level experience they will have at your facilities when they visit.

The cost of duplicating short videocassettes, about 15-minutes in duration, from a master copy is approximately $2-$3 per tape. Usually the cost per tape is the same regardless of how many copies you purchase. So once you have master tape, you can pick up the phone and order as few or as many videocassettes as you like. You can keep your duplication costs low by ordering a few at a time, and give them to select clients and local leaders, then expand the distribution of the tapes as you need to. Locally, you can produce a good quality video for approximately $100 to $1,000 per minute depending upon which video production company you use. But if you use some of the production footage for your commercials, you can re-edit for both purposes. Make sure that your local production company is willing to work with you to produce both at the same time to save you money. About 85% of your market probably has access to a VCR, therefore you can be assured that when you send video tapes to people in your market, most will be able to view them.

Make sure your video is not so professionally over-produced that it contrasts with your target market. Make certain that the essence of your empathy for your clients clearly comes through on tape in addition to the information on the video. Put as much warmth into the videos as possible. Talk to viewers as you would your best friend, always giving your best professional advice. Talk one-on-one and feel the emotions you are stirring in your viewers as you speak during tapings.

You can offer your videos free through your ads—direct mail, local magazine and newspaper ads, local publicity, etc. Give them to local video stores to rent out as free public service videos. Give them to pubic and private libraries, and to the local association chapter office' lending libraries. Consider ending your video with a short tour of your office and testimonials from actual clients depicting what you have done for them. Remember that you add tremendous value for the viewer by helping the people in your target market attain their primary goals.

−79−

USE BANNERS AND SIGNS
TO PULL TRAFFIC TO YOUR BUSINESS

Your accounting or bookkeeping business can benefit tremendously by using banners and signs to attract attention to your offices, which in turn will generate a higher volume of walk-in traffic.

Several months ago, I was driving on a crowded Los Angeles freeway and I noticed the scope and volume of businesses that had turned large portions of the city's buildings into billboards by displaying huge banners on windows and ledges of the tall structures. I was astounded by all of the different types of businesses using them. I saw insurance agencies, hair salons, accounting firms, cellular phone-service companies, and many other types of businesses using the banners.

Some businesses located along freeways in large US cities can have as many as 25,000 to 60,000 cars drive by their buildings per day. This is a large captive audience. Most of the banners had the name of the company, the product, or a service coupled with an offer to call a phone number for more information. One of the purposes of the banners and signs was clearly to influence car passengers to pick up their cellular phones to schedule appointments.

If your office is set in a prime location, try this idea. Ask your retail leasing agent or landlord for permission to put a large banner on your office building. Call the Highway Commission of your state and ask them for average traffic counts on all of the streets and highways your building faces. Use the information on the "average number of cars per day" to decide if the roads near your office have enough consistent traffic to warrant the extra effort. Most accounting businesses in prime locations find banners to be very helpful in increasing business. If your building faces one main highway, all the better, because your banner's exposure to traffic will be extremely high. Smart marketers use the large banners and flags, or other attention-getting items, to attract passers-by and draw them in. If you are opening a new office, use the banners and signs to tell people about your grand opening and the benefits you are offering. Use your graphics and no more than a three or four-word special offer to spark interest in your services. Consider putting your web site address and your telephone number on your banner to make it easy for people to contact you.

In the chapter about using point-of-purchase (POP) displays, we talked about using VisionQuest Display Holders to put banners on your sidewalk or in front of your door to lead people to your office. This is a great option for foot traffic and other smaller banner applications.

QUICK TIPS FOR USING SIGNS AND BANNERS

- Keep your message short and to the point. Try to encapsulate your entire message in a few words. Always remember to include the name of your business and contact information.
- Make a sign that you feel proud of displaying. Make sure it is one that ties into your entire marketing effort, your USP and image building strategy.
- Use lights and flags on signs and banners.
- Make sure that your signs and banners are mistake-free. Proofread carefully. Typos will turn off everyone who reads your sign. Such errors often make your business seem like a budget enterprise.

Consider using multicolored flags or renting a searchlight after dark for special events you hold at your offices. People love to hunt down these stimulating devices.

If your office is located on a busy street, consider using "messaging signs." Use signs that allow you to change your message everyday. People driving by become accustomed to seeing messages and will look forward to reading them. This can be a great way to bond with potential clients - draw them into your offices with your clever or unique messages.

–80–

USING POSTER POWER
IN YOUR MARKETING

Full-color posters can pack a "wallop" to your promotional punch. Marketers of successful bookkeeping businesses have tested the use of posters and many like them because they look more like art than advertising. The best part is that computer technology has made posters very inexpensive for marketers. And you can make up a few dozen posters for a very low cost.

You can use posters in a variety of ways. We have discovered that the best way to use them is through cross-promotion. Find one or more good business cross-promotion partners who are willing to promote your business to their clients as you promote their business to your clients. Try to partner with a business who targets the same kind of market you do, but one that doesn't compete with you directly. The best cross-promotion partners for accounting firms will be attorneys, marketing consultants, small banks, business services firms, and any other business that shares your specific kind of clients. Agree to put posters and other promotional materials inside each other's office locations. If you choose an attorney as your cross-promotion partner, put a very large poster, highlighting the expertise of their team, with their pictures in your waiting area. In exchange, they can put a large poster that promotes your accounting services in their waiting area. Create an offer on the poster to give people a reason to call or visit each of you. Each partner should also cooperate by giving each other's business cards out to clients. This is instant cross-promotion. Agree to do this for a month to test your compatibility with your partners. Perhaps you can build a team of cross-promotional partners throughout your community who agree to help you promote your business throughout the year in unique ways.

CREATIVE WAYS TO USE POSTERS TO MARKET YOUR BUSINESS

- Hang the posters on the walls of your Business and use them as visual demonstrations of the benefits you offer. Your poster will create a sense of excitement.
- Hang posters on poster boards in your city to announce your grand opening, Christmas party, or other public events you sponsor.
- Consider making up calendars because they are like monthly posters advertising your business. Send them to small business owners and others who will hang them in places where others will see them. Remember: The theme of the poster must be related to the prime advantage (USP) that your business offers.
- Use a small poster as a freestanding insert in your local newspaper or magazine.
- Two nevers: Never mail a poster unless you use a mailing tube. And never create a poster unless you commit to doing it in at least two colors, preferably in vibrant colors.

If you decide to produce a large quantity of posters, use a conventional printer. Once you pay for the negatives, the posters should cost you as little as 25¢ per poster. Larger quantities of 5000+ can reduce costs even more.

–81–

USE DIRECT MAIL AND POSTCARDS TO BRING IN MORE CLIENTS

Direct mail can be a very powerful tool for promoting your accounting and bookkeeping business. It is an incredibly powerful means for you to follow-up with clients with whom you have had initial contact. By thinking "outside of the box" you soon begin to realize that you have permission to play your version of the business marketing-game any way that you choose. This is especially true and most evident in the way you use direct mail to promote your business. Mailings offers you so much flexibility and diversity because you can target people directly. When you send a full-blown letter, a brochure, or a response card that people send back to you, you may not get everyone to read it. However, you will influence enough of the right people to respond. Many will call you for more information or to respond to your offer for a free consultation, or whatever else you are offering.

One of the most powerful mailings that you can create requires sending a postcard making a special statement about your service attempting to persuade your past and potential clients to contact you. You can use a "tent postcard," which are two postcards connected by perforations. One of the postcard sides makes a proposition, the other is to be torn off, filled in with name, address, and other pertinent information and mailed back to you "postage paid." You can create a self-mailer or self-contained single proposition mailing with no envelope covering it. Whether you choose a single postcard or a four-page brochure to promote your business, you can create a very rich, high-profile sales presentation if that is what you think your market will respond to—otherwise, you can scale it down. Show it to as many potential clients as possible to gauge their reaction before mailing out a large number of postcards.

The cost of creating full-color printed material is very competitive, and the cost of full-color printing is not that much more of an investment. For the investment of a few extra pennies per postcard, a richer looking full-color postcard highlighting your business will give you more of an upscale image.

> HOT TIP: One of the best uses for a postcard promotion is to put three power-packed elements on it. First, you need an arresting, irresistible headline in a bright contrasting color. Some of the best headlines include: "Stop Overpaying Taxes Now!" or "Reduce Your Expenses, Increase Your Spendable Income... We'll Show You How. Guaranteed!" Or "Our Advice is FREE!" Second, You need to have a full-color picture that connects emotionally with your market. If you are attracting homebased business owners consider using a picture of a home-business owner inundated with bills (there are many stock-photo houses you can use, i.e. www.photodisc.com). Third, you must influence your recipients to take action. I feel that one of the best actions that you can suggest on the postcard is to call or have clients visit your web site for more information on a specific offer you are extending. For example, "Come to our web site www.taxsolutions.com for a free report or plan that shows you how to instantly stop overpaying taxes."

I know of a prominent accountant whose business was built using direct mail. You can follow her example. She obtained a mailing list from a magazine, a local business journal, which targeted small business people in her local market. She knew that readers of the journal had a greater chance of being attracted to their services. All she did was send very rich looking, four-color, postcards offering recipients a wonderful benefit, and a bonus if they would bring the card into her office. The promotion was very successful.

Another accountant was very inventive in his approach to growing his business. I shared with him how much more business he could be doing using direct mail. He really surprised me when he took the simplest application and parlayed a $650 investment into $36,000 of extra business in 9 months.

How did he do it? He took his new service, summarized it on the front of a postcard, and made an irresistible offer. He obtained new clients at break-even—at his cost—just to entice clients into the buying stream of the service. He sent a postcard to clearly communicate his offer. He identified one thousand clients earning over $50,000 per year who were in closest proximity to his office. He made one very powerful and very simple offer on the back of the postcard, and 75 people responded to the first mailing. He reused the postcard five more times and earned thousands of extra dollars from this effort, all from an initial $650 investment.

Does this give you any fresh ideas? I am sure you have received more than one subscription offer for a business magazine. Have you ever felt compelled to respond to it? The magazine usually gives you lots of reasons why you need to subscribe to it. You are told all about the benefits received from reading the articles. They attempt to place you in the position of what it would be like in your life or business after you subscribe, then they make you an irresistible offer. All the magazine marketers requires is that you take the simple action of returning the card without sending any money with it, or they request that you pick up the phone and call an 800 number to order it. I am willing to bet that you have subscribed to more than one magazine this way. Am I right? Ask yourself why you decided to subscribe.

You can test the same tactics and strategies on a small scale. When you obtain the desired response rate—one that yields a profit—roll it out on a larger scale. The biggest factors influencing the success of your mailing will be: the quality of your mailing list, the headline, your offer, the presence of an action statement and the design impact of the piece to get enough attention to be read. Most other factors are subordinate to those just listed.

THE BEST AND LOWEST PRICED RESOURCE FOR PRINTING POSTCARDS:

1-800 Postcards
50 West 23rd Street-6th Floor
New York, NY 10010
1-800-POSTCARDS Toll-free
212-271-5505 X600 Phone
212-271-5506 Fax
www.1800POSTCARDS.com

–82–

PROMOTE YOUR BUSINESS TO NEWCOMERS IN YOUR AREA

Did you realize that there is a tremendous opportunity for you to build loyal clients in your local market by targeting people who have recently moved into your city? There are hundreds, possibly thousands, of people moving into your area every one month who are potential clients for you. If you have ever relocated to a new area, you will instantly recognize the opportunity for your business, because you will remember how strange and unfamiliar everything seemed to you at first. Your marketing opportunity lies in your ability to make newcomers feel welcome and at home in your neighborhood.

When people move to a new area they do not always have contacts for the special services they need. Many times they will rely on the advice and opinions of neighbors, friends and relatives because they have nowhere else to turn. Your city hostess or welcome wagon provides a referral service to newcomers who want to learn about businesses existing in their new location. Welcome committees will offer free packages, gift certificates and samples to newcomers. You might want to create a $30 to $40 tax-service package to be given at a reduced cost to newcomers through your local city hostess. New residents will appreciate your special offers. About one-quarter to one-third of them will become loyal customers for your investment of time and energy. It will be well worth your time test marketing this idea in your local area.

HOT TIP: I know one exceptionally astute accountant who obtains a list of newcomers from his local city hostess. He segments this list geodemographically. This means that he compares the list of newcomers to demographic information—ages and incomes mostly—and then filters that information by zip code. He sends the best token gifts he can afford as "welcome presents" to a small critical mass of newcomers whose neighborhoods closely match the geodemographic profile of his best clients. He sends his best prospects items, such as, Godiva Chocolates and fruit baskets with offers for reduced cost accounting services. To prospects that do not match his criteria, i.e. people in lower income areas, he sends postcards and less costly items. (See session in this book on analyzing your geographic marketing for additional ideas)

If you want to connect with newcomers in your area, consider having your local city hostess personally provide a gift certificate to newcomers with a special offer (i.e. half off specific services; visit your office for a special gift, etc). You can require the newcomer to fill out a postage-paid request card that the hostess mails back to you. By doing this, you will accumulate a prequalified list of names and addresses of those most interested in your service. You can mail several reminders to them to visit you in the months ahead.

You could also create your own special direct promotion to newcomers in lieu of using your city hostess. Think about the main organizations in your area that relocate the most employees in your city—businesses, schools, institutions. Your city may have a high population of college students and that may be the key factor that draws new residents. Your town may have a high number of new homeowners or renters who have relocated to your neighborhood because certain industries or new large corporations have increased employment opportunities.

If you are not informed about new resident trends, you can call your local Chamber of Commerce, Economic Development Council, Small Business Development Council (SBDC), or Senior Core of Retired Executives (SCORE) and discover the pertinent local trends. This information helps you tap into this aspect of your market. All of these help centers are listed in your local phone book.

Once you have figured out what is bringing newcomers into your area, your next step is to find and target the specific individuals. To do this, as I mentioned above, you can contact your city hostess or find a mailing-list broker in your city who specializes in newcomer lists.

Another way to target new residents in your neighborhood is with direct mail. It is a great "blanket strategy." One of the best ways to obtain a mailing list of new residents is to find a local mailing-list broker specializing in newcomers, which can usually be found in your local yellow pages. Your aim is to find several experts providing lists of new local residents. Before you call the list broker, create a clear profile of whom you want to target— perhaps by looking at incomes and the kind of neighborhood dwellings that matches your clients.

You may decide that your primary target market of new residences may very well be in the areas that are closest to your office. You may want to drive around your area and become familiar with the residences and zip codes matching your best clients. The more you know about the specific geographic areas that you want to target by zip code, the better off you will be when you talk to a list broker. You will then be able to check the accuracy of the information he or she gives you and make better decisions with greater confidence. Network with other noncompetitive business owners who are targeting the same market that you are, and ask them about their experiences with these clients. I recommend that you find three or four list brokers, purchase a "test quantity" of a few hundred names from each one, and perform a test mailing, perhaps by including a welcome letter and gift certificate. If you find that one list out-performs the others by a significant factor, rest assured that the lesser performing lists are seeded with older names.

Take some time right now to open your local phone book and begin making contacts with all of the organizations I have mentioned above. Consider calling your city hall and ask for the number of your city hostess. You should use your yellow pages to locate at least one good newcomer list broker. Consider begin sending gift certificates, postcards or letters to newcomers in your market with a compelling incentive to call of visit you. Always test all of your offers on a small scale first.

-83-

USE "ON-HOLD" MARKETING TO PROMOTE YOUR SERVICES

If you're like most people, you probably really hate being put on hold when you call a business for an appointment. Most clients who are put on hold for too long feel that they aren't being respected and that their time is being wasted. Some entrepreneurs contend that they are so busy that they have no other choice. Studies have proven that people will wait longer on hold if pleasant music is played.

The Ritz Carlton Hotel in Boston, Massachusetts has won awards for excellent service. When they train their employees, they tell them that if customers complain about being put on hold for more than 15 seconds, the employees will be reprimanded. The reason for this is that the hotel knows that even the slightest bit of suffering a client endures—in the form of an employee lacking empathy by ignoring the client for a few extra seconds—is so disrespectful that it is unforgivable. They insist that if their employees put a client on hold for more than 15 seconds, they are to apologize for the inconvenience, take the client's name and phone number, and promise to call them back within 5 minutes. Employees follow through by calling the client back with a solution to their problem. After the problem is resolved, the employee calls back to confirm that the guest is completely satisfied. Take a lesson from the Ritz Carlton and restructure the way you treat your clients on the telephone.

You may be wondering how you can effectively handle the phone that is constantly ringing off the hook. If you don't already have one consider hiring a receptionist to greet clients and make them feel comfortable. They can also offer clients refreshing drinks as they arrive and keep them occupied, making their waiting time a pleasurable experience. A host or hostess can add that extra warm and pleasurable touch. They can handle all of your scheduling for call-in appointments. In the event that your phone lines are tied-up, I suggest that you keep clients on hold for no more than 15- to 45-seconds. And when they are on hold, use a combination of music and messages that are appealing.

You should have a periodic business consultation with your local phone company to determine how many phone lines you need to handle the volume of calls that you receive.

ON-HOLD MARKETING SUGGESTIONS

- Choose a type of music that is compatible with the image that you are trying to create (see USP). Perhaps you will play relaxing instrumental music intermixed with the gentle voice of an announcer giving suggestions and descriptions about certain kinds of services that you offer.
- Consider using companies that specialize in helping your business create an appropriate image. Muzak and AEI can provide you with customized recordings and equipment that can provide music for your telephone system.
- Interrupt the music once in a while (not too often) with a voice telling clients that someone will be right with them so that they won't hang up. Try to break up the time on hold to keep clients distracted.
- Use a five-minute endless-loop tape to give listeners specific information about special-needs areas (review session on Take One Technologies). Give them tips to show them how much you empathize with them and their problems. Tell them how to best use the services that you sell.

–84–

USE PUBLICITY POWER TO SPREAD NEWS ABOUT YOUR BUSINESS

I define publicity, for our purposes, as editorial mention that highlights you or your accounting business in some significant way. The coverage is not paid for and may appear in local, regional and/or national media. The most important aspect of publicity is that you must take initiative to generate it in most cases. The media rarely comes to you seeking to do an article about your specialized expertise unless an editor or producer hears about you through your own publicity efforts. Those with a wise, but more aggressive strategy tend to get more of the best ink and airtime consistently.

I know a bookkeeping service that successfully used publicity in a unique way. The firm put out a great publicity release, in which they talked about the changing climate for out-sourcing accounting services and they helped readers to understand the advantages and the cost-effectiveness. They are leaders in their field nationally. The publicity release got picked up by 30 different business publications and the firm gained over 100 new clients in the process.

I know a highly successful tax attorney. He started writing articles in trade columns 30 years ago. Each and every month he writes a column which has been picked up in over 90 individual trade and business publications throughout the globe on a specialized tax-subject related to estate planning. His expertise involves the transfer of ownership of a privately owned business from the owner to their children, their heirs, or their employees with the lowest possible tax consequences. He has written articles each month for 30 years. As a result, his firm went from a nondescript, little-known entity that was ranked about 12,000[th] in the nation to the number 33 largest private accounting firm in the United States. His success is primarily attributed to the familiarity and prominence achieved through the publicity his written articles has earned for him.

Publicity provides two wonderful and consistent benefits for your accounting business. First, it gives you a powerful, and highly credible, objective message vehicle with which to attract attention. Second, it is a low-cost way of reaching infinitely more people.

In planning your publicity strategy, you will primarily be appealing to editors and media people who are interested in the information needs of their readers and audience members. The audience members are, of course, primarily interested in things that benefit them. This is the self-serving basis of human nature that you must catering to in your news releases.

Your aim is to convert your specialized knowledge into specific information bulletins that the audience uses to make or save money in some significant way. You will send that information to all of the media sources that people in your target market are exposed to. This will significantly promote your business.

If you're not already aware of it, one of the most valuable tools you will use in your marketing arsenal is your publicity release. I know many professionals who send 650- to 1200-word articles to media sources in their field each month. Some of the media sources will publish the articles on a one-time basis. Some of the editors request a continuous supply of articles from the professionals.

Let's look at your initial options for developing publicity for your business in your local market. You must begin boldly by sending regular press releases to the formal local press. This includes newspapers, magazines, trade magazines, specialty publications, radio stations, television stations, cable channels covering local news, and public broadcasting media. You should also send your press releases to trade organizations. This includes associations, such as trade publications that influence business-related industries in or beyond your local area. Your press releases should also be sent to all kinds of local civic or community organizations. Your publicity efforts simply keep important people informed about the significant accomplishments of your resulting professional expertise and experience.

Obtaining consistent publicity requires developing an awareness of where the best public relations opportunities reside and then placing your name and the name of your firm in the midst of those happenings. It also means committing yourself to doing public service and associating yourself with the causes of good charitable organizations.

One of my clients, for example, created two local golf tournaments with the Make-a-Wish foundation. A local cable news source picked up the story and gave them a full five minutes of coverage, which aired on the local CNN Headline News for weeks in the local market. Needless to say, my client was literally the talk of the town for months after the story appeared on TV.

Never hesitate to become involved in recreational, social, and charitable activities and use your involvement to leverage publicity for your business.

You have at your disposal numerous traditional and nontraditional ways of obtaining publicity. You may discover one or more areas of hidden opportunity by taking a moment to develop your own extensive answers to the following questions:

- How can I extend my business deeper into the community by creating a cause larger than my business that will connect well to my business efforts and promote that cause?
- How can I provide increased advantages, education, news or special little-known information through the press and obtain attention for my accounting business?
- What important public service issues can I research to make special information available to local media contacts? For example, information about Internet scams, changes in tax laws that are vital to consumers, information about trends to watch out for during an IRS audit, etc.

You will gain a tremendous bonus when you become involved in local community charities, or recreational activities through your involvement on media-relations committees. There you will make precious contacts with valuable players in your local media, with whom you will reconnect after the event is over to promote your business. Doors will open to you perhaps for late-breaking local news interviews, or writing newspaper articles, in the event that the local media will be covering a story in your field of expertise.

I know of one accountant who used his post-event contacts with a local upscale magazine to suggest that the editor feature his newly built dream home in the magazine, if she ever needed extra editorial material. The editor was in need of additional story ideas and did the story the same week that he initially contacted her. The pictures and articles had nothing to do with his accounting expertise, but the status of the panache publication and his fancy luxury home positioned him as one of the most successful young entrepreneurs in his community.

Becoming connected with local organizations as a committee volunteer and helping with upcoming events is a great way to begin creating a winning public relations strategy. Your local Chamber of Commerce and Board of Trade can give you information on every business and civic group VIP in your area. Simply obtain a listing of the organizations, select one, and volunteer to use your new skills to create a budget, add value to a committee, or promote an event. Network as you go, and soon you will have a long list of powerful media connections and other influential contacts.

Through your community involvement, your life touches the lives of others and this can be a very fulfilling experience. You'll receive feedback of what others think of you, and most of the time this is an overwhelmingly positive experience. Have fun expanding your business by making more high-quality contacts with your local media.

−85−

USE A PUBLICITY KIT TO MULTIPLY YOUR PUBLICITY POWER

During the course of your career you will undoubtedly create some very special and interesting news and events that will warrant your efforts to obtain local publicity. Perhaps you will run special events, speak at local business association meetings, perhaps work with local charities, or develop unique new business approaches. When you do anything that is newsworthy, send out a release and slant the publicity in favor of your business.

The vehicle you must use to inform the local media about your most newsworthy activities is in the form of your publicity kit. Your publicity kit consists of

- A Cover Letter
- Suggested Copy Or An Article
- A Black & White Glossy Photo
- An Envelope
- Postage Or Other Delivery Method (I.E. Fed-Ex)

Sending your publicity kit to the media will provide you with a great deal of exposure. I suggest that an updated version of your publicity kit be distributed to your local media at least once per quarter. You can generate all of the documents on your computer, print them on your laser printer and mail them out yourself. Let's look at all of the documents which should be included in order to create and arrange a successful publicity kit.

I have created countless successful national and international publicity campaigns for clients and myself. I write regular magazine columns for many international publications for various industries, all of which arose as a result of my publicity efforts. I have been fortunate enough to have received editorial mention over the years in publications such as Woman's Day, Natural Health Magazine, Teen Beat Magazine, Potentials In Marketing and hundreds of other well-known magazines. I am very proud to say that my collective efforts have created editorial that has reached tens of millions of readers. I did all of this with a simple publicity formula that anyone can create in a few hours. So can you. Significant local publicity can be obtained by making a little extra effort to present your publicity kit to the media.

Throughout this chapter I will create a sample publicity kit for an accounting and bookkeeping business that you can use a model.

STEP ONE:

Write your cover letter. Your cover letter should be addressed to the specific editor that you want to appeal to. You must quickly and briefly introduce the purpose for sending the publicity. You must instantly compel that editor to run a story about the information you are presenting, therefore it must be highly relevant to the audience of the media source. Telling the editor that you have been thinking about his or her readers and that you have exclusive information that will save or make them money, reduce their time, or raise a highly interesting issue. You must create a story idea that the editor wants to instantly run in his newspaper, magazine or that a producer will air.

If you are sending hundreds of publicity kits, I suggest "mail merging" a customized sentence into the last paragraph of the cover letter from a database program that tells the editor exactly why readers of his specific magazine will benefit from running your story. I always customized the last paragraph of the letter to focus on sharing the benefits of the information I am offering to the audience of that specific publication. Write it to slant the letter in favor of audience of the media source you're sending to.

STEP TWO:

Write your news release. This is a printed story on plain paper. It should have a compelling headline and consist of 100 to 150 words of descriptive copy (it can be longer if you are submitting an article), and double-spaced. Include the release date, your name, and your contact information at the top of the page. Read different articles that highlight accounting businesses and special interests topics related to your market in trade journals and newspapers, and think about why they were selected for publication. You will discover that most of the "news stories" you read usually emanate from publicity releases.

When writing your news release, use the "Five W's" to jog your thinking:

- Who are you talking to?
- What is the specific advantage that you are giving to the readers?
- When is your newsworthy item or special event occurring?
- Where is your event being held or where is your business located?
- Why are you sharing this information with the reader? Discuss the newsworthiness of the piece.

Remember to use the inverted pyramid when you write your release: put the most important information first (at the very beginning of the release). This is vital because when editors decide to publish your release, they will often begin by trimming the final few paragraphs or last few words to make it fit into their publication.

Make sure to include your name, address and phone number for editors to contact you.

STEP THREE:

Include an inspiring photograph. You can create photographs by hiring a local photographer with an excellent reputation for quality. Make sure your photographer uses format-sized film (not 35-millimeter film). Have your photographer use black & white, two-and-a-quarter-inch format film. If you are promoting a special seminar that you will be putting on locally have the photographer take a simulated and inspiring photo depicting some aspect of the event so that readers feel a part of it. Editors will be less likely to publish a photo of your office building. If you will be speaking at a luncheon, have the photographer create a few animated and exciting podium shots of you. Try to capture the look and feel of the experience you will be promoting through your news release.

In my experience, editors still tend to publish releases with photos containing the three "Bs"—beauties, beasts, and babies—more than any other photos. So if you are co-sponsoring an event with the local SPCA or the Make-a-Wish Foundation, be certain to show an inspiring photo of the animals or the children, who are the focus of the event. This will greatly increase the odds of your photo and news release being published.

The best labs I know for making duplicate photographs are based in Hollywood, California. Do not use a local photographic service that creates cheap looking "mechanicals." Mechanicals are photographs of the lowest quality you could provide to a media source. One of the best sources for photo duplication I know is:

Duplicate Photo Labs
1522 N. Highland Ave.
Hollywood, CA 90028
(213) 466-7544 phone
(213) 446-0106 fax
(800) 520-7544 toll-free

Duplicate Photo Labs will charge you under half-a-dollar per high-quality black & white print, which can cost as much as $2.50 locally. So it is well worth the effort to use them, even if they are out of state. All you have to do is send them your photo or negative and they will take care of the rest. Order as many as you plan to send out. Call them toll-free for a price list by fax.

STEP FOUR:

Compile your publicity lists to editors. You can easily obtain a list of local media by asking your local Small Business Development Council (SBDC) or local Chamber of Commerce for a list of local media contacts. Trade associations in your field, both local and national, are another great resource for contacts you can use to compile your publicity lists. You should also look up media directories in your local library, which will list local media contacts by city and state.

As soon as you have your list, log the contact information in your personal computer using a database or contact management program. Don't forget to list each contact by the type of media that they represent. Include addressing your letters to the editors by name. You can use this list to personalize each letter using the mail merge function (see your word processing software manual) and create envelopes as you laser print each mailing.

I suggest mailing your publicity kit in a plain white 4-inch by 9-inch envelope without a return address. This will guarantee that the editor will open the mailing because he or she will not know if it is a business letter or a card from his Aunt Dolly. In addition, always use first-class postage (preferably a stamp or metered insignia).

STEP FIVE:

Have a follow-up plan. After mailing out your publicity kit, if you have submitted a well-written, noncommercial, short and to-the-point release with a strong local slant that impacts readers with tremendous human interest, you can expect between 2% to 30% of the media to print your news idea. Some may contact you for an interview for local radio or television coverage, if you send releases to the electronic media.

Be sure to follow-up on every mail-out within 10 working days because some editors will fit your idea into a master schedule, which may require you to plan ahead for an interview or to submit a larger story idea three- to six-months from your release date.

On one occasion a Texas-based client contacted me regarding her massage product, called the "Doodleybopper." I created her news release and it was picked up by Runner's World Magazine, Runner's World Online Internet site, Woman's Day Special Interest Publications, Natural Health Magazine, Massage Magazine, Chiropractic Journals, and many more magazines and trade journals. The total response to our publicity effort was 45%. Each of these magazines placed the equivalent of a one-quarter to one-half page advertisement into their publication at no charge to us. We gained tremendous exposure for this product.

STEP SIX:

Say thank you. Always thank the editor and reporter covering your event or publishing your editorial. Send a personal "thank you" note on a card or a business letter. Never forget to show your gratitude for your editor's wonderful effort to help your business grow.

STEP SEVEN:

Use your publicity in every promotion. After you have received the publicity, use it in a variety of ways. If you received a print editorial, ask the issuing publication if you can buy a slick from them, which is reprintable artwork of the piece, from them. If you received a radio or television interview, ask for a copy of the piece. Reprint and use the materials in your next mailing. Highlight your print exposure in your television commercials. Quote it and mention it in your radio ads and other interviews. Be proud of the publicity you that have achieved. Flaunt it. Have a local graphics agency blow up your slick to 11-inches by 17-inches and hang it in your waiting area. Use reprints as handouts when you speak in public. Showing others that you have been blessed by the media will cause people to respect you and your business at a higher level.

There are ten reasons why the media may not publish your news release:

1. It was received too late to meet their most recent deadline.
2. There wasn't enough media space to work it into the publication or broadcast.

3. It was not considered to be newsworthy.
4. There was no local angle or slant.
5. The idea you submitted lacked timeliness, or an abundance of other news overshadowed your story idea.
6. The release you submitted was poorly written or it was not written in a style acceptable to the medium you are soliciting.
7. News release was too long and the editor didn't have enough time to edit it.
8. The release you submitted was too commercial. If the news release is an obvious attempt to plug your business, it won't be published. The release you submit must give readers news, such as a new way to alleviate a problem. If the release only contains facts about you or your business and not information the reader can use to receive an advantage, it won't be published.
9. Sneaking business names or addresses into inconspicuous places. Usually any name or address information about your business will appropriately be put at the end of your article in a "bio-box." If you erroneously "seed" the article with information about how clients can find you, then, the editor will assume you are publishing for some other reason other than to help the reader obtain information that is newsworthy—the editors' primary concern—and will then discount the value of your entire release.
10. Creating releases in order to influence editors to print the idea rather than to provide valuable material to readers or viewers.

SAMPLE OF CUSTOMIZED COVER LETTER FOR PUBLICITY KIT

Ben Gable
Tax Advisor

February 27, 2003

Ms. Betty Shuman
Editor
Small Business Journal
17 Station Street
Box 1200
Brookline Village, MA 02147

Dear Ms. Shuman:

I am available for interviews and to write articles in my area of specialization: Estate Tax Planning. I would enjoy sharing information about how the new local and federal government administration may impact the tax situation of your readers.

I espacially would enjoy outlining a simple checklist of year-round tax-saving tips that your small business readership will value.

I look forward to hearing from you soon.

Sincerely,

Ben Gable
CPA

BG/kl

Enclosure: Photo, news release copy

—86—

ALWAYS REMEMBER TO SAY, "THANK YOU"

When I was finishing my Masters Degree in marketing, one of my professors stopped me and looked me straight in the eyes and said, "Allen, last week when you left my class you turned to me and said 'thank you.' Do you know how much that meant to me? It made my whole week." Then he said, "Never forget how much of a difference a heartfelt thank you means to people." From that day forward, I made a promise to myself to remember to say "thank you" to others for every kind deed. Now, when I consult with business professionals, I make it a point to tell stories that I have gathered along my journey about how to really connect with people—and the biggest way I know how to connect with clients is to say, "thank you."

Remember that the simple things in life usually mean the most to us because they have the power to touch us in basic ways. Often the smallest and simplest positive experiences that we have with others can change our lives. As humans we tend to get so caught up in ourselves, our own lives and daily existence, that we forget the joy we can give to others and receive ourselves by remembering how important a simple act of kindness can mean to someone else. Simple little experiences in life can transform us and enrich us by connecting us more deeply to ourselves and others. And it is so easy to do.

Can you remember a special date that you had, or a special relative or friend that you loved to be around? Wasn't it like magic when you did simple things together, or when you talked about simple things that brought both of you joy? Didn't you laugh more frequently? Didn't you feel freer when you were with them? Think back about your most memorable experiences in life — a wedding, graduating from school, a vacation you took. When you look back, ask yourself, "What meant the most to me about that experience?" I bet your most pleasurable memories are about people you loved and things they may have said to you. I'll bet that the feeling of love and acceptance means the most to you because it signals to you that someone has taken the time to make you feel special or has flown three thousand miles to share your experience with you. And I'll bet that this meant more to you than earning some sum of money. Remembering the small things has the power to connect you with others in meaningful ways. It makes others feel accepted and loved for who they are, not just what they do for you. Your aim should be to make everyone (clients and staff) feel that way every day at your office.

When did you last take the time to thank one of your clients (and staff) for supporting your talents and efforts to give quality service? Genuinely reaching out beyond yourself is scary because it requires a measure of selflessness. Selflessness is the price that you have to pay to communicate from the heart. Most marketing consultants will never tell you that. And you will never learn it for yourself by staying inside an insulated world. You have to venture out of your cocoon every day. You must take some risks and reach out to others in simple ways.

A sincere "thank you" is one of the very best marketing tools you have. Sending thank you notes written from your heart can quadruple your business in the next 12 months. That sounds too good to be true, but it can happen for you.

Our world is becoming more technologically advanced every day, and because of the constraints of time and the speed of technology, people take less initiative to connect with clients in meaningful ways. Those who take time to care and touch others' lives stand out from countless millions. People who take time to write a little note to say something like, "Thank you, Sue, for coming in this week" are always the most successful in their profession. They always have the highest clientele and the most energy in all their endeavors.

IDEAS FOR SHARING "THE LITTLE THINGS" THAT MEAN A WHOLE LOT TO YOUR CLIENTS

- Send a thank-you note or card to every client you have ever served. Show them how much you care. It will take time and effort and a lot of stamps, but there is no time like the present to do it and your clients will love it.
- Send a short thank-you note to each client after every office visit. Personalize each note by remembering special things you chatted about. After each visit, send a thank-you note saying something like, "thank you and

good luck in your business. Let me know how well things go for you."

If you ever learn that a client receives a job advancement, becomes sick, becomes a Mom or Dad, graduates, retires, becomes engaged, becomes a Grandmother or Grandfather, or experiences anything else that is significant or potentially life-changing, share the experience with them. Run to a card shop and buy a special card for that person.

- Always keep a record on index cards or on a computer database of every card mailed. If you do it on a computer, you can print out a list of client names and addresses and sort them in order of their birthdays. So at the middle of each month, you can print out the list for next month and begin sending cards to make your clients feel special.
- Make a special list of clients who have not visited in a while. Use your computer database for sorting by the date of their last visit. If a client has not been in for two or three months, ask if anything went wrong during any of the visits, or at any other time. Sometimes clients are afraid to hurt our feelings when things go wrong, so they do not say anything to us. But we need to know so that we can correct whatever it is.

By following these guidelines consistently, you can expect to retain and attract lots of clients, fill an entire appointment book, and make much more money. The most important point to emphasize is that you are extending yourself to make client relations and customer service an important part of the future of your business.

Try to buy thank-you notes and cards that are related to the business. Scan stores looking for cards that are accounting-related or have to do with business in a fun way. When you find cards you like, buy them and use them.

−87−

MAKE YOUR BUSINESS TOTALLY ACCESSIBLE TO YOUR CLIENTS

You must make your business totally accessible to your potential clients. You must find creative ways to make it easier and quicker to use your service. You must create a frictionless pathway to your door. Once clients find your offices, you must make it easy for them to communicate to you what they want. Did you know that accessibility and convenience are often the factors that make people choose to use some businesses over others? Use the following ideas to improve your client's ability to find you and do business with you. See if you are hitting your accessibility targets:

TARGET NUMBER ONE: HIRE A MYSTERY CLIENT TO MEASURE YOUR EASE OF SERVICE

To find out how easy it is for clients to do business with you, hire a mystery shopper or mystery client. Since you're the owner or manager of your business, you are probably too involved in your business to objectively measure how accessible your office is and how well your staff is servicing clients. There are local and national firms that you can hire to patronize your business and document their experiences. Look in your yellow pages under "shopping services." If you cannot find a consultant offering mystery-shopping service in your area, hire a local marketing consultant to spend a few hours analyzing your service according to the guidelines outlined here.

Have your mystery client call your business randomly to book an appointment with members of your staff, or perhaps they will meet with you, if you're a one-person operation. Have them analyze how courteous, empathetic, and responsive you and/or your staff is to their call. They will look at some simple things, such as many times the telephone rang before the call was picked up? How long were they put on-hold? Did the receptionist ask how the potential client heard about your business? Were they (and/or you) responsive to the client's expressed needs and empathetic to their concerns for waiting times, if asked? Did your receptionist give reasonable estimations? How far away did the mystery shopper have to park and walk from your door? Were your signs clear? Was the office easy or difficult to find once inside the building? Is your office accessible to the physically challenged? When they call you after hours do they get caught having to listen to a long message that gives them few options for receiving the vital information needed to visit you during regular business hours?

TARGET NUMBER TWO: GIVE YOURSELF AN ACCESSIBILITY AUDIT

Use this list to stimulate your thinking about how your approach to the following critical service issues separates you from your competition. Do you make it easier for clients to conduct business at your office, or do you need to change how you handle these issues?

- Your Hours of Operation. Who wrote the rules that say you can only be open from Monday to Friday? If I opened a new accounting office, it would be open from 8:00 a.m. to 12:00 midnight, seven days per week during peak season and from 8:00 a.m. to 5:00 p.m. during non-peak seasons. (Unless Blue Laws of the state dictated Sunday restrictions.) And we would never be closed during lunch hours because I know that many people like to conduct errands during their lunch hour, so I would want to be there for them.
- Your Parking Situation. Have you ever decided not to shop at a store because it was too much trouble to park? Make sure that your employees do not take up precious parking spaces in front of your facility. If your parking situation is limiting your business, try implementing a valet service at certain times of the day.
- Accepting Credit Cards. This could boost your sales up to 80%. Having "merchant status," which is the right to accept and to process credit cards at your business is a valuable way to make it easier for clients to pay for their service. When you obtain merchant status, you can run client

credit and debit cards. Your electronic credit card terminal will batch your merchant service provider the transactions at a time you specify. The money from those transactions will most likely be deposited in your account the next business day. The best place to obtain merchant status is with your local bank. Sometimes, smaller accounting offices have trouble receiving merchant status locally. By the way, make sure you are able to accept as many different kinds of credit cards as possible, because many people tend to max out the primary ones—MasterCard, Visa, and American Express — and want to use others such as Discover.

- Accepting Checks. One small business owner I visited had a large sign on the front window that said "No Checks Accepted." I was shocked to see this because this limits the number of ways that clients can pay them. Instead, they should have had a bold sign that read, "We will happily accept checks," and include a list of available credit- and debit-card options.

- Accessibility for the Physically Challenged. Please make sure no one feels alienated or intimidated about difficulties in walking, wheeling, or visiting your business by any other ambulatory method. If you are on the second floor, try to position your office near an elevator. Make sure that the elevator is not too far from the parking lot. Several years ago I sprained my ankle very badly and had to use crutches for two weeks. Prior to this, I had never realized how challenging some buildings could be. By the end of the two-week period, I vowed to help as many people who were physically challenged as possible to access doors and buildings when I had the opportunity. And I do every chance I get. I hope you will, too.

—88—

EXPAND YOUR VISION—CREATE A PROTOTYPE FOR YOUR BUSINESS

Perhaps you want to increase the effectiveness of your accounting business without spending all your time working in your business. As an accountant you give service to clients by investing your time and energy — converting your most personal resources and talents — into service. You may have discovered that your work has become life-consuming. This is why putting practical systems into place to handle repetitive tasks is so essential. It frees you to work productively. The solution to your most pressing business challenges lies in converting your business into a well-oiled machine. Your business grows as you begin to add practical systems that replace your own repetitive efforts.

Try imagining that your business is a model for other businesses. Your aim is to look at the business objectively and determine which actions will help your business and staff operate more autonomously, allowing you to spend more time focused on the important things while turning the details over to others.

Imagine that your accounting business is the model for 200 identical accounting businesses. Picture what it would look like. Ask yourself questions that generate vision and a mental image of your improved or ideal business, such as:

- What would the sign in front of your business look like?
- How would your staff answer the phones?
- How would your office look?
- What systems would your people have to develop to anticipate a larger clientele or to better service existing clients?

Think through every aspect of your accounting business from this new visionary perspective. Take a few moments to daydream about how you would orchestrate the kind of business that operated like a well-oiled machine. This simple game of using your imagination will help you make a powerful shift in the way you think about how you market your business. You will also discover the kinds of people you need to help you work your business system from all angles.

You must challenge yourself to look more closely at your philosophies. Is your aim to spend more or less time working in your business? Maybe your goal is to turn your administrative and billing tasks over to a small team and spend your time only with clients. Perhaps you would wish to hire a new team to generate new clients in special market segments, such as consulting with start-up or home-based businesses. The bottom line is that you have the capability of creating systems that enhance your strengths, make up for your weaknesses, or just make your day more fun and enriching. You can run your business any way you want to enhance your life.

Now, take some time by sitting down and making a list of the systems you can create to enhance your business. Think *through* your business. Think about all the marketing activities you must have in your business to maximize your success. Here are some idea stimulators:

- A very successful accountant hires people to work from their homes for him. He has one woman who works as a telemarketer. He pays her $7.50 per hour to call his clients periodically. He installed a telephone in her home with a toll-free number. She also takes incoming calls for certain market segments. The accountant e-mails and faxes her scripts and a database of clients. She calls clients to set up appointments, conducts surveys and stays in touch with potentially lost clients. The accountant receives the phone bills and knows when she is working and how many calls she is making.
- Many accountants raise their fees enough every year to farm out more services to other companies. Hire mailing services, small telemarketing companies, outside sales reps, quality control people, and new accountants to perform a carefully charted client-needs analysis for you.
- Lean on technology. For almost any business task requiring human effort, there is usually a powerful technological equivalent, and a way to automate communications by using broadcast e-mail and faxing to reach larger groups

of people with similar messages. Your Internet site can be useful to help clients self-educate, fill out electronic evaluation surveys, and for prescreening clients with self-paced surveys at the start of a relationship. You need at least one "techie" — someone who is knowledgeable enough about computers and telecommunications technology to systematize your tasks for you.

There are endless arrays of communication systems that can be created to improve your delivery of services. Only you can decide which systems are best to add to your business. Document your systems. Describe how you will plan and execute them. Write step-by-step procedures for important tasks so that when you delegate them, your staff can work the system in a self-sustaining way.

—89—

USING E-ZINES

E-zines are e-mail newsletters. Just like printed newsletters, they contain valuable information that people subscribe to. If you send a newsletter to your clients now, consider also sending it by e-mail. If you have never sent out an e-zine consider doing it because it gives you one more point of contact with prospects and clients. Here are the steps you should take to start an e-zine:

STEP ONE: FIND SOME EXAMPLE E-ZINES

The best way to get a flavor for what e-zines are all about is to subscribe to a number of them. There is a free great e-zine that you can subscribe to about Internet marketing at "http://www.liszt.com."

STEP TWO: SUBSCRIBE TO E-ZINES IN YOUR SPECIFIC MARKET

Next subscribe to e-zines in your target market. Again, the "www.liszt.com" web site lists many resources you can use to find thousands of e-zines. So that you can get a feel for what they are all about and how others are using them.

STEP THREE: CHOOSE A TOPIC

You must select a topic that you are going to write about. Give this very careful thought. Perhaps there is a very important subtopic in your specific field that is very profitable. Is there something that you know more about than your competitors that you can use to position yourself as an expert by sharing your ideas or research on it?

STEP FOUR: CHOOSE A FORMAT

You may want to use one of many formats for your e-zine: news factoids, site reviews, question-and-answer, short paragraphs, lists of resources, articles, transcribed interviews.

STEP FIVE: CHOOSE HOW OFTEN YOU'LL SEND IT OUT

This is critical. The web never sleeps and if you over-promise and under-deliver then you may never sleep either. You do not need any more stressful deadlines than are necessary. So if you think you will want to create it twice per month, promise yourself that you'll do it once per month. If you cut your objective in half you will thank yourself later because those deadlines creep up very quickly.

SPECIAL POINTS TO NOTE ABOUT E-ZINES:

- Make your e-zine free to entice people to sign up for it. People will always notice if you miss an issue. If e-zine providers are ever a week late people will e-mail them to ask for it. People will align their expectations with your e-zine and make mental notes of when they are due.
- E-zines help to build relationships. If you invest time and effort to create relationships with people by broadcasting your e-zines to your house e-mail list, then never risk blowing it by not performing. Promise less and over-deliver.

HOW TO FORMAT E-ZINES:

- Be certain that each line in the e-mail document is no more than 65 characters long. Put in your own "hard returns" so that you won't exceed this guideline. If not, it will look odd in some e-mail programs.
- Try not to use special characters. The rule here is if you cannot type it with a regular key, or using shift or alt , etc. then do not use it.
- Try to use a fixed width font when your create your copy. Use the font Times Roman because it is an all platform-friendly font.

STEP SIX: CREATE YOUR FIRST ISSUES

Now you are prepared to create your first issue of your e-zine. Create more than one before you start sending. Always have at least three issues finished before you promise to send out Issue One.

STEP SEVEN: GET SUBSCRIBERS

When you start sending the e-zine I suggest that you use a simple e-mail program. I use Eudora. You really don't need anything fancy in the beginning. Eudora Light is fine.

HOW TO GET SUBSCRIBERS TO YOUR E-ZINE:

- Write articles for other e-zines related to your primary target market needs. At the bottom of the article, provide a free offer to readers to subscribe to your e-zine. This is a powerful way to do it.
- Upon receiving 1,000 subscribers, approach other e-zines and ask their webmasters to work with you on an "ad swap." This is a trade out or a barter, whereby you run their ad in your e-zine sin exchange for them running your ad. It is important to find out where your ad will be positioned in their e-zine—beginning, middle or end—and how many ads will be running alongside of yours on each issue. If they run 5 ads per issue and you run one, account for this in your exchange. You might decide to partner with local consultants, local news publications and other local organizations who target your market, but who are noncompetitive to you.
- When doing a trade out for advertising: If they have 3,000 e-zine subscribers and you have 1,000, then do a three to one trade. You can run their ad three times and they will run your ad once.
- Always test your ads before doing a trade out on your e-zine. One great test is to try different sig file offers. Your sig file (signature file) is a small identification that your e-mail program puts at the bottom of your e-mail telling your company name, who you are, address etc. Sig file offers are special inducements placed onto the bottom of each outgoing e-mail message. You will notice that some offers out-pull others, sometimes by a significant difference. Try testing different sig files on the same discussion list with a different mention of the benefits of receiving your e-zine. Remember, these posts are an incredible source of new subscribers. Continue to test sig files until you discover one that pulls best and use that as the foundation of your ad. You can find a list of discussion lists at "http://www.deja.com"–go to "Power Search" and search for accounting-related discussion lists.

- E-mail other e-zines related to your field, but not directly competitive to yours, and tell them you would like to advertise. About 65% of the e-zines that exist today do not have any formal advertising programs or rate data associated with them. So you might receive a quote back from them by e-mail and you can negotiate with them. Remember, many web site and e-zine owners really do not understand the value of their traffic. So you can get a large volume of traffic for cents on the dollar compared to traditional advertising. Plus, your reach is highly targeted.
- Banner ads are also highly negotiable in many cases. Try obtaining the best deals for yours because you will find them week in and week out resulting in a great deal of traffic for your site and e-zine.
- The value of general e-zine advertising—not well targeted—is around $29 per thousand subscribers. I know of a site that charges a little over $200 per thousand. Strange as it may seem, some sites are only $1 per thousand. Never pay more than $4 to $6 per thousand. Shop and negotiate.

HERE ARE SOME IMPORTANT TIPS FOR SENDING E-ZINES:

- Make certain that you put all of the e-mail addresses from your list in the BCC: field in your e-mail program. Never use the CC: fields. Using BCC: ensures that your subscribers do not see the e-mail addresses of everyone you are sending your e-zine to, thus you are protecting their privacy.
- When your subscriber list grows to over 1,000 people, then you can start using a list server. You web host probably already has the resources to do this and you may find out that your web fees already cover this. Talk to your webmaster.

HOW ABOUT CHARGING FOR E-ZINES:

- We have tested this thoroughly. In most cases it is very difficult getting people to pay you for e-mail newsletter subscriptions. However, though people are much more willing to pay for highly specialized information, even this can be difficult to do.

- Creating a free e-zine gives you an opportunity to sell advertising, which is a far better way to generate revenue using your e-zine. As your e-zine list grows there will be many people who will desire to connect with your target market in more intimate ways. Chances are that you will receive a lot of subscribers in a short time who will generate ad revenues that "more than cover" what you would otherwise charge for the subscription.

HOW TO DETERMINE IF A PARTNERING E-ZINE IS SUCCESSFUL ENOUGH TO ADVERTISE WITH THEM:

- You can tell by how large their subscriber base is. If an e-zine has a base of 30,000 subscribers, it is probably doing well. Unless the list is a broadcast list and the subscribers do not "opt into it." Stay away from any e-mail lists whose subscribers do not "opt in."
- If the e-zine goes to a small tightly-targeted market, then 800 to 1,200 subscribers indicates success.
- Consider the quality of the material of the partnering e-zine. Take time to read many issues. If the information is high quality, then be certain that the subscribers value and read it. This makes the e-zine more credible. This tends to increase the response rates of the e-zine.
- Always check references from other past advertisers.

Always start with your client base and start your e-zine by offering to provide clients with valuable information. At the same time you can start to attract general subscribers from all over the nation whether in your local market or not. Once your e-zine subscriber base is large enough (over 1,000 e-mail addresses) you will be in a position to sell advertising to other noncompetitive web site providers, local consultants, and many other people who want to reach your readers.

—90—

MAKE YOUR WEB SITE IRRESISTIBLE

It is so important to use good marketing principles when you work with your webmaster to design your web site. Perhaps you will be brave and try to design your own web site. In either case, you must compel people to visit your site. Once visitors do click to your site, you must have a very clear and specific goal for each web page a visitor views. Some of the goals of the most successful web sites on the Internet include:

- Selling products and services on the site. The site www.etrade.com sells securities on-line.
- Bringing buyers and sellers together. The site www.ebay.com brings buyers and sellers together in an online auction. Each pays a small fee for the privilege of selling and buying on the site.
- Attracting a large number of clients. Some sites make little or no profit on the things that they sell in order to attract a lot of web site traffic. They make money on the advertising that they sell to other noncompetitive vendors. They generate hundreds of thousands to millions of page visits per month. Amazon.com is one site that has used this strategy for several years.
- Attracting a niche audience. Some sites use their sites to serve their best clients, perhaps making it easier to do business with the firm. Many service organizations have private web sites that are intended only for this purpose.

As a successful accounting firm the goal of your site will be to serve your niche market well, by giving them valuable information about your firm and what makes your business different. If you want to get fancy, consider having your webmaster set up your site to receive downloadable Quickbooks and Quicken files for you to work with. Try to put online mortgage calculators, tax estimators and other tools that make your site valuable to your clients.

Most businesses with an on-line presence know very little about good marketing. You must offer people the things that they want. One survey reveals the reasons that people tend to use the Internet (in rank order from most to least popular reasons):

- Browsing
- Entertainment
- Education
- Work-related
- Shopping

Heavy users of the Internet tend to seek out news and information sites. Business users hunt for information. Light users tend to look for education and training-related sites.

The key to creating valuable web site "content" that makes your visitors return time and again is to focus on you're client's key interests in a very self-serving way. For example, if you provide accounting services and also provide securities investment advice to your clients, consider creating a specialized web site that gives very personal investment information, which relates investment decisions to logical tax implications. If you provide services to entrepreneurs who have home-based businesses, then consider creating a web site that gives them very specialized news and information. If you want to look at a great site that has developed an entire presence around the hot interests of people go to "www.wz.com."

By becoming dedicated to creating a web site that has a lot of tasty, easily downloadable reports and customizable information for each client's specific interests, you create exceptional value for site visitors. That value perception reflects positively on your business.

TEN WAYS TO MAKE YOUR WEB SITE MORE IRRESISTABLE

Here are some great strategies that you can present to your webmaster before creating your web site. You can use this list of web site ideas as a discussion and planning tool because there will be multiple ways to technically execute each of them.

Use this as an idea stimulator in discussing your site with your webmaster:

STRATEGY ONE: FOCUS ON YOUR INTENDED CUSTOMER

What are they going to get when they get here? What's of value to them? Make a list of the needs and interests of your clients. Make this list as comprehensive as possible. If your clients consist of wealthy working moms think about their need for planning and information on how present choices will impact future tax decisions. Create your site around the most compelling informational needs that your market possesses.

After you have figured out what kind of information — categories and sub categories —that you want to put on your site, ask the "what else question?" Determine what other vital pressing and important needs your clients have for decision-making tools and information that you can give them on your web site.

Perhaps you could license software from a software provider and offer that free to your clients as a gift and valuable decision-making tool. I know an accountant who licensed software that helped young families set budgets and stick to them. He offered this to any one who visited his site for free. Word-of-mouth enhanced his effort by 1000% and he had over 25,000 web site visitors per month, many of whom downloaded the free software. His next step was to sell ads on his site to 20 other businesses at $200 per month each. In addition, he generated a lot of new non-Web-based business from surrounding cities just from the web site visits.

Look at each page on your web site. You must have a clear, definable goal for each page that a visitor sees. Imagine yourself being the person coming to see your site. Ask yourself, "What valuable things can I obtain on this web site and on each page?" You should have a good answer to that question. There should be a reason they would care about what's on your Web site. Often 90% of the time there is no answer to that. Think from your client's perspective.

STRATEGY TWO: USE YOUR SITE AS THE ULTIMATE EDUCATIONAL TOOL

What makes a web surfer chose one web site over another? Usually it is because the important information they are seeking can be found, or be used immediately. So by giving people something that they are looking for and doing it in an educational way you will enhance the success of your web marketing effort.

Here are the best ways to attract people to your site and educate them simultaneously:

1. Give Valuable Information — Timely news, helpful checklists of tips, survey results, and expert advice is valuable to your web visitors.
2. Provide a Lot of Free Stuff — People love free software, interactive spreadsheets, contests, giveaways, surveys that generate customized reports that enhance decision making.
3. Create a Social Environment —   People want to chat in a chatroom setting about their challenges, they like to post specific questions to discussion groups, they like to submit e-mails to your staff experts for guidance. People want to interact in a community. Create community on your web site.

You can easily apply one element from the above list in some way on your web site. At least consider having a clickable e-mail question submission form to enable people to connect with your staff.

People are on the Web to get information in all kinds of different ways. You want to provide useful free information in multiple formats. The more useful information you provide, the more successful your web site will be. Providing useful information is the heart of a successful web site.

STRATEGY THREE: MAKE YOUR SITE FUN TO VISIT

Humor is a great thing to use. In many other kinds of direct marketing, people tell you to stay away from humor. It's hard to pull off. When you're doing stuff on the Web, humor works extremely well. People tend to appreciate it.

Examples: "Don't click here if you have a life" and "Don't click here." Those kinds of things get people's attention.

STRATEGY FOUR: BE DIFFERENT

Be a little bit different. I suggest trying to look at the world from the perspective of *thinking outside the box.* Look at your web site creation from different angles, slants, viewpoints and perspectives. Find your point-of-difference, look at the fun side of your specialty. When you look at your field in a way that's a little bit different, people will come to your site just because you bring a different perspective to their world. You want to stand out. Just remember, being a bit outrageous is not as important as providing useful information.

STRATEGY FIVE: USE STRONG HEADLINES AND SUBHEADS

This is clearly the one crucial factor that contributes to the sustainable success of web sites. You really need to have a good headline. The best example of the use of excellent headlines is at the web site http://www.bizchallenge.com/accountant. There you will discover a web site that is not filled with senseless graphics, just a lot of very valuable information about improving your web site marketing. Look at the headlines they pull you into the site. The site compels you to want to learn more about the valuable ideas that are presented there.

Never use your company name and logo as your headline. Almost 95% of all companies do this. Company names and product names may be better used as subheads. Make your headlines and subheads especially interesting and self-serving to the client.

Good web site copy writers think of their headline as the ad for the ad. People are going to leave your web site instantly if the headlines and subheadlines do not attract them enough to read on. Some people call headlines on a web site "grabbers."

By simply adding more valuable information that will stop web visitors in their tracks, you will have improved your web site tremendously. You can also add special reports on your web site that people can download as Microsoft Word® files or as Adobe Acrobat Files®. Perhaps you could offer a report entitled :"Five Simple Steps To Saving 15% On Your Federal Income Tax Burden," or "TAX STRATEGY 2001: How To Stop Overpaying Taxes."

You should also inform your local press about the availability of your special reports on your web site. Many of my clients have received free blurbs about their web site in countless national and local publications just by sending out news releases to the attention of the editor mentioning the very valuable free report on a cutting-edge topic.

–91–

FOUR SIMPLE WAYS TO INCREASE WEB SITE MARKETING RESULTS

There are many valuable strategies that you should employ in your web site marketing. Below you will find the four strategies I have discovered work better than all others after significant amounts of testing. If you are new to web publishing (and even if you are not) hire a webmaster to help you with the technical aspects of your Internet marketing effort.

STRATEGY ONE: FREE INFORMATION

People go on-line for information. You need compelling information to spark their attention. Information that's not sales pitch or hype. The two main goals for offering free information are to offer something useful to your target audience and to promote your business products or services.

> HOT TIP: Teach people something new and interesting. This will differentiate you from your competition. You could offer special free reports. You could offer newsletters. You could offer a booklet that you have published. You could offer a tax planner and organizing kit that is sent by mail, with checklists that are sent by e-mail. Give people the tools they can use to get a result.

If you publish a newsletter, offer a small free sample of your tax-saving consulting advice. One example of offering newsletters is one that was published in a book called *Marketing On The Internet.* It's a success story about a publisher of a financial newsletter. It took him 15 years to build a subscriber base of about 10,000 people. Then it took him just five months to *double* that base on the Internet. And the best part is, he's now growing at 20% a month. So, you definitely can market newsletters on the Internet. Free samples are a very good way to do that.

- You can offer e-zines
- You can offer article reprints—obtain the copyright approval (permission) if somebody writes an article about you, then display it on the Internet
- You can offer survey information on the Internet
- You can offer tips on the better use of products, or how to accomplish any task using the Internet.
- You can exhibit frequently asked questions (FAQs)
- You can create catalogs

STRATEGY TWO: PROVIDE RESOURCE LISTS AND DIRECTORIES

People have complained that information on the Internet is very hard to find. So, if you are an expert in a special area, compile directories of resources that tie into your products or services. You can have a list of Internet-related resources and also non-Internet-related resources, whatever it might be.

HOT TIP: I know an accountant specializing in start-up business consulting. He obtains a lot of clients by conducting free seminars at his local Small Business Development Council and Chamber Of Commerce. He has compiled a step-by-step list of web sites, including all of the resources and to-dos — state and local business licensing agencies, and local SBA friendly banks — that business people need to start up their businesses. As soon as first-time visitors log on to the web site for his accounting office, they are given instructions on how to access this valuable checklist of agencies, and how to create their new start-up page. Almost 55% of the first-time visitors make his web site their start-up page. The site is filled with valuable information that also explains how his accounting firm can save them time and money at key points along the pathway of their start-up venture.

STRATEGY THREE: EXCHANGE VALUABLE LINKS

Links are what make the Web so powerful. Links are simply underlined text in a Web page; when you click on a link, your browser will take you to some other resource on the Internet some where in the world, or elsewhere on your Web site. The one great thing about this is you can trade your links with other web site providers, even with competitors who are willing to do so. Or collaborate with synergistic businesses. Consider trading links with local consultants, attorneys, business advisors, local small business newspaper columnists, small banks, etc. Links are a very powerful tool that can drive more traffic to your web site over night.

I know a company who created payroll software. The marketer of that company traded links with other companies that 1) deal with accounting software but don't have payroll software, and 2) accountants that work with small to medium-size businesses. These clients will tend to be non-competitive and interested in payroll issues. The links drive people with an interest in payroll software to the site. And when they come to the accountant's site they click on the link to the software and go to that site. This is called "click-through traffic."

STRATEGY FOUR: DELIVER NEWS

Provide real news. This can be general news, like CNN. Or the ESPN sports page. It is best for the news to be exclusive to the special groups of clients you are targeting (for that very specific market you are interested in attracting to your web site). A very good example is *Financial Planning,* the largest magazine for financial planners. They put up a Web site, and every day articles are included which are of interest to financial planners. They are attempting to sell subscriptions to their monthly magazine by becoming a news and information resource for financial planners, and by providing news stories that are of specific interest to that specialized group. You can post updates on special tax laws that impact your clients and many other pertinent valuable news items that directly influence their bottom line.

The aim is to become a recognized source. You must become a treasure trove of valuable information in your subspecialty. Then people will flock to your web site for the money-saving and money-generating advice that you give.

–92–

THINGS THAT SHOULD NEVER APPEAR ON YOUR WEB SITE

This chapter is meant as a checklist for your webmaster and web site designer to use before officially putting your web site up onto the Internet. It comes from Internet marketing expert Audry Lanford. If any of the terms seem confusing, your web technicians will know what to do to ensure that none of the below-mentioned problems never occur on your site. The things we have listed here will annoy, frustrate and disempower your web visitors excessively. Make certain that your web site is free of the following bugs and annoyances:

1. UNDIFFERENTIATED PRODUCTS OR SERVICES

A surprising number of sites offer products and services with no "online ordering advantage." This is especially true of health-related items, business services, book and information sellers and Multi-level Marketing reps. You must give your visitors a compelling reason to buy from you online, make an appointment, or order your free report, etc. Always list multiple ways you may be contacted on each of your web pages, not just a toll-free number and e-mail.

2. LARGE USELESS GRAPHICS

Web surfers have the need for speed. Yet far too many home pages open with large useless graphics (LUGs) that load slowly and make no contribution to the effectiveness of the page. Your "home page" should be 30K or less in file size—"including graphics." Spinning globes, unrelated stock photos, massive company logos, etc., take up precious real estate that could be better utilized for benefit-related information.

3. WELCOME TO MY SITE

Phrases like this, repetition of your company name and other self-serving statements only cloud your message. Your home page and virtually every other page on your site should begin with a compelling, stimulating, interest-generating "headline" or opening equivalent that answers your viewer's basic question, "What's in it for me if I read this page?"

4. BLINKERS, SPINNERS, SCROLLING MARQUEES, COUNTERS, ETC.

There was a time (that lasted about fifteen minutes) when these things were new and unusual. Now they are passe — and in many cases, distracting and annoying. Counters, especially, have lost their usefulness. They are self-serving devices that have no purpose because most visitors really don't care how many alleged hits your site has received.

5. EXTERNAL LINKS — ESPECIALLY ON YOUR HOME PAGE

This is equivalent to having an office or storefront with a choice of doors leading to other businesses. When a potential customer arrives, why give that person an immediate opportunity to leave and never return? If you must link externally, do it on a page that's buried deep in your site that can only be accessed after viewing the important pages.

6. JUST ABOUT ANY AWARD LOGO/BANNER

Most Internet awards are dubious at best, and meaningless to most of your visitors. Awards are self-serving space-wasters that should be replaced with visitor-focused information which gives people a reason to stay at your site and not leave it to investigate the award sponsor.

7. TYPOGRAPHICAL OR GRAMMATICAL ERRORS

It seems obvious, yet many, many web pages contain common spelling and grammatical errors. Your copy is a reflection on your professionalism, your attention to detail, and your commitment to excellence. Why give visitors any reason to doubt you? Use spelling and grammar checkers to make sure your copy is first-rate.

8. OVER USE OF THE WORDS "WE, OUR, US, MY, ME, MINE"

These are self-serving words that turn readers off. Instead, you should use words like "you" and "your." Before you post copy to your site, run a "find and replace" utility and check for the number of "you-words" against the number of "us-words." The ratio should be 15 "you words" for every "us-word."

9. NAME, RANK AND SERIAL NUMBER INFORMATION

It's amazing how many home pages begin, "The Nesterman Conference Company is a family-run business located in Cornfield County, Nebraska..." Who cares? What does this have to do with the benefits of your products or services? If you must include boring vital statistics like these, put them on an "About Us" page and give some reasons why these things are important to readers.

10. FRAMES

Many older browsers don't support frames. Many search engines do not index them properly. Many frames require scrolling to read the text and activate links. Frame scrolling bars take up precious real estate.

11. UNDER CONSTRUCTION SIGNS/NOTICES

What good does a page that isn't finished do for your visitors? It just wastes their time and could possibly frustrate or annoy them. Every page on your site should have a purpose or reason why it's there. Every page should also have a "call to action"— what you want the visitor to do after reading the information.

12. BROKEN LINKS

This should be obvious, but broken links are all too frequent. Broken links are annoying, frustrating and unprofessional. Why make your visitors mad?

13. MISSING GRAPHICS

This should also be obvious, but missing graphics are all over the Web — even on professional sites whose principals should know better.

14. INCOMPLETE CONTACT INFORMATION

It's amazing how many companies try to remain anonymous and then expect people to do business with them. To maximize your credibility and believability, you should include complete contact information on every page. Use a physical street address, not a P.O. Box. Provide a live phone number, not a voice mailbox. List your fax number, and toll-free ordering number if you have one. And, of course, list an e-mail hotlink to you, not your webmaster.

15. HOME PAGE THAT SCROLLS INTO OBLIVION

Despite the universal quest for information by web surfers most of them will not read long home pages that scroll into oblivion. You should break up your home page to a maximum of three complete vertical-page scrolls on a 14" monitor. Give visitors links and benefit-related teasers that lead to separate pages.

16. COOKIE NAGS THAT APPEAR MORE THAN ONCE

Many people believe "cookies" are an invasion of their privacy. If you must use cookies, don't nag your visitors more than once per visit to allow you to set a cookie.

17. FREE OFFERS THAT ARE NOT IMMEDIATELY FULFILLED

You should make some kind of free offer on your site that will allow you to capture visitor names and e-mail addresses. But you should only do this if you can immediately fulfill your offer. Many sites offer free consultations or information, but often fail to deliver. This can permanently damage your credibility.

18. NON-SECURE OR CONFUSING ORDERING PROCEDURES

Many sites have non-secure or confusing ordering procedures. Better to not request credit card info, etc., if you can't do it securely. Offer a mail-in, call-in or fax-in alternative. If you have more than a few items for sale, invest in a shopping cart ordering system. Make it easy for customers to buy from you.

19. PLUG-INS AND JAVASCRIPT POP-UP WINDOWS

Most people will not take the time to load plug-ins to view or do something at your site. They'll just click away. JavaScript pop-up windows can be annoying. Why make it difficult for visitors to see what you offer?

20. PLAGIARIZED MATERIAL

This should be obvious, but many people take copyrighted material from other sites and pretend it's theirs. Doing this will eventually bite you and could lead to serious legal problems. The good news is, most people are flattered to let you use their material, if you give them proper attribution.

–93–

12 STEP CHECKLIST FOR EFFECTIVE WEB MARKETING

Here is a quick summary of the best ideas about Internet Marketing we have presented in this book. Good luck with your entire Internet marketing effort.

1. Understand the Internet and the Internet culture.
2. Use email with a good grabber signature file so that when you send email, it intrigues people and they want to go visit your site.
3. Create a compelling web site.
4. Provide lots of free useful content on your site.
5. List your web site everywhere. Use those electronic yellow pages and search engines.
6. Trade links with others so that when people go to their pages they will be directed to your page.
7. Promote your site using good public relations. Send out lots of local and regional news releases announcing survey results from your site, news and valuable information.
8. Change your site frequently so people are interested in coming back and seeing what is new. And remember to label what is new by using the words "new" or "updated" next to the headlines and links.
9. Be a good Internet citizen and develop a good reputation on the Internet.
10. Figure out ways to save money on the Net, such as using your web site to facilitate customer service.
11. Develop strategies to leverage both your traditional and your Internet marketing so they compliment each other. Put your Web address or URL on your brochures, your business cards, and on everything you use to market your business through traditional means.
12. Test everything—from headlines to offers, links and

banner ads. Always use the results that you obtain from testing to make better, more astute marketing decisions.

–94–

FREE WAYS TO DRIVE TRAFFIC
TO YOUR WEB SITE

One of your goals in establishing an Internet presence for your organization is to make it fun and easy for potential and existing clients to visit your Home Page. When you influence people to log onto the Internet and type in the name of your site in their browser then you are generating response-based traffic. When you generate more traffic, then more people will interact with you as a valuable source of information. Here are the best ways that you can generate more traffic on your site:

INTERNET TRAFFIC GENERATORS

ONE: LEVERAGE THE POWER OF SEARCH ENGINES

Take a look at "GoTo.com." GoTo.com is a search engine that accepts bids on the placement of your site based on key words. Millions of people use GoTo.com to get better search results to find the kinds of sites that they want faster. The best thing about GoTo.com is that you only pay when someone clicks into your site. This is what you want. Here's how GoTo.com works:

- Bidding starts at "one-cent" per key word that you list with them. People submit bids similar to an auction at the GoTo.com web site for certain key words. If you're in a business with few competitors on the Internet, then you may often get new visitors for a few cents per "hit" on your site. The more you pay, the higher up on the list you are.
- Calculate the value of each new site visitor. Then you will know how much you can afford to pay to ensure that your site will be profitable.

TWO: PARTICIPATE IN KEY E-MAIL DISCUSSION LISTS

Participate in e-mail discussion lists. You can go to www.deja.com to obtain discussion lists related to your field or business.

- Join as many discussion lists in your field as possible. Post something to the list when you have something interesting to say to contribute to the usefulness of the list. This builds your credibility among list participants. When you are taken seriously, then that leads to traffic, sales and contacts.
- Lurk (read others comments) on the list for a while to scope out the tone. Then you can answer the questions of other people, or pose an excellent question that is relevant. Make certain that you share only enriching content and ideas.
- At the end of your posting to the discussion list include your sig file. This is like a short advertisement. Keep it no longer than six lines. Put a compelling offer there to influence readers to visit your site and subscribe to your e-zine.

Most of the sig files that I see online are poorly done. Create a very compelling reason for people to take action to visit your site in the sig file. If the information you are sharing in discussion groups is excellent—well thought out, researched, relevant, and gives fast and complete facts, then you've captured them and you're on your way. The sig file completes the job and reels them in because you will give them a reason to take action.

Hot Tip: Your E-mail contains a signature also, that automatically attaches itself to the end of every e-mail you send. Many e-mail programs such as Eudora will allow you to create signatures — short, six lines max— containing your contact information and a short advertisement describing what you do.

THREE: CREATE E-ZINES

Create "e-zines"—mini-magazines that you send out through your e-mail program. We've talked more about this in another section because it is so powerful. They're the most powerful method of encouraging repeat traffic to your site. Write articles for your e-zines that are highly interesting to your target market. Allow other people to reprint your articles when they ask to generate extra traffic, e-zine subscribers and credibility. Put offers for your free e-zine and your URL (web domain name) in all the publicity you receive.

FOUR: EXCHANGE LINKS

Exchange links with owners of non-competitive sites. Begin by creating descriptions that entice people visiting those sites to come to your site. My wife owns a company that designs books covers exclusively for publishers. Her Internet home page is www.bookcovers.com. One of the first ways we drove traffic to her site was to create alliances with other sites that attracted publishers and self-publishers. We exchanged links with compelling banners and descriptive copy to and from her site with publisher associations, famous authors who wrote books on publishing, and many other non-competitive businesses. The result was lots of traffic and many extra clients per month. Brainstorm a list of non-competitive sites that are good matches for your business. To make this link exchange work well do the following:

- Create matches with sites that host discussion lists related to your business.
- Do not just settle for a dull link at the site—this will waste your time.
- Put snappy copy in the link that describes what you are all about.
- Once you find a site that fits, e-mail their webmaster and request to exchange links. Explain the benefit to them, related to the additional traffic they will receive from your site.
- Have the link text prepared in html format (enlist your Internet specialist to do this for you). Tell their webmaster where on your site you have added mention of their site, This saves them some time and signals to them that you are serious and considered them extensively in creating this offer.
- Choose your potential link partners wisely. One highly targeted visitor to your site is 100 times more valuable than random surfers.

INDEX

ABOUT THE AUTHOR

Allen D'Angelo M.S. is a marketing consultant to many small, medium and large businesses. His insights lead clients to find the most practical and highest results-bearing marketing applications that profoundly improve their businesses. Allen has spent years studying and testing marketing strategies using highly controllable direct marketing applications in order to isolate methods that give his clients realistic results that are appropriate for their industry, businesses and budget. The result of Allen's work has been the development of creative and low cost marketing solutions that can be successfully embraced by companies of any size and budget.

Printed in the United States
122410LV00010B/200/A

9 781574 723502